Overcoming Depression

The aim of the **Overcoming** series is to enable people with psychologically based disorders to take control of their own recovery program. Each title, with its specially tailored program, is devised by a practising clinician using the latest techniques of cognitive behavioral therapy – techniques which have been shown to be highly effective in changing the way patients think about themselves and their problems. The series was initiated in 1993 by Peter Cooper, Professor of Psychology at Reading University and Research Fellow at the University of Cambridge, whose original volume on overcoming bulimia nervosa and binge-eating continues to help many people in the USA, the UK and Europe.

Other titles in the series include:

Overcoming Anger & Irritability
William Davies

Overcoming Anorexia
Christopher Freeman

Overcoming Anxiety
Helen Kennerley

Bulimia Nervosa and Binge-Eating
Peter J. Cooper

Overcoming Childhood Trauma
Helen Kennerley

Overcoming Compulsive Gambling
Alex Blaszczynski

Overcoming Low Self-Esteem
Melanie Fennell

Overcoming Mood Swings
Jan Scott

Overcoming Panic
Derrick Silove & Vijaya Manicavasagar

Overcoming Social Anxiety and Shyness
Gillian Butler

Overcoming Traumatic Stress
Claudia Herbert & Ann Wetmore

To order further *Overcoming* books
please see order form at the back of this book.

OVERCOMING DEPRESSION

New revised edition

A self-help guide using cognitive behavioral techniques

Paul Gilbert

Robinson
LONDON

To my family

Constable & Robinson Ltd
3 The Lanchesters
162 Fulham Palace Road
London W6 9ER
www.constablerobinson.com

First published by Robinson Publishing Ltd 1997

This revised and expanded edition published by Robinson,
an imprint of Constable & Robinson Ltd 2000

A copy of the British Library Cataloguing in Publication Data for
this title is available from the British Library.

ISBN 1-84119-125-6   2306884

Important Note

This book is not intended to be a substitute for any medical advice or
treatment. Any person with a condition requiring medical attention should
consult a qualified medical practitioner or suitable therapist.

Printed and bound in the EU

10 9 8 7

Contents

Acknowledgments   vii

Foreword   ix

Introduction   xiii

Preface to the Revised Edition   xvii

Preface to the First Edition   xix

PART I: Understanding Depression

1   What is Depression?   3

2   Causes of Depression: Biology and Stress   12

3   Causes of Depression: How Evolution
May Have Shaped Depression   29

4   Causes of Depression: Early Life,
Psychological and Social Aspects   48

PART II: Learning How to Cope

5   Initial Steps   69

6   Thoughts and Feelings   84

7   Challenging Negative Thoughts and Feelings   99

8   Styles of Negative Thinking   121

9   Self-Bullying and How to Challenge It   139

10   Calling Ourselves Names: How Negative
Labels Affect Us   156

11   Further Methods to Challenge Negative Thoughts   171

PART III: Special Problems Associated with Depression

12 Approval, Subordination and Bullying 187

13 Confronting Shame 210

14 Coping with Guilt and Caring Too Much 234

15 Coping with Anger 263

16 From Anger to Assertiveness and Forgiveness 284

17 Dealing with Frustration, Disappointment
    and Lost Ideals 302

18 Perfectionism and Competitiveness, or
    How the Secret of Success is the Ability to Fail 320

19 Summing Up 343

Appendix 1: Monitoring and Challenging Your Thoughts 348

Appendix 2: Quick Guides 355

Appendix 3: Antidepressants 363

Appendix 4: Useful Books and Addresses 369

Index 374

Extra Monitoring Sheets 383

Acknowledgments

Many people have contributed enormously to the writing of this book. At times depressed people read some chapters and gave very important feedback and views of their own. Sadly, in order to protect confidentiality, I cannot name them but my heart-felt thanks goes out to them. They have saved me from some insensitivities and obscurities and have helped clarify certain points. I am also indebted to the many depressed people who have shared their stories with me and shown me the many faces of depression.

Many colleagues have, over the years, shared discussions on treating depression. Steven Allan, my research colleague, needs special mention for his preparedness to read the whole book and spend many evenings discussing ideas, and for sharing his therapeutic experience. Special thanks also go to Professor M. Perrez for his encouragement and many helpful comments on the text. Other colleagues who have read sections include Ken Goss, Liza Monaghan, Phil Brewin and Mia Gregory. To all these I owe my thanks.

I also owe my thanks to those who tried to educate me. Professor Ivy Blackburn started me off in cognitive therapy many years ago. Dr William Hughes introduced me to psychoanalytic approaches, Dr E. MacAdam to family therapy and Dr H. Ghadiali to group therapy from a Jungian perspective. Special thanks go to Dr John Price who has had a deep impact on my thinking about depression, especially in regard to some of the theories outlined here. He has also shared many therapeutic ideas with me. His theories on depression, put forward in the 1960s and 1970s, are now gaining research evidence. He deserves credit for being one of the first to see depression as a state of defeat.

I am forever amazed at the patience of my own family. Jean, Hannah and James all allowed me the time to write but also rescued me from over-involvement. I have no doubt at all that much of my current contentment with life resides in their loving support – not to mention the tea and sympathy.

I would also like to thank Professor Peter Cooper for asking me to write this book and as editor giving me the freedom to write it as I saw best. Gratitude also to Mark Crean of Robinson Publishing for his encouragement and hard work on the manuscript. Special thanks must go to the original copy-editor, Nancy Duin, who toiled with my English. Of course, any confusions, bad spellings and other annoying things are obviously my responsibility. For these I apologize in advance.

Foreword

Many, perhaps the majority, of those who go to see their family doctor have some type of psychological problem which makes them anxious or unhappy. There may be a fairly obvious reason for this – the loneliness of widowhood or the stresses of bringing up a family – or it may be that their mental state is part of their personality, something they were born with or a reaction to traumatic experiences in their lives. Despite being so common, I soon discovered after starting in general practice over ten years ago that this type of mental disturbance (usually described as a *neurosis* to distinguish it from the *psychosis* of those with a serious mental illness like schizophrenia) is particularly difficult to deal with. What are the options? Well, there are always drugs – minor tranquillizers, antidepressants and sleeping pills. It is certainly easy enough to write a prescription and more often than not the patient feels a lot better as a result, but there is no getting away from the fact that drugs are a chemical fix. Sometimes this is all that is necessary to tide someone over a difficult period, but more usually the same old problems recur when the drugs are discontinued.

The alternatives to drugs are the 'talking therapies' ranging from psychoanalysis to counselling that seek to sort out the underlying cause of anxiety or unhappiness. Psychoanalysis is out of the question for many, being too prolonged – often lasting for years – and too expensive. Counselling certainly can be helpful for no other reason than that unburdening one's soul to a sympathetic listener is invariably therapeutic. But once the counselling sessions were over, I got the impression it was only a matter of time before the psychological distress reappeared.

Here, then, is one of the great paradoxes of modern medicine. Doctors can now transplant hearts, replace arthritic hips and cure meningitis but, confronted by the commonest reason why people seek their advice, they have remarkably little to offer. And then a couple of years ago I started to hear about a new type of psychological treatment – cognitive therapy – which, it was claimed, was not only straightforward but demonstrably effective. I was initially sceptical as I found it difficult to imagine what sort of breakthrough insight into human psychology should lie behind such remarkable claims. The human brain is, after all, the most complex entity in existence, so it would seem unlikely that someone had suddenly now at the end of the twentieth century found the key that unlocked the mysteries of neuroses – a key that had eluded human understanding for hundreds of years.

The central insight of cognitive therapy is not, it emerges, a new discovery, but rather is based on the profound observation originally formulated by the French philosopher Descartes that the essential feature of human consciousness was 'cogito ergo sum' – 'I think therefore I am.' We *are* our thoughts and the contents of our thoughts have a major influence on our emotions. Cognitive therapy is based on the principle that certain types of thought that we have about ourselves – whether, at its simplest, we are loved or wanted or despised or boring – have a major effect on the way we perceive the world. If we feel unloved, the world will appear unloving, and then every moment of every day our sense of being unloved is confirmed. That, after all, is what depression is all about. These types of thoughts are called 'automatic thoughts' because they operate on the margins of our consciousness as a continual sort of internal monologue. If these thoughts are identified and brought out into the open then the state of mind that they sustain, whether anxiety or depression or any of the other neuroses, can begin to be resolved.

So this type of therapy is called 'cognitive' because it is primarily about changing our thoughts about ourselves, the world and the future. The proof of the pudding, as they say, is in the eating and the very fact that this type of therapy has been shown to work so well, in countless well-controlled studies, is powerful confirmation that the underlying insight that our thoughts lie behind, and sustain, neurotic illnesses is in essence correct.

Nonetheless, some may be forgiven for having misgivings. The concept of cognitive therapy takes some getting used to and it is certainly hard to credit that complex psychological problems can be explained by such an apparently simple concept. There is perhaps an understandable impression that it all sounds a bit oversimplified or trite, that it fails to get to the root cause of the source of anxiety or depression.

So it is necessary to dig a bit deeper to examine the origins of cognitive therapy and perhaps the easiest way of doing this is to compare it with what for many is the archetype of all forms of psychotherapy – psychoanalysis. Psychoanalysis claims to identify the source of neuroses in the long-forgotten and repressed traumas of early childhood, so it is less concerned with thoughts themselves than with the hidden meaning which (it claims) underlies them. The important question, though, is whether psychoanalysis does make people better, or at least less unhappy. Many people certainly believe they have been helped, but when Professor Gavin Andrews of the University of New South Wales reviewed all the studies in which the outcome of psychoanalysis had been objectively measured in the *British Journal of Psychiatry* in 1994, he was unable to show that it worked any better than 'just talking'.

In cognitive therapy, the importance of human thoughts lies precisely in their content and how that influences the way a person feels about themselves, a point well illustrated by one of its early pioneers, Aaron Beck. Back in the sixties, while practising as a psychoanalyst in Philadelphia, Beck was treating a young woman with an anxiety state which he initially interpreted in true psychoanalytic fashion as being due to a failure to resolve sexual conflict arising from problems in childhood. During one session he noticed that his patient seemed particularly uneasy and, on enquiring why, it emerged she felt embarrassed because she thought she was expressing herself badly and that she sounded trite and foolish. 'These self-evaluative thoughts were very striking,' Beck recalled, 'because she was actually very articulate.' Probing further he found that this false pattern of thinking – that she was dull and uninteresting – permeated all her relationships. He concluded that her chronic anxiety had little to do with her sex life but rather arose from a constant state of dread that her lover might desert her because he found her as uninteresting as she thought herself to be.

Over the next few years, Beck found that he was able to identify similar and quite predictable patterns of thinking in nearly all his patients. For the first time he realized that he was getting inside his patients' minds and beginning to see the world as they experienced it, something he had been unable to do in all his years as a psychoanalyst. From that perspective he went on to develop the principles of cognitive therapy.

Compared to psychoanalysis, cognitive therapy certainly does appear much simpler, but we should not take this to mean that it is less profound. The central failure of the founders of psychoanalysis was that they did not recognize the true significance of thoughts in human neurosis. Once that significance was grasped by those like Aaron Beck then human psychological disorders became more readily understandable and therefore simpler, but it is the simplicity of an elegant scientific hypothesis that more fully explains the facts. It can't be emphasized too strongly the enormous difference that cognitive therapy has made. Now it is possible to explain quite straightforwardly what is wrong in such a way that people are reassured, while allowing them to be optimistic that their problems can be resolved. Here, at last, is a talking therapy that works.

Professor Gavin Andrews in his review in the *British Journal of Psychiatry* identified cognitive therapy as 'the treatment of choice' in generalized anxiety, obsessive compulsive disorders and depression. It has in addition been shown to be effective in the treatment of eating disorders, panic attacks and even in the management of marital and sexual difficulties, in chronic pain syndromes and many emotional disorders of childhood. Its contribution to the alleviation of human suffering is remarkable.

James Le Fanu, GP

Introduction

Why cognitive behavior therapy?

Over the past two or three decades, there has been something of a revolution in the field of psychological treatment. Freud and his followers had a major impact on the way in which psychological therapy was conceptualized, and psychoanalysis and psychodynamic psychotherapy dominated the field for the first half of this century. So, long-term treatments were offered which were designed to uncover the childhood roots of personal problems – offered, that is, to those who could afford it. There was some attempt by a few health service practitioners with a public conscience to modify this form of treatment (by, for example, offering short-term treatment or group therapy), but the demand for help was so great that this had little impact. Also, whilst numerous case histories can be found of people who are convinced that psychotherapy did help them, practitioners of this form of therapy showed remarkably little interest in demonstrating that what they were offering their patients was, in fact, helpful.

As a reaction to the exclusivity of psychodynamic therapies and the slender evidence for its usefulness, in the 1950s and 1960s a set of techniques was developed, broadly collectively termed 'behavior therapy'. These techniques shared two basic features. First, they aimed to remove symptoms (such as anxiety) by dealing with those symptoms themselves, rather than their deep-seated underlying historical causes. Second, they were techniques, loosely related to what laboratory psychologists were finding out about the mechanisms of learning, which were formulated in testable terms. Indeed, practitioners of behavior therapy were committed to using techniques of proven value or, at worst, of a form which could potentially be put to test. The area where these techniques proved of most value was in the treatment of anxiety disorders, especially specific phobias (such as fear of animals or heights) and agoraphobia, both notoriously difficult to treat using conventional psychotherapies.

After an initial flush of enthusiasm, discontent with behavior therapy grew. There were a number of reasons for this, an important one of which was the fact that behavior therapy did not deal with the internal thoughts which were so obviously central to the distress that patients were experiencing. In this context, the fact that behavior therapy proved so inadequate when it came to the treatment of depression highlighted the need for major revision. In the late 1960s and early 1970s a treatment was developed specifically for depression called 'cognitive therapy'. The pioneer in this enterprise was an American psychiatrist, Professor Aaron T. Beck, who developed a theory of depression which emphasized the importance of people's depressed styles of thinking. He also specified a new form of therapy. It would not be an exaggeration to say that Beck's work has changed the nature of psychotherapy, not just for depression but for a range of psychological problems.

In recent years the cognitive techniques introduced by Beck have been merged with the techniques developed earlier by the behavior therapists to produce a body of theory and practice which has come to be known as 'cognitive behavior therapy'. There are two main reasons why this form of treatment has come to be so important within the field of psychotherapy. First, cognitive therapy for depression, as originally described by Beck and developed by his successors, has been subjected to the strictest scientific testing; and it has been found to be a highly successful treatment for a significant proportion of cases of depression. Not only has it proved to be as effective as the best alternative treatments (except in the most severe cases, where medication is required), but some studies suggest that people treated successfully with cognitive behavior therapy are less likely to experience a later recurrence of their depression than people treated successfully with other forms of therapy (such as antidepressant medication). Second, it has become clear that specific patterns of thinking are associated with a range of psychological problems and that treatments which deal with these styles of thinking are highly effective. So, specific cognitive behavioral treatments have been developed for anxiety disorders, like panic disorder, generalized anxiety disorder, specific phobias and social phobia, obsessive compulsive disorders, and hypochondriasis (health anxiety), as well as for other conditions such as compulsive gambling, alcohol and drug addiction, and eating disorders like bulimia nervosa and binge-eating disorder. Indeed, cognitive behavioral techniques have a wide application beyond the narrow categories of psychological disorders: they have been applied effectively, for example, to helping people with low self-esteem and those with marital difficulties.

At any one time almost 10 percent of the general population is suffering from depression, and more than 10 percent has one or other of the anxiety disorders. Many others have a range of psychological problems and personal difficulties. It is of the greatest importance that treatments of proven effectiveness are developed. However, even when the armoury of therapies is, as it were, full, there remains a very great problem – namely that the delivery of treatment is expensive and the resources are not going to be available evermore. Whilst this shortfall could be met by lots of people helping themselves, commonly the natural inclination to make oneself feel better in the present is to do precisely those things which perpetuate or even exacerbate one's problems. For example, the person with agoraphobia will stay at home to prevent the possibility of an anxiety attack; and the person with bulimia nervosa will avoid eating all potentially fattening foods. Whilst such strategies might resolve some immediate crisis, they leave the underlying problem intact and provide no real help in dealing with future difficulties.

So, there is a twin problem here: although effective treatments have been developed, they are not widely available; and when people try to help themselves they often make matters worse. In recent years the community of cognitive behavior therapists have responded to this situation. What they have done is to take the principles and techniques of specific cognitive behavior therapies for particular problems and represent them in self-help manuals. These manuals specify a systematic program of treatment which the individual sufferer is advised to work through to overcome their difficulties. In this way, the cognitive behavioral therapeutic techniques of proven value are being made available on the widest possible basis.

Self-help manuals are never going to replace therapists. Many people will need individual treatment from a qualified therapist. It is also the case that, despite the widespread success of cognitive behavioral therapy, some people will not respond to it and will need one of the other treatments available. Nevertheless, although research on the use of cognitive behavioral self-help manuals is at an early stage, the work done to date indicates that for a very great many people such a manual will prove sufficient for them to overcome their problems without professional help.

Many people suffer silently and secretly for years. Sometimes appropriate help is not forthcoming despite their efforts to find it. Sometimes they feel too ashamed or guilty to reveal their problems to anyone. For many of these people the cognitive behavioral self-help manual will provide a lifeline to recovery and a better future.

Professor Peter Cooper
The University of Reading, 1997

Preface to the Revised Edition

The first edition of *Overcoming Depression* was written in 1995–6 and appeared in 1997. Since then a number of people have read it and have offered much useful advice on what was helpful and what was not. I have taken these views to heart and, in addition to some minor and stylistic changes, have revised this edition in the following ways.

There are now three chapters covering theories of the causes of depression. In the earlier edition I had not made clear enough the relationship between our life situation, the meaning that we give to it and the bodily responses of stress. I hope I have been more successful this time. I have also clarified some of the evolutionary ideas on depression, which considers how nature has allowed for human depression.

A number of people felt that I hadn't offered enough advice on the use of thought forms. I have therefore written a new section at the end of Chapter 7 on how to use thought forms and also design your own. Over the last few years work that we have done looking at compassionate challenges have suggested that they can be very helpful in overcoming depression and I have slightly expanded that section in Chapter 7.

The biggest addition to the book, however, is the chapter on guilt (Chapter 14). Many patients and colleagues felt that was an important omission and I am delighted to be able to cover this theme in the new edition.

Sadly, there is no indication that the rates of depression have been falling in the five years since I began to write the first edition of this book. Life remains tough for many people. However, people are gradually becoming more prepared to recognize that they are depressed, or at least emotionally exhausted, and to seek professional help. Currently, most family doctors will offer medication. This book can be used in conjunction with medication and may well help you to make the best of it. In Appendix 3 you will find a short section on the use of St John's Wort, a herb for which there is increasing evidence of an antidepressant effect.

I hope that the writing style remains accessible. I am grateful to Di Woollands for all her secretarial support and to Gillian Bromley for her expert help in copy-editing. Many thanks also to all at Constable & Robinson Publishing who have made this series the success it is. Above all, I hope this volume provides you with insight into the nature of depression and the various ways in which you may try to overcome it. I wish you well with your efforts.

Paul Gilbert
Derby, November 1999

Preface to the First Edition

Depression is a horrible state to be in. Having worked with depressed people for many years and having heard many different stories, the thing that stands out is the sheer misery of it. Another way I encountered depression was personally, nearly twenty years ago. In the context of some major set-backs in my life, I suddenly found myself caught up in one. Even though I had studied depression, I was not as prepared as I thought I would have been to deal with it. My depression was of the milder kind but even so it was associated with panic attacks, many sleepless nights, a terrible sense of having failed in important areas of my life and a deep dread. Researchers rarely talk about dread, but I think it is a good word to sum up what people feel when they are depressed. I can't say I felt particularly sad, as you might if you lose a loved one, more frightened, irritable and joyless. Hence, I would choose the word dread or 'living in dread' to describe it. I also discovered that one does strange things when one is depressed. Occasionally, I would sit in lukewarm baths at four in the morning to try to reduce the agitation. I would take taxis to work because I couldn't face the bus, and if I had to give a talk or lecture you'd have to drag me out the loo! However, I was not so knocked out by it that I couldn't function, as some people can be. And on the whole I chose to see it as a 'brain state change' brought on by stress. Indeed, my first book on depression was called *Depression: From Psychology to Brain State*. Not the most inspiring of titles, perhaps, and it is now out of print, but my own experience had convinced me that something had 'happened in my brain' and I wanted to explore how social and psychological factors could produce biological changes.

Sadly, some people seem at risk of certain types of depression, and we now know that genes appear to play a role. However, while I do not want to underplay the biological dimension of depression, some forms are surprisingly common and genes probably play a major role only in a minority of cases. Life events and early childhood experiences seem by far the more common sources. I suspect this was true for me. My early years were spent in West Africa. It was a place of tremendous freedoms and I would roam happily in the outback. For nearly a year we lived in the 'bush' with no running water or electricity – and no school! My memories are still vivid of that time and when the skies are dull and cold I remember with great fondness the excitements, the blue skies and expansiveness of Africa. When I came home to England to go to boarding school I found the confinement and harshness of it difficult. I also found that I was behind in my education and had serious problems with the English language. To this day I do not like confinements and can easily feel trapped in places. The life events that triggered my depression were all related to feeling trapped and failing.

I see depression as a state of mind that we have a potential for, just as we have the potential to feel grief, fear, sexual arousal and so forth. And like any state of mind, depression is associated with very real changes in the brain. In my own work I have explored the reasons for this by thinking about the typical things that tend to trigger depression. This led to a consideration of whether the capacity for depression might be something that evolved along with us as we plodded the conflict-ridden trail from reptiles to monkey to humans. I won't go into the details of that except to say that depression probably affects animals. As with humans, depression seems to strike mostly when an animal loses status (is defeated), loses control and/or is trapped in adverse environments. When these things happen the brain seems to switch into depressed-like states. In humans, signals of being valued as a person have evolved as important mediators of mood states.

The other thing to consider, if we stay with an evolutionary view for a moment, is that although the brain is a highly complex organ it is also something of a 'contraption'. Deep in our brains are structures that evolved with the reptiles. Neuropsychologists even called this part of the brain 'the reptilian brain'. Evolution does not create totally new designs. Rather, old designs are adapted, added to or altered as a species evolves. It is rather like developing a car, but each new design must include the old – you can't go back to the drawing board and start afresh. So the brain has various structures within it that stretch way back many millions of years. This is why we can see the brain as a cobbling together of different bits that do different things. We have the potential for great violence, terror, lust, love and compassion. We are a mosaic of possibilities arising out of this jerry-built brain of ours.

Provided these various parts of the brain work together then it functions reasonably well, but if they get out of balance then it functions less well. Due perhaps to childhood trauma or difficulties and later stressful life events, we sometimes find it difficult to keep this mixed array of possibilities under control. They start pulling in different directions. The brain may tell us that there is far more danger than there is, and we panic; it may tell us that we are inferior, worthless and to give in, and we feel depressed; it may tell us that we need to get our own back, and so we seethe with the desire for revenge. Each of these parts has its own job to do, but they must work in harmony. In depression we lose this harmony and have thoughts and ideas that lead us to feel more defeated, inferior and worthless, and thus more depressed.

What we find in depression is that people experience all kinds of thoughts and feelings coming from different systems within the brain, and these can be difficult to control or make sense of. Another way to think of this is that we have different parts to ourselves and can play different roles, e.g. child, hero, lover, parent, friend, enemy, helper and so on. Evolution has provided many brain systems that enable us to enact different roles. Each part tends to see the world in its own way. For example, the hero part strides out and risks all. The coward part says, 'You must be joking. I'm not going out there.' Now if the two work together then they will make a sensible compromise and evaluation of risk. But if the hero does not listen to the coward then the hero puts the self in danger. On the other hand, if the coward does not listen to the hero, the coward just hides in the corner. In reality, of course, there are no actual 'parts' as such; what we experience is the activation, to a greater or lesser degree, of different brain systems. When we pay attention to our thoughts and feelings we can actually recognize which brain systems are turned on. Our thoughts and feelings are windows on these different systems in us.

So what to do if you feel depressed? The first thing to say is that the thoughts we have when we are depressed tell us that the depression system is switched on. That may not seem very helpful, until we realize that there may be ways to turn it off again and bring ourselves back into balance. For example, when we are depressed we may think in ways that seem right 'to the depression', but which may seem very wrong to other parts of ourselves. The rational and compassionate parts of ourselves may have a very different view of things. The more we can say, 'OK, my depression is a part of me; one of my many brain systems, but it can't be relied on to be accurate or helpful', the more we can step in to try to take control of it.

Secondly, as we get depressed the depression system tends to throw other systems out of balance. For example, we may become more irritable or anxious. And as a result we may judge ourselves and/or others more harshly, which feeds the depression. Typical of depression is to devalue things, usually ourselves and accomplishments, but we may also devalue others. We may start to believe that things are darker than they are.

Thirdly, depression is about how the brain is operating at any particular time. So depression is very much felt 'in the body' and is about feelings. Depression was designed (evolved) to slow us down, to weaken self-confidence and make us more sensitive to possible social losses and threats. It does this by changing the way our bodies work. However, if we can get other systems to challenge the depression, by learning how to think differently about ourselves and events, then we have an opportunity to get things back into balance. This book will discuss how to recognize important depressing thoughts to work with and how to challenge them.

This book is for people who would like to know more about depression – what it is and how to help oneself. It is not a cure-all, nor a substitute for therapies like drugs or psychotherapy, nor can a book like this change the painful realities of living. It is simply one approach. Each person's depression is, in part, similar to other people's and in part unique to that person. What understanding can do is to offer a way to move out of depression rather than plunge further into it. There are many ways to challenge some of the negative thinking of depression. I will try to point out some pitfalls to watch out for and suggest some methods that will enable you to develop a more rational and compassionate approach to yourself.

The book is divided into three parts. The first is the most technical. I have included this because many of the depressed people I see say that they would like to know more about depression itself. If it seems too technical, you can skip those bits you find difficult to follow; in fact, you can skip the whole of Part I if you like. Part II outlines some basic approaches to self-help. Here we will explore the role of thoughts and feelings, and how to challenge some of the thoughts and feelings that lead to a downward slide. There is a chapter devoted to how depressed people treat themselves (which is often very badly) and how to treat yourself more kindly. The more you learn to value yourself (or at least to stop devaluing yourself), the greater the chances of turning the depression system off. Each chapter in Part II is followed by a series of exercises you can try. In Part III the basic approaches covered in Part II are applied to special problems. These include the need for approval, anger, shame, lack of assertiveness, disappointment and perfectionism.

You will read of many other people's depression. All names have, of course, been changed. Also, to avoid any chance of identification, the details of all the stories have been altered. Sometimes two or three cases have been rolled into one, again to avoid identification. The focus of each problem is on the specific themes that reveal the dilemmas and complexities of depression.

Our journey together may be a long one, but I hope it will equip you with some ideas of how to move out of depression. Recovering from depression usually requires time, effort and patience, but if you know what you are trying to achieve, and have a way forward, you are likely to be more successful in your efforts. So let's begin.

PART I

Understanding Depression

1

What is Depression?

If you suffer from depression, you are, sadly, far from being alone. In fact, it has been estimated that there may be over 300 million people in the world today who suffer from it. Depression has afflicted humans for as long as records have been kept. Indeed, it was first named as a condition about 2,400 years ago by the famous ancient Greek doctor Hippocrates, who called it 'melancholia'. It is also worth noting that although we cannot ask animals how they feel, it is likely that animals also have the capacity to feel depressed. Animals can certainly behave as if they are depressed. So, to a greater or lesser degree, we all have the potential to become depressed, just as we all have the potential to become anxious, to grieve or fall in love.

Depression is no respecter of status or fortune. Indeed, many famous people throughout history have suffered from it. King Solomon, Abraham Lincoln, Winston Churchill and the Finnish composer Jean Sibelius are well-known examples from history. What is important to remember is that depression is not about human weakness.

What Do We Mean by 'Depression'?

This is a difficult question to answer because a lot depends on who you ask. The word itself can be used to describe a type of weather, a fall in the stock market, a hollow in the ground and, of course, our moods. It comes from the Latin *deprimere*, meaning to 'press down'. The term was first applied to a mood state in the seventeenth century.

If you suffer from depression, one thing you will be aware of is that it is far more than just feeling down. In fact, depression affects not only how we feel, but how we think about things, our energy levels, our concentration, our sleep, even our interest in sex. So depression has an effect on many aspects of our lives. Let's look at some of these.

Motivation   Depression affects our motivation to do things. We can feel apathetic and experience a loss of energy and interest – nothing seems worth doing, everything is so pointless that it's hopeless even to try. If we have children, we can lose interest in them and then feel guilty. A work project that we might have been very keen about becomes boring. We have to drag ourselves around. Each day can be a torment of having to force ourselves to perform even the most minor of activities.

Emotions   People often think that depression is only about low mood or feeling fed-up – and this is certainly part of it. Indeed, the central symptom of depression is called 'anhedonia' – derived from the ancient Greek meaning 'without pleasure' – and means the *loss of the capacity to experience any pleasure*. Life seems empty; we are joyless. But – and this is an important but – although we lose the ability to have positive feelings and emotions, we can experience an increase in negative emotions, especially anger. We may be churning inside with anger and resentment that we can't express. We might become extremely irritable, snap at our children and relatives and, at times, lash out at them. We may then feel guilty about this, and this makes us more depressed. Other very common symptoms are anxiety and fear. When we are depressed, we can feel extremely vulnerable. Things that we may have done easily before seem frightening, and at times it is difficult to know why. So the two 'A's' – anger and anxiety – are very much part of depression. Other negative feelings that can increase in depression are sadness, guilt, shame, envy and jealousy.

Thinking   Depression interferes with the way we think in two ways. First, it affects concentration and memory. We find that we can't get our minds to settle on anything. Reading a book or watching television becomes impossible. We also don't remember things too well, and we are prone to forget things. However, it is easier to remember negative things than positive things.

The second way that depression affects our thoughts is in the way we think about ourselves, our future and the world. Very few people who are depressed feel good about themselves. Generally, they tend to see themselves as inferior, flawed, bad or worthless. If you ask a depressed person about their future, they are likely to respond with: 'What future?' The future seems dark, a blank or a neverending cycle of defeat and losses. Like many strong emotions, depression pushes us to more extreme forms of thinking. Our thoughts become 'all or nothing' – we are either a complete success or an abject failure.

Images When we are depressed, the imagery we use to describe it tends to be similar. We may talk about being under a dark cloud, in a deep hole or pit, or a dark room. Winston Churchill called his depression his 'black dog'. The imagery of depression is always about darkness, being stuck somewhere and not able to get out. If you were to paint a picture of your depression, it would probably involve dark or harsh colours rather than light, soft ones. So darkness and entrapment are key internal images.

Behaviors Our behavior changes when we become depressed. We engage in much less positive activity and may withdraw socially and want to hide away. Many of the things we might have enjoyed doing before becoming depressed now seem like an ordeal. Because everything seems to take so much effort, we do much less than we used to. Our behavior towards other people can change, too. We tend to do fewer positive things with others and are more likely to find ourselves in conflict with them. If we become very anxious, we might also start to avoid meeting people or lose our social confidence.

Depressed people sometimes become agitated and find it extremely difficult to relax. They feel like trapped animals and pace about, wanting to do something but not knowing what. Sometimes, the desire to escape and run away can be very strong. But where to go and what to do is unclear. On the other hand, some depressed people become very slowed down. They walk slowly, with a stoop, their thoughts seem stuck, and everything feels 'heavy'.

Physiology When people become anxious about something, their bodies can produce a surge of adrenaline. And depression can result in other biological changes, affecting our bodies and our brains. Now, there is nothing sinister about this. To say that our brains work differently when we are depressed is really to state the obvious. Indeed, any mental state, be it happy, sexual, excited, anxious or depressed, will be associated with physical changes in our brains. Recent research has shown that some of these are related to stress hormones such as cortisol, which indicates that depression involves the body's stress system. Certain brain chemicals, called neurotransmitters, are also affected. Generally, these chemicals are reduced in the brain when we are depressed, and this is why some people find benefit from drugs that allow the monoamines to build up. The next chapter will explore these more fully.

Probably as a result of the physical changes that occur in depression, we can experience a host of other unwanted symptoms. Not only are energy levels affected, so is sleep. If you are depressed, you may wake up early, sometimes in the middle of the night or early morning, or you may find it difficult to get to sleep. There are some depressed states, however, in which sleep is increased. In addition, loss of appetite is quite common and food may start to taste like cardboard; as a result, sometimes there is weight loss. Other depressed people may eat more and put on weight.

Social relationships   Even though we might try to hide our depression, it almost always affects other people. We are less fun to be with. We can be irritable and find ourselves continually saying 'No'. The key thing here is that this is quite common and has been since humans first felt depressed. So we need to acknowledge these feelings and not feel ashamed about them, for if we do, it will just make us more depressed. There are various reasons why our relationships might suffer. There can be conflicts that we feel unable to sort out. There might be unvoiced resentments. We might feel out of control. Our friends and partners might not understand what has happened to us. Remember the old saying, 'Laugh and the world laughs with you. Cry and you cry alone'? Depression is difficult for others to comprehend at times.

Are All Depressions the Same?

The short answer to this is no. There are a number of different types. One that researchers and professionals commonly refer to is called 'major depression'. According to the American Psychiatric Association, one can be said to suffer from major depression if one has at least five of the following possible symptoms, which have to be present for at least two weeks.

- Low mood
- Marked loss of pleasure

⎫ You have to have one of these symptoms

- Significant change in appetite and a loss of at least 5 percent of normal body weight
- Sleep disturbance
- Agitation or feelings of being slowed down
- Loss of energy or feeling fatigued virtually every day
- Feelings of worthlessness, low self-esteem, tendency to feel guilty
- Loss of the ability to concentrate
- Thoughts of death and suicide

⎬ You must have at least four of these symptoms

Such a list of symptoms is important to professionals, but it does not really capture the variety and complexity of the experience of depression. For example, I would include feelings of being trapped as a common depressed symptom, and many psychologists feel that hopelessness is also one. I have included this list here to give you an idea of how some professionals tend to think about depression.

Researchers distinguish between those mental conditions that involve only depression and those that also involve swings into mania. In the manic state, a person can feel enormously energetic, full of their own self-importance and confident, and may have great interest in sex. And if the mania is not too severe they can accomplish a lot. People who have swings into both depression and (hypo) mania are often diagnosed as suffering from *bipolar illness* (meaning that they can swing to both poles of mood – high and low). The old term was manic-depression. Those who only suffer depression are diagnosed as having *unipolar depression*.

Another distinction that some researchers and professionals make is between *psychotic* and *neurotic* depression. In psychotic depression, the person has various false beliefs called 'delusions'. For example, a person without any physical illness might come to believe that he or she has a serious cancer and will shortly die. Some years ago, one of my patients was brought into hospital because she had been contacting lawyers and undertakers to arrange her will and her funeral as she was sure that she would die before Christmas. She believed that the hospital staff were keeping this important information from her to avoid upsetting her, and she tried to advise her young children on how they should cope without her (causing great distress to the family, of course). Sometimes people with a psychotic illness can develop extreme feelings of guilt. For example, they may be certain in their minds they have caused the Bosnian war, or done something terrible. Psychotic depression is obviously a very serious disorder, but compared to the non-psychotic depressions it is, on the whole, rare.

Another distinction that is sometimes made is between those depressions that seem to come out of the blue and those that are related to life events, e.g. when people become depressed after losing a job, the death of a loved one or the ending of an important relationship. Today, however, although we recognize that people clearly differ in the exact nature of their depressions, and the patterns of their symptoms, this distinction is less credible. In psychotherapy, one often finds that, as one gets to know a person in depth, what looked like a depression that came out of the blue actually had its seeds in childhood. Sadly, this does not mean that some of us are not more biologically vulnerable to depression than others, only that distinguishing between depressions in terms of cause is fraught with problems.

Clearly some depressions are more serious, deep and debilitating than others. In many cases, depressed people manage to keep going until the depression eventually passes. In very serious depression this is extremely difficult, and getting professional help is important. Depressions can vary in terms of onset, severity, duration and frequency.

Onset   Depression can have an acute onset (i.e. within days or weeks) or come on gradually (over months or years). It can begin at any time but late adolescence, early adulthood and later life are particularly vulnerable times.

Severity   Individuals can vary as to whether their symptoms are mild, moderate or severe.

Duration   Some will come out of their depression within weeks or months, whereas for others it may last in a fluctuating, chronic form for many years. 'Chronic depression' is said to last longer than two years, and 10–20 percent of depressed people suffer from it.

Frequency Some individuals may only have one episode of depression, whereas others may have many. About 50 percent of those who have been depressed will have a recurrence.

The fact that depression can recur may seem alarming, but this should really come as no surprise. Suppose, for example, that since a young age you have always felt inferior and worthless. One day this sense of inferiority seems to get the better of you and you feel a complete failure in every aspect of your life. Now, it may be that a drug will help you to recover from that episode, but even if you become better, you may still retain, underneath, those feelings of failure and inferiority. Drugs do not retrain us or enable us to mature and throw off these underlying beliefs.

How Common is Depression?

As I have already indicated, depression is, sadly, very common. If we look at what is called major depression, the figures look like this.

	Women	Men
Suffering depression at any one time	4–10%	2–3.5%
Lifetime risk	10–26%	5–12%

What this suggests is that about one in four or five of us could have some kind of depressive episode at some point in our lives. It also implies that depression is about three times more common in women than in men. Depression is also found more often in certain deprived sections of society – e.g. in areas of high unemployment. New research also indicates that rates of and risks for depression have been steadily increasing throughout the twentieth century, but the reasons for this are unclear. Socio-economic changes, the fragmentation of families and communities, the loss of hope in the younger generation – especially the unemployed – and increasing levels of expectations may all be implicated.

Key Points

- Depression, in its various forms, is very common and has been for thousands of years.
- Depression involves many different symptoms. Emotions such as anger and anxiety are common and at times more troubling than the depression itself. We can also have a strong desire to escape – for which we may feel guilty.
- There are different types of depression.
- Some depressions are quite severe, while others are less so but still deeply disturbing and life-crippling.

My key message to you, if you suffer from depression, is that if you feel a failure, if you have a lot of anger and hatred inside, if you are terrified out of your wits, if you think life is not worth living, if you feel trapped and desperate to escape, whatever your feelings, you are not the only one. Millions of depressed people throughout the world feel like you do. Of course, knowing this does not make your depression any less painful, but it does mean that there is nothing bad about you because you are in this state of mind. These feelings are sadly often

continued on next page

---

part of being depressed. True, some people who have not been depressed may not understand it or may tell you to pull yourself together, but this does not mean that there is anything bad about you. It just means that they find it difficult to understand.

Importantly, there are many things that can be done to help people who are depressed. There are some good drugs (antidepressants) available and many effective psychological treatments.

2

Causes of Depression: Biology and Stress

The next three chapters explore theories about the causes of depression. If you are feeling depressed, you might find these chapters a bit tough because they are somewhat technical in places, and it can be difficult to concentrate when one is depressed. Don't worry about that. To help yourself, you can if you prefer go straight to Part II, 'Learning How to Cope'. When you feel better, you might want to come back to these chapters, or dip into them. I have expanded them from the first edition partly because depressed people and their relatives have often asked to know more about what causes depression.

The Mind–Body Link

Now, when you feel depressed the last thing you want to hear is that 'it's all psychological' or 'only a state of mind'. After all, you probably feel tired and aimless, you may not be sleeping well and so you may feel exhausted. You may feel *physically* unwell compared to your normal self. One patient said, 'My whole system seems stuffed with black cotton wool.' This is because when we become depressed there are very real changes in our bodies and brains. The fact is that our brains *are* working differently when we are depressed. Depression is as much a physical problem as a psychological one. Although we sometimes still tend to think of the mind and body as separate, they are not. The mind and body are one. Over 2,000 years ago, the Greeks thought that depression was caused by too much 'black bile' in the body. Indeed, 'melancholia', another word for depression, means 'black bile'. But, as they were well aware, this raises another question. What causes the black bile to increase? The Greeks had rather good ideas about this. They thought that there were people who 'by their nature' had more black bile – melancholic types. But they also believed that stress, diet and seasonal changes could affect the amounts of black bile in the body. The Greeks recognized that we can be upset by things that happen to us and that these upsets can affect our bodily processes – that is, affect the black bile. Their approach to depression was the first truly *holistic* one, taking body, mind and social living into account. Today, we call this holistic approach the *biopsychosocial* one. This simply means that we need to understand not only the bodily and mental aspects of depression but also the *interactions* between our *biology* and bodily processes, our *psycho*logy (how we think and cope) and the kinds of *social* circumstances in which we live.

Today we no longer think in terms of 'black bile' but in terms of chemical changes in the brain and other bodily processes. But the idea that some people are sadly 'by their nature' prone to certain types of depression because of internal factors such as genes has been confirmed by research. However, research has also shown that the majority of depressions can arise from combinations of early life experiences, current life events, lifestyles and the way we cope with them. Our central task in this chapter will be to try to understand how these interact to produce the bodily and mental states of depression. The more we understand these interactions, the more sense it will make to try to help ourselves by using some of the methods outlined later in this book.

Biological Aspects

The brain is affected by depression in many ways. The sleep system is disrupted; the areas of the brain controlling positive feelings and emotions (joy, love, pleasure, fun) are toned down; and the areas controlling negative emotions (anger, anxiety, jealousy, shame) are toned up. In other words, when we are depressed, not only does life stop being enjoyable, but we are also more anxious, sad, irritable and bad-tempered. These changes in our feelings happen because there are changes in the way messages are relayed between one nerve cell and another in the brain.

Chemicals that operate as messages between nerve cells are called *neurotransmitters*. Now, there are very many different types of neurotransmitters in the brain. One type is called *monoamines*. These include dopamine, noradrenaline and serotonin. These three neurotransmitters control many functions in the brain including appetite, sleep and motivation. They are also especially important for moods and emotions. They are, if you like, our *mood chemicals*. In depression these 'mood' neurotransmitters (dopamine, noradrenline and serotonin) are believed to be depleted and not working efficiently.

If this seems a little complex, just hold on to the key point: that *our moods and feelings are affected by certain types of chemical systems in the brain*. Antidepressant drugs work by boosting the parts of the monoamine system that control positive emotions and toning down those areas that control negative emotions. Different antidepressants do this in slightly different ways (see pages 363–8).

So, we know that there are important chemicals in the brain that affect our moods, and that the trick of all treatments is to help these to work more efficiently. The key question for people suffering from depression is: why have these changes occurred in the brain, and what can we do to help us to recover?

In fact, there are various ways in which our *mood chemicals* can be affected to make us vulnerable to depression. The three most important are our *genes*, our *history* and *current stress*. Let's look at each of these in turn.

The Genetic Blueprint

Genes are segments of DNA that control a vast number of chemical processes. Genes are essential for life. Genes dictate whether an organism will be a fish, a rabbit or a human. They are the blueprints for life forms and the blueprints for the key characteristics of each individual person. Our genes are the blueprints from which you and I were created. We inherit our genes from our parents, and these genes control the colour of our eyes, skin and hair. They also trigger developments so that, as we grow, our sexual organs develop.

Genes also play a role in personality, including susceptibility to anxiety and depression, because they are one of the things that influence our brain systems – our neurotransmitter systems. Research with infants has shown that differences in temperament can show up in the first days of life: for example, some infants are inhibited and cautious, while others are keen to explore; some infants are very active, while others are passive. Everyone, except identical twins, is genetically unique – we are not exact copies of each other.

The first possibility, then, is that there is an *inherited* biological sensitivity to depression. For this view to be accepted, depression must be found to run in families. The strongest evidence in its favour would be if identical twins, separated at birth, were in adulthood found to have a similar risk of depression. This has, in fact, been found to be so: if one identical twin becomes depressed, the chances of the other twin developing depression are much higher than for any individual selected at random from the general population. The more severe the depression – if, for example, it is psychotic or bipolar – the greater the risk. For non-identical twins, the risk is higher than for the rest of the population, but not so high as for identical twins. On the basis of this evidence, it does seem that for some forms of depression there is a genetic or inherited risk. Genes may affect the threshold, that is to say, the ease with which depressed brain states are activated by life events, and recent evidence suggests that they may also affect how we cope once we become depressed.

We must be careful not to draw from these findings conclusions that are too simplistic, such as 'all depressions are inherited diseases.' In the first place, much depends on the definition of depression. Some depressions (especially bipolar or manic depression) do have a high 'genetic loading'. In addition, some people appear to have an increased risk of certain types of depression if some of their close (genetic) relatives suffer from certain disorders, including anxiety and alcoholism. However, although depression may run in families, this does *not* mean that there is always an inherited genetic risk involved. There are many reasons why depression can run in families. It may be because people are under the same pressures over time: for example, the stress of poverty can affect many generations, as can certain types of parenting. A parent who is cold and indifferent to his or her child may raise a child who has problems with expressing feelings, is vulnerable to depression and thus is cold and indifferent to his or her own children. We should also remember that the mild to moderate depressions (the most common kinds by far) are so common among some groups of people (e.g. the poor or otherwise disadvantaged; those traumatized by war) that the causes are most likely related to life circumstances and lifestyles. But we should not underestimate the power of our genes either. Over the years there have been studies on thousands of twins, and genes seem to affect many behaviors and personality traits – right down to preferences in clothes and food!

Early Life and How the Brain Develops

What else might lay the foundations for depression, other than genes? Can there be factors in a person's life that affect the mood neurotransmitters? Indeed there can. First we need to note that the human brain is quite immature at birth and develops enormously thereafter. So, although genes give us a blueprint, the brain is not a closed system following a pre-set pattern irrespective of what is happening in the outside world. Indeed, the quality and forms of our early relationships actually help to shape the various types of connections that nerve cells make in the brain. We now know that the brain is very 'flexible' in this regard. The way the brain matures during infancy and early childhood depends on social input: that is, various types of experience shape the brain and our mood chemicals. The brain of a child who is loved and wanted will mature differently from that of a child who is abused and constantly threatened. Indeed, research has shown very clearly that love and affection, in contrast to coldness and abuse, affect the way areas of the brain that control moods and emotions develop. For instance, there is increasing evidence that many of those susceptible to chronic forms of depression have histories of abuse, and that the stress systems of some of these people have an increased sensitivity.

So, a biological sensitivity to depression might result from early experiences that affect the way the brain grows and matures. Again, we should not be too pessimistic about these findings; even in these cases, medication and psychological intervention can still be very helpful. As individuals come to recognize their own personal sensitivities, psychological understanding and training can do much to help them cope better and change their sensitivities. However, prevention is of course better than cure, and the more we understand about the role of our early relationships in how our brains mature, the more seriously, as a society, we must take child care.

Stress and Depression

So far we have seen that genes and development may affect our biological sensitivity to depression. What about current stress? Can stress make us biologically sensitive to depression? The answer is yes – indeed, stress is probably the most common influence on our mood chemicals. Many depressions are triggered and maintained by stress, so it is worth spending a little time exploring the connection here.

Now, stress can be, and has been, blamed for just about all our woes and difficulties. However, a connection between stress, how we handle it, and depression is now well documented. In fact, understanding the linkage between our thoughts, our behaviors and our stress systems is one insight that might help you really focus on changing the way you think. The psychologist Richard Lazarus has done much to advance our understanding of how the meanings we give to things, and how we to try to cope, affect our stress systems and emotions. His new book, called *Stress and Emotions: A New Synthesis*, published by Free Association Press in 1999, offers an excellent overview of this work for those who would like to read more on the subject.

Stress can be related to lots of different psychological problems, including anxiety, irritability, fatigue – and depression. The way we cope with stress, too, can give rise to different psychological problems. Some people under stress are able to recognize it and back off from what is stressful to them. Others, however, are not able to escape from things that are stressful; for example, if one is in a job or a relationship that is 'stressful', it may not be easy to simply walk away. We will look at the issue of 'being stuck' in stressful situations that we can't get away from, and how this is related to depression, in Chapter 3. Other ways of coping with stress may cause problems of their own: for example, drinking too much alcohol. But before we look at how our thoughts and coping efforts can make stress worse, let's explore what happens in the body when we are stressed.

The first thing to note is that over millions of years systems in the brain have evolved to help the body respond to *threats*. How do they work? Well, imagine you are walking home one night and someone jumps out on you. The body will fly into action. Your heart rate goes up, you breathe faster, a knot tightens in your stomach, you start to sweat and you feel 'afraid'. Notice how there is both a bodily response (heartbeat, sweating) and a psychological one (fear, wanting to run away). This is the body's *defence systems* working. They are fairly automatic, and are geared to preparing you to run like hell or stand and fight. Now, there are many different types of stress that can mobilize the body and its defence systems: for example, hearing about a threat to your child, discovering you failed an important examination, believing you have a serious illness, or hearing that a lover you were keen on has left you. Lots of different types of *threats* and *losses* activate the defence and stress systems. Importantly, some threats, while serious (like someone jumping out on you) are short-lived (you run away). You may be shaken up for a while, but the stress settles down. However, other threats – like failing an exam, having a serious illness or ending a relationship – may have long-term implications.

So, we know that we have defence systems that will mobilize the body in certain ways when we are under threat or have suffered a loss. And we know that some threats and losses are short-lived and pass, while others do not. Next, we need to think about how quickly our body detects and responds to threats and losses, *and* how quickly the defence/stress systems will settle down again. Is depression a state in which the stress system has not settled down but is in a constant state of high or chronic arousal? Quite possibly; depression is often associated with long-term stress arousal.

Stress and Our Bodies

As noted above, stress requires the body to mobilize for action and you can guess which neurotransmitters are involved in this. It is our old friends dopamine, noradrenaline and serotonin – the same neurotransmitters that control our moods. The basic story is that long-term stress adversely affects our mood chemicals. Let's look at this more closely.

In recent years there has been growing interest in how one aspect of our stress/defence systems works in depression. This system is called the hypothalamic–pituitary–adrenal system – or HPA for short. It works like this. Sitting at the base of the brain are two small but very important organs call the hypothalamus and pituitary. Now, when the brain detects and responds to threats and losses the hypothalamus sends a signal to the pituitary (by release of a hormone called CRH for short). The pituitary picks up the message from the hypothalamus and sends a signal to the adrenal glands (which lie just above the kidneys). The message to the adrenals is sent by release into the bloodstream of a hormone called adrenocorticotrophic hormone –ACTH for short – which tells the adrenal glands to step up the release of the stress hormone, cortisol. So the hypothalamus signals to the pituitary, and the pituitary signals to the adrenal glands, and the basic message is: 'We are under threat – mobilise for action.'

Cortisol is an important hormone that circulates in the body all the time, increasing and decreasing over each twenty-four-hour period. This hormone does some useful things. It mobilizes fat for use as energy; it is an anti-inflammatory agent; it is involved in the functioning of the liver; and it may also increase the sensitivity to and detection of threats. All well and good. Except that, under stress, there is an increase in circulating cortisol; and it turns out that *prolonged* elevation of cortisol is bad for us. It is bad for the immune system (indeed, the effects of cortisol may be one of the problems in those who suffer from chronic fatigue syndrome), and it can cause undesirable changes in various areas of brain function which are involved with memory. Problems with memory and concentration may well be symptoms of excessively high cortisol levels. Cortisol also affects the mood chemicals – especially serotonin. And it can make us hypersensitive to threats, which is not necessarily useful if it makes focus too strongly on the negative aspects of situations and events.

Research has revealed that many depressed people have hyperactive HPA systems with elevated cortisol levels. There is a substance called dexamethasone which normally suppresses the production of cortisol for twenty-four hours or so in non-depressed people. However, if we give this to depressed people, we find that some of them show what is called *early escape*; that is, their HPA system over-rides the inhibiting effects of dexamethasone and continues to produce high levels of cortisol. In other words, the stress system is in overdrive.

What we have, then, is a stress system that may be useful for dealing with short-term threats and losses but can become a real disadvantage in the long term. In the next chapter, we will consider how evolution could have allowed such a poor design to develop, so that we have ended up with stress systems that can actually cause damage to other bodily processes. For the moment, though, let's think about another important aspect of stress: control. Can we control the stress on us, and what happens if we can't?

Uncontrollable Stress

Some years ago, the American psychologist Professor Martin Seligman found that, if animals were put under stresses that they could not control, they would become very passive and behave like depressed people. This did not happen if animals could control the stress. These extremely important findings were later taken up by other researchers who wanted to see what changes took place in the brains of animals subjected to uncontrollable stress. It was found that some of the changes were similar to those associated with depression – for example, activity in areas of the brain that control positive emotions and behavior was reduced, stress systems went into overdrive and our old friends the mood chemicals of dopamine, noradrenaline and serotonin were depleted. However, if other animals were subjected to the same stress *but had the means to control that stress*, different changes took place – the areas of the brain that control positive emotions and active (rather than passive) behavior were toned up and the mood chemicals were enhanced. This tells us something very important. The same stress, but with different levels of control, can produce quite different changes in our bodies and brains. If you are stressed and can do something about it, your brain will react in one way; but if you can't do something about it, it will react in a different way. The way you cope with stress is a key issue.

We can see, too, that our ability to cope affects how stressful a particular event or experience will be. Remember the example of someone jumping out on you, mentioned above? Suppose you are the world's best karate expert: you may be startled, but you know exactly how to get the better of your assailant. Or you fail an exam; but you tell yourself, 'Never mind, I'll sit it again next year.' Coping can change the implications of events for us, and this can increase or reduce their stressful impact. These findings are very important, for they strongly imply that the more control we can take over the stresses in our lives, the less likely it is that our mood chemicals will take a dive and stress systems spiral out of control. As we note below, though, this is not always easy.

The Straw that Breaks the Camel's Back

We often talk about 'the last straw' because we know that stress can build up and be cumulative. Take Nicky. Her firm had come under financial stress and she believed she would be likely to lose her job, leaving her with a very uncertain future. The threat of redundancies had been hanging over the office for a couple of months and the atmosphere at work was very gloomy. Then, driving home late one evening, she was involved in a car crash. Responsibility for the accident was unclear, but she felt that it had been partly due to a lapse in concentration on her part. She was not seriously injured, but her car was damaged and she was shaken up for quite a while. As she was recovering from this, her mother had a heart attack. Nicky had not been sleeping well for a month or so, and shortly after her mother became ill the problem became even worse. She began to brood more and more on the car accident and her responsibility. She also thought that maybe the worry of all that had contributed to her mother's heart attack through stress. She felt she should do more to help her mother, but found the burden of visiting taxing on her time and energy. She began to feel very low in mood, increasingly anxious and irritable, and personally inadequate; she found it difficult to get out of bed in the morning, and prone to thinking 'there is not much point because things just happen out of my control.' Not being able to 'get her old energy back' was itself depressing.

In many cases of depression there is a combination of stresses and setbacks. There may be financial worries, worries over jobs (or lack of them), conflicts at home or in work, children having problems, health worries and so forth. Over time these cumulative stresses increase stress arousal and edge us closer to maladaptive feedback, where we begin to ruminate on all the problems and spiral down into depression.

The Small Things Get More Difficult

One of the things that many people notice as they become depressed is that small things, or things they would formerly have done easily, like calling the garage to have the car fixed, or having friends over for dinner, get very hard to do. They start putting these things off, and at the same time worrying because they have not been done. Suddenly, small things become big things. If this happens, then try as best you can to do those small things and not let them build up and get on top of you. You will feel better for it, even though it may take a lot of effort; whereas if you do put things off, you may then start to brood on them and that will increase the stress on you. Also, recognize that your experience is a common one, and not evidence of your being 'personally useless'.

Thoughts Can Generate (More) Stress

Is it possible to become even more stressed by the way we think about our problems and about ourselves as people? Is it possible that one of the drivers of our stress systems is what we dwell on and ruminate about? And, more importantly, if we can learn how to stop going over and over the negatives in our lives (especially negative thoughts about ourselves as being useless and out of control), would this allow our stress systems to settle and heal? For many depressions, the answer to all these questions is almost certainly 'yes'.

One of the reasons why our thoughts can amplify the bodily stress response, with its various changes in hormones and brain chemicals, is because our conscious thoughts are plugged into older bits of our brains. Take sex, for example. Humans (and possibly only humans, to any significant extent) can generate internal fantasies of sex and get themselves 'hot'. We can lie alone in our bedrooms and simply fantasize. When we do this we trigger our pituitary to release sex hormones that flood the body, giving rise (excuse the pun) to erections or vaginal lubrication. *Our imagination alone can release sex hormones from the pituitary.* Isn't that amazing? Well, when I was an adolescent I never thought about it – just took it for granted. But it is amazing, and in the context of depression it is really important to understand the way our thoughts and images can influence our hormones.

To show the power of conscious negative thoughts, consider the following hypothetical situation. Suppose you are lying in your bath on Friday evening, relaxing and planning a nice quiet weekend. Then suddenly you remember you were supposed to be at an important meeting where your job prospects were going to be discussed. At that moment of recall you may become flushed, aroused, anxious, annoyed with yourself; and you may be uptight for the whole weekend. 'How could I forget?' you keep saying to yourself. Until you remembered the meeting and it came into your conscious mind, you did not feel anxious. So, our conscious thoughts and memories are powerfully linked to our feelings and moods. If you then dwell on the damage your failure to turn up might have done to your job prospects, you will be more stressed than if you pick up the phone, explain the situation to your boss and decide that this is not such a terrible thing to have happened. You see how conscious thoughts of an event and how we cope with it both interact with our stress responses?

This capacity for our thoughts, images, memories and coping efforts to stimulate our emotional and physiological responses is profoundly important. When people start to work on their depression, it is not uncommon for them to say: 'But surely my thoughts can't make me feel so bad?' or: 'Surely changing my thoughts can't make that much difference?' The answer is 'yes', they can. Of course, there is much more to depression than negative thinking; but imagine walking around in the world thinking that you are unlovable and worthless. What do you think will happen to your stress or mood systems? Imagine that you dwell on all the negatives in your life and your feeling that things just can't be changed. Unfortunately, if you do this your stress system will read those thoughts as threats. Just as your sexual images and fantasies will be read by the brain as a signal to release sex hormones, so negative thoughts are likely to send signals to the stress system to release stress hormones. And the more stress hormones that are released (on top of the other physiological changes associated with stress), the more you are likely to focus on your negative thoughts and feel worse – and thus you slip into unhelpful spirals of negative thinking and more stress. Stopping this feedback is one of the things this book will try to help you do. However, as I have said before, and will say again, if your mood chemicals have become too low and stress systems too overactive, you may need some extra help in the form of medication.

Stress Spirals

A lot of what we try to do when helping people cope with depression is to stop spirals of stress. All kinds of events can happen to us at any time – our plans and aspirations may not be working out; our relationships may be falling apart; we may be involved in car accidents, financial reverses and health changes. And we may simply be overworking, trying to cope with the demands of a job, children or both, caught up in the 'hurry, hurry' society. All these experiences can be stressful to the extent that they tax our stress systems, raise cortisol levels and deplete mood chemicals. As the amount of cortisol in our system goes up, we become more focused on the negative, more fatigued and more stressed. This is shown in Figure 1.

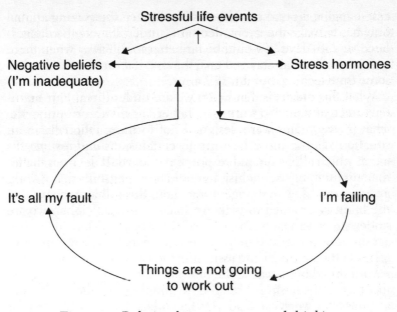

Figure 1   Relation between stress and thinking

Stress and Built-in Irrationality

There are many times in life where our decisions are not based on rationality. Falling in love, choosing this career over that one, wanting children, liking this movie but not that one – all are based on what things *feel* like to us. Our feelings can be automatically triggered and affect how we think about things and what we do. So there is another reason we can become more focused on the negatives and locked into the kind of loops described above. This has to do with the way our brains work. Basically, *our brains are built to be irrational at times!* Consider an animal in an open field having lunch. Suddenly its attention is drawn to a movement in the grass. What should it do? Should it ignore it? Wait to find out what it is? – Or get the hell out of there? Now, in many cases in the wild, the best thing to do is 'get the hell out of there', because the movement could mean the presence of a predator, in which case hanging around could be costly. In fact, the grazing animal only has to make the wrong decision (underestimate the danger) once, and it's dead. It would be far better to run away when there was no need to than stay and take the risk. If it runs away it has lost some time feeding, but it is still alive.

What this means is that when we are under threat, our brains have been designed to work on a 'better safe than sorry' principle. That is, our brains were designed not to think rationally in all situations, but at times to jump to conclusions *and assume the worst*, which allows a rapid response if needed. It does not matter that this jumping to conclusions could be wrong, only that it works and protects us. The strange thing about this is that it means that the brain is designed to make mistakes, especially when we are under stress: to lead us to assume the worst and take defensive action unnecessarily. It helps to recognize that when we find ourselves being irrational and assuming the worst, this is not because we are stupid but because the brain has a natural tendency to do just that – to catastrophize. Today, jumping to conclusions and assuming the worst can lead us to feel pretty miserable and lock us into stress loops (see Figure 1), so we need to bring our rational minds to bear on the situation to help us gain more control over our feelings.

With insight and effort, we can learn to go some way towards correcting the false assumptions the brain makes. In fact, this is what people who are able to control their stress often do. They may have the same kinds of negative thoughts to start with; but they then break out of that kind of stress loop above by say things like, 'Well, I know things look bad for me now, but they will likely improve. Three months from now, this will be past and sorted. I can probably get X to help me. I'll go and have a cry on Y. Life can be a bitch to many people. It's not my fault.' And so on. Look back at Figure 1: you can see the difference in these kinds of thoughts from the loop.

Of course, breaking out of the loop may not be easy. People who are vulnerable to depression may not have anyone from whom they can seek emotional support, or may feel it is shameful to ask. We will discuss this later; but you can see that at some point we need to break this loop that will lead into a downward spiral. If you are so exhausted that you can't sleep and life has become very black, you may need to try some medication. But we also need to stand back and look at how we think and how we cope, and recognize just how much damage our negative thoughts (natural though some of them might be) can do to us.

Parts II and III of this book offer ways to do this. For the moment I hope that you can see that depression is not just psychological, or 'all in the mind', or a sign of a weak character. Depression is about how our bodies and brains respond to stress. Depression is about genetic and developmental sensitivities. And, of course, being depressed and tired can itself be stressful and depressing. If you feel ashamed of being depressed, remember that you did not design your body to respond as it does – you'd much rather not be stressed and depressed. If you don't like the term 'depression' then tell yourself you are exhausted or burnt out or in cortisol overdrive, and seek help – but recognize that there are things you can do to help you regain some balance and get your stress spirals under control.

Now, you may be asking: 'Why has nature allowed our brains and bodies to become so easily overtaxed by the way we live?' It's a good question: and it takes us into another journey – a journey into the reasons why our capacity for getting depressed may have evolved. It's an interesting story, as we will see in the next chapter.

Key Points

- Depression involves changes in body and mind.
- For some people there is a genetic risk of depression, but biological sensitivity can also arise from early life experiences.
- As we become stressed, biological changes take place in the brain, and these can lead us into downward spirals.
- Some of our negative ways of thinking are due to the way stress works to make us focus on the negative and assume the worst.

continued on next page

- Learning to exert more control over our lives and our thoughts can help us in many ways, not least by giving our brain chemistry a chance to recover.

3

Causes of Depression: How Evolution May Have Shaped Depression

In Chapter 2 we looked at some of the 'mechanics' of depression – that is, how it seems to work on the inside. We saw that depressed states may be associated with genetic dispositions, and with various forms of stress. Is it possible that, like some of our emotions, depression evolved to have some useful *functions*? In other words, are there innate mechanisms in the brain that produce depression? Evolutionary theory suggests that the answer is 'quite possibly' – or at least, that *some aspects* of depression may have an innate basis for all of us.

Emotions and Their Uses

To get a feel of this, let's first think about emotions. Different emotions evolved because they help us to see and react to the environment in different ways:

- *Anger* tends to be brought into play when goals are blocked – it makes us try harder. It can also be used to retaliate against another person if he or she is the source of the blocking or threat.
- *Anxiety* is focused on threats – it gives us a sense of urgency, prompting us to do something to escape or reduce the potential harm of a threat.
- *Disgust* makes us want to expel noxious substances or turn away from them.
- *Jealousy* may be useful to ensure that actual or potential lovers stay loyal.

- *Love* cements bonds and makes people support and care for each other.
- *Guilt* makes us wary of exploiting or harming others, and prompts us to try to repair the relationship if we do.

Emotions, then have certain functions, even if they are unpleasant and painful to us. Imagine what a person would be like who did not have the capacity to feel anger, fear, love or guilt. These emotions are part of our being; they have evolved as part of our human nature. So evolutionary theory suggests that we can suffer various painful states of mind because we have innate potentials to switch into them. For example, if someone we love dies, we can find ourselves in a deep state of grief. And very unpleasant it is too, with its associated sleep problems, crying, pining, anger and feelings of emptiness. We might have learned to share these feelings or to keep a stiff upper lip, but there is, in most of us, a potential grief state of mind. As another example, we all have the potential for aggressive, vengeful fantasies and attitudes: if someone harmed your child, your inner desire for revenge could be intense. And, of course, we all have the potential for feeling sexually aroused or anxious. All these possible feeling states are in our genetic blueprint. And there may be genetic and developmental differences among us that affect just how easily or intensely these emotions can be triggered in each individual.

We can, however, have innate potentials for many negative (and positive) emotions but never (fully) activate them. Suppose nobody you love dies before you? In that case there might never be an occasion for profound grief, and even though you almost certainly have the innate capacity to experience grief, you never actually feel it. And if no one does you or your family serious wrong, you may never experience the urgent and repetitive nature of vengeful thoughts and feelings. The fact that many people don't suffer certain states of mind (e.g. grief, sadistic vengefulness, depression) does not mean they do not have some capacity for them.

But, you may well ask, what is the point of depression? The adaptive value of anger, anxiety and love is easy to see from the examples given above, but depression seems so unhelpful – and, to be frank, it often is.

One way to answer this question is to think about what exactly depressed people feel, think and do, and wonder if aspects of these reactions might have been useful as humankind was evolving in the past. We know that depressed people often lose energy and give up on things; they see themselves as inferior, even worthless; they lose confidence and behave submissively rather than assertively and dominantly; they become irritable and hide away; they want others to give to them rather than having to give to others. So just as we can ask, 'When was it useful to get anxious or angry?' we can ask, 'When might it have been useful for our ancestors to give up on things, to see themselves as inferior and to behave submissively?' In other words, what is the possible value of these states of mind?

Stopping Us Chasing Rainbows

One view of the adaptive function of milder depression is that it helps us to give up aspirations that we are unlikely to fulfil. Because a depressed mood reduces the pleasure derived from certain things, we are more likely to turn away from them. Without any internal signal that could prompt us to give up pursuing the unobtainable, we could well continue to pursue it and so waste a lot of time and energy. Low mood, on this interpretation, is basically a 'give it up' signal. If this is the case, we would expect to become mildly depressed when we have to give up things we value because we realize we're unlikely to succeed in gaining or keeping them. Frustration may be one consequence of this; low mood may be another. In other words, lowness of mood can be both the stimulus to, and the response to, renouncing something we desire. Whether the mood is a mild dip or more serious depression may depend on whether we are able to accept giving up and come to terms with our loss, or whether we keep pursuing the unobtainable and failing. We will explore this question is in some detail in Chapter 17 on coping with frustration and disappointment.

Reactions to Loss: Depression as Grief-Like

It has been suggested that some forms of depression are like grief.

Many animals become stressed when they lose contact with close others. Many very young creatures, including rat pups, baby monkeys and human infants, can show a protest-despair response to separation from, or loss of, the mother. Commonly, at first the infant protests and becomes more active (restless, angry and anxious, and in humans tearful) but if the mother does not return the infant can become quite withdrawn. This condition has been called a *despair state*. It is believed to help the infant conserve resources and stop drawing attention to itself as an unprotected juvenile, which would attract predators. Interestingly, there are genetically determined variations in the 'despair' reactions of different infant animals: some become seriously incapacitated by such losses and separations, while others are less affected.

The reason we need closeness and feel good when we feel connected with others (and bad when we feel disconnected) is biological; it is an evolved need, especially in children. The mechanisms for coping with loss, which have evolved over millions of years, seem to be the rough blueprint for many of our human responses to serious personal loss. We too can go through a protest stage of feeling angry and looking for the loved one, followed by numbness and despair. Of course, most grief in humans is complex, and people can move back and forth through several phases, so I do not mean to oversimplify it, only to indicate that there are evolved mechanisms at work. Acute grief is a stress state associated with elevated cortisol levels. 'Attachment losses' are painful and stressful because we are biologically set up for them to be so.

In some depressions the protest–despair mechanism works in very subtle ways. It is as if there is a continuous background sense of not really feeling close enough or connected enough to others, and yet desperately wanting to. Sometimes people become depressed even though they have not *recently* experienced any actual major loss, but in the course of therapy it may turn out that they have never felt loved or wanted by their parents or partners, and are in a kind of grieving state for the closeness they lack. Some people want to be close to others, but in their early family life have experienced closeness as associated with punishments or threats, or as something withheld or not available. Thus we can have a deep yearning for closeness with others (it's part of our nature) but also a basic belief that we are unlovable and/or that other people are unreliable and will severely disappoint us. The depression has to do with our being in a state of wanting closeness but being unable to get it. And, of course, feeling like this is also a chronic form of stress that ticks away in us.

How We Relate to Others

In everyday life we develop different styles of relating to others. Some people experience what is called *anxious attachment*. They are frightened of being rejected or abandoned; they become anxious if left on their own and angry at separations. In contrast, other people may decide that attachments to others are just too painful and difficult, and so they *avoid* closeness. Others move between anxious and avoiding styles: sometimes they seem to want a lot of closeness and reassurance that they are loved (and lovable), but at other times they are aloof and distant. This style can be difficult for partners, who can't always make sense of the person who is needing closeness today but wants to escape tomorrow. So (stressful) conflicts can arise. All of us can have these various relating styles to varying degrees, and stress can affect them. For example, when we are under stress, we may want more reassurance and closeness from our loved ones; but when our jobs are going well and we feel good, we may want less closeness and more freedom to come and go.

Lonely, despair-type depressions can arise when it seems that we cannot get close enough to others; we feel cut off and solitary. When people are depressed they often feel emotionally alone and isolated – this is part of the depressive experience. It can feel as if there is a barrier between oneself and others. But depression can also arise from too much closeness. We may feel trapped and weighed down in relationships and can't get away, or don't have enough space or distance from others. And we might feel guilty about even wanting to get more space. The common theme in too much and too little closeness is the stress they cause (see Chapter 2).

Helping Us to Avoid Fighting
Against Overwhelming Odds

Another evolutionary approach looks at why some depressed states are associated with feeling *inferior to others, subordinated* and *defeated*. The grief model described above does not really tell us why depressed people would feel like that. So we need to consider the fact that depression makes us give up attempting all sorts of challenges and reduces our aspirations; it knocks out our optimism and 'go for it' attitude; it can leave us with feelings of inferiority and shame. How could this have been adaptive?

According to this approach there are biological differences between animals who have high rank and those who have low rank. It is now known that animals that have been subordinated or have suffered a lot of attacks from others show similar behavioral and biological changes to those humans who suffer from depression. Very subordinate animals have low levels of the mood neurotransmitter serotonin and raised levels of cortisol compared to higher-ranking animals. In some very subordinate animals their stress systems are in overdrive. Some of this stress is caused by the harassment of subordinates by higher-ranking animals. But there is another aspect to it. If an animal is highly subordinate then it might not be a good idea to stroll around the place as if it were powerful, competent and dominant – to do so will only invite attacks that it will lose, probably being injured in the process. So it is in the subordinate's interest to keep a low profile, not be ambitious and look out for trouble. Toning down the mood chemicals and raising the level of stress hormones is one way the brain enables an animal to behave like a subordinate: that is, stay out of trouble and be socially on guard.

Now, humans evolved from primates, all of which have for millions of years lived in groups where some are dominant and (most) others are more subordinate and wary. So the inner mechanisms for living like this (submitting and keeping a low profile) are part of our nature. Some depressions, then, may be related to potential states of mind that can be triggered by certain no-win situations and/or where there is *enforced subordination* (feeling you have to do things you don't want to, often because of fear; feeling that others seem to have more power over you than you want). There is a kind of 'stay low' mechanism. This may be a reason why depressed people often feel inferior, worthless, and at the bottom of the pile (like a low-ranking animal) and find it difficult to be assertive.

Subordinate Thinking

'Subordinate thinking' or 'thinking of oneself as a subordinate' is very much a part of how many depressed people think about themselves. Depressed people may label or judge themselves and/or feel judged by others in ways that not only are negative but also suggest they have been allocated a low rank or status. In extreme cases, they might actually be ostracized and excluded by other people. Judgments such as 'inferior', 'unlovable', 'worthless', 'bad', 'inadequate', 'useless' and so on are, in effect, assignments of status that assign the individual a low rank in the social order. Mood, then, is partly an energy control system that signals status and confidence. Basically, the better our mood the more confident we feel and the more we seek out those things that are important: friends, sexual partners, good employment, etc. Like our primate cousins, the more confidence we feel the more we stand tall and display that confidence. As our mood goes down, our confidence slips away as if we are becoming subordinate in a potentially hostile or rejecting world, and we take a low profile. Indeed, depressed people don't stand tall but tend to slouch with head down and eyes averted. We may put on a front, but as our mood drops further this deception is harder to keep up; we lose enthusiasm for trying to 'go for it' and want more and more to get out of the way and hide.

Of course, if we are happy being subordinate (and often we are), and we feel the 'higher ranks' will help us rather than just look down on us, then being subordinate is not stressful. Letting others take the strain can be a good choice. The kind of subordination that is stressful and is related to depression is the kind that is forced and/or unwanted. Many kinds of unwanted subordinacy are easy to see: in being bullied, for example, and/or criticized and unsupported, individuals are being treated by others like inferior subordinates. Other cases are more subtle. Darren's wife had an affair with another man. Darren concluded this was because she preferred this other man; therefore, in his wife's eyes, he was inferior to her lover and as an inferior would lose any 'battle' to win her love. He became depressed, with an acute sense of being in a subordinate position (to the other man) and not able to do anything about it except be angry (and risk driving his wife away) or leave someone he loved.

To show you how, for humans, thoughts are often involved in our sense of (stressful) inferiority, consider two women of, say, sixteen stone. One says, 'Well, I would like to be thinner for health reasons – but hey, "big is beautiful" and I am a really nice person.' For this person her weight is not related to feeling inferior. But the other woman says, 'Oh God, I am so fat nobody will love me. When I look at the magazines I see how fat I am. I can't let others see me like this. I will just hide away and not go out to night clubs or parties.' This woman has an acute sense of inferiority and being subordinate to other (less weighty) women. And because she hides away, she will get more depressed.

So, we can feel inferior for many reasons; but the important point to note here is that unwanted inferiority (which often comes from how we see and think about ourselves) is stressful and can make us behave like subordinates: we lose our confidence and want to hide at the edges rather than be in the centre of things. This may be rooted in evolutionary mechanisms, where being in an unwanted inferior position can trigger subordinate behavior and sap confidence. It also affects the mood chemicals we noted in Chapter 2. And note how, feeling like this, one might behave in ways that make the situation worse. Hiding away and not going out much just makes you more lonely and isolated.

You have probably noticed yourself how your moods make you behave more or less like a fearful, unconfident subordinate. One day you might just feel down. The confidence that was previously there feels as if it has suddenly gone, and you don't feel like facing the world. Or think of the extrovert man who loves parties but then gets depressed. An invitation for a party drops through his door: he feels anxious about it, and thinks it is all just too much effort. He does not go. So you can see that mood seems to be strongly linked to feeling subordinate in some way, and prompts us to keep a low profile and stay on the edge of things even when we don't really want to be like this.

If you can learn to challenge those inferiority thoughts and break the link between subordinate feelings (e.g. anxiety, unhappiness) and behavior (hiding away, loss of confidence) and stress, you will feel better.

Feeling Defeated

Feelings of exhaustion and defeat often pervade our experience of depression. The key feature of defeat is having engaged in some kind of struggle to do or achieve something, and feeling one has lost. *Defeat states* are designed by evolution to make losers tone down their efforts and pleasure. Think of how losers in competitive sports behave, in contrast to winners. The winners go out on the town to celebrate; the losers may slink off home, not wanting to socialize much. Although some losers are more graceful and resigned to the outcome than others, these are pretty universal reactions, though of course they vary from very mild to severe.

It is very important that we learn to cope with defeats and setbacks, because unfortunately many of us won't get through life without them. However, there are ways of thinking that make accepting defeat very tough. Some people take setbacks or defeats as evidence of some personal inadequacy. This eats away at the inner sense of oneself. We may set ourselves up for this by thinking that being an 'OK person' depends on being successful. If so, what happens if you try for something and fail? Then, by definition, you are not an OK person. So, by thinking in certain ways, we can allow a defeat to make us feel like failures: subordinate and inferior. Below are some other examples of this kind of thinking, most of which we will meet many times later in this book.

Unrealistic standards   We are often taught, 'whenever things don't work out, try, try and try again'; or, 'you can do anything if you really want to'; or, 'if X can do it, so can you.' Sometimes this is encouraging, at other times it is just silly advice. Sure, these slogans can inspire us to put in effort; but they can also set us up for impossible dreams and expectations which cannot be met and so will end in defeat for us. A subordinate animal that kept challenging a dominant would sooner or later get seriously injured. It might be better for it to accept its position and set realistic expectations.

We can set ourselves up for feelings of defeat when we aim too high, trying to be perfect and/or never to make mistakes. Since this is impossible to achieve, we will feel constantly defeated due to the high standards we set ourselves (see Chapters 17 and 18). And our tendency to fall into a low mood when things go wrong may make our endeavours even more difficult.

Others are better than me   It is often said these days that we are more vulnerable to depression because our expectations are too high, and so we are inevitably going to get disappointed and feel defeated. I agree that this is the case for some people. They can get carried away by what they think they should have or should be. But the problem is also one of social comparison (and relative inferiority). It is because we think that others can be a certain way (cope with stress and troublesome kids) or have certain things (good jobs, fast cars, fashionable body shapes and lots of sex) that we – with the help of the media – develop these expectations in the first place. It is the sense that we are 'not making it' while other people are that causes the pain and can leave us feeling defeated. 'They can do it; it's only me who can't.' This is also a theme of shame, a subject we shall consider in detail in Chapter 13.

I must be better than others   Oliver James, in his TV program *Britain on the Couch* (and his book of the same title) interviewed boys from a wealthy private school and found that few of them would be happy unless they got straight A's in their exams. Their expectations and need to 'compete at the highest level' were such that they had lost all sense of perspective and were terrified of failure. Women compete to look like the dolls of the catwalk and the media. The greater the intensity of competition and the more extreme the standard aimed at, the greater the risk of depressing defeats.

Self-criticism on top of a sense of defeat   Our anger at the disappointment of a defeat can turn into an attack on the self. Depressed states of mind often focus on feeling worthless, inferior, not up to it and inadequate compared to others. The messages that others, or we ourselves, are giving us are not messages of love, acceptance and value, just when we need these things most, but of criticism and put-down. The more hostile the criticism, the more the stress system is activated. In many depressions there is a connection between feeling defeated, feeling subordinate and inferior, and continually knocking ourselves further down.

Chronic conflicts Feelings of defeat can come from chronic conflicts in our relationships that we never seem able to win. Often these involve much (usually unexpressed) anger, accentuated by a feeling that we always lose these battles, or 'can't afford' to say what we 'really feel'. For Fran, the conflict was with her mother. Whatever she did, her mother would always find fault and tell her how she should have done it. Fran never felt able to tell her mother what she felt about this, and developed a deep sense of being no good, and that whatever she tried to do it would never be good enough. If they did have arguments, it always felt to Fran that her mother was by far the stronger person, and exerted a hold over her. Fran often felt like a defeated subordinate in many of her relationships.

Losing sight of the positive The sense of anger and loss associated with a major setback can make it seem like a defeat when it is not. This then can make us lose perspective on the things that are good in our lives. We can overestimate the damage a major setback can actually do. This may be because (as we saw in Chapter 2) the biology of stress tends to make us focus on the negative. A student had to do a major rewrite of his PhD. Feeling defeated, a failure, angry and overwhelmed, he killed himself. The fact that he had a job that would have supported him financially, many friends, and considerable sporting talent, and that he might well have got his PhD if he had put in the extra work, was all of no avail when he was faced with what he saw as a major defeat *in one area* of his life. He believed that if he had been good enough this would not have happened to him; and now he felt too exhausted to pick himself up to do the work necessary.

One of the themes we will look at in this book is how defeat and disappointment can so easily make us lose perspective, and how as a result we can become extremely negative (angry and more stressed). Rather than allowing this to happen, it is important not to let our evolved brains dictate what we will feel.

Entrapment

The 'defeated depressed brain state' is particularly likely to be activated in situations of enforced subordination and entrapment. Someone in an unhappy marriage or a terrible job, or living in a place that he or she hates but can't get away from, can easily come to feel stuck, with no way out. This kind of perceived entrapment is a chronic stressor. Here are two examples.

- When David, a highly paid executive, had to put in increasingly long hours at work, he came to hate his job; and the situation was made worse when a new, overly critical boss arrived. However, David had a big mortgage, had got used to a certain lifestyle, and could see no way of getting another job. He felt trapped in a position where he was being constantly pressured and criticized.
- Cathy lived in a poor area with high unemployment. With an abusive husband and little money of her own, she felt totally responsible for her two children. She felt trapped, put down and unsupported.

My colleagues and I have been exploring feelings of entrapment in depression, and we have found that many depressed people feel trapped. This is often associated with wanting to run away or get away. Sometimes people are simply not able to do this because they don't have the resources or there is nowhere to go; or they may stay because they feel guilty about leaving or moving away from others. Sometimes actually getting away is helpful, but at other times exerting more control or becoming more assertive reduces the desire to escape. The key point is that strong desires to escape means that the fight/flight system is active, and this is part of the stress system. So the more people want to get away, the more they are likely to be a state of high stress. And, of course, the more they brood on their entrapment, the more stressed and depressed they will be.

Overview

It is clear, then, that certain states of mind can be turned on by certain situations. There are two particular reasons for exploring these ideas with you here. First, it will help you to make sense of some of your experiences of depression. It is not just *any* stress that can trigger depression, but *certain kinds* of stress – it is stress that is related to (perceived or actual) losses and defeats, which often cause people to feel inferior, worthless and trapped. These seem the most crucial aspects of the stress–depression linkage. Second, and perhaps more important, if you grasp the essentials of this approach you will see that what happens to people when they are depressed has to do with the activation of potential inner states. If you think of depression as being a part of you that has been triggered, you may be able to exert more control over it. Your depression is one of many potential states of mind; it is no more the 'real' you than any other state of mind you might be in.

When and Why Depression is Not Adaptive

It is important to emphasize that although we can understand the underlying mechanisms of depression and how some of these mechanisms may have had adaptive functions in the past, this does not mean that depressions today are adaptive. Often they are not. So why can depression be maladaptive? Well, in the first place, evolution cannot go back to the drawing board and redesign systems from scratch. It has to work with what is already there. For example, think of most of the animals you know about. How many of them have a *pair* of lungs, *one* heart, muscles to move *four* limbs, *two* eyes located above *one* nose and *one* mouth, *two* ears on the outside of the head, a blood supply, an immune system, a digestive system that takes in food one end and expels waste the other, and so forth? Humans and many other animals are all based on the same general design, with added and modified differences.

The brain is included in this general pattern: the areas of the brain that process threatening information and release stress hormones are fairly similar in rats, monkeys and humans – and the pituitary is a key player in all these species.

Although life has got much easier in many ways for a lot of us (we in the West suffer less disease, famine and war than our ancestors) there are also many stresses and strains on us now that were not present as we evolved which can overtax our systems. Some researchers think that the rising levels of depression in modern societies could be attributable in part to aspects of our society overstressing emotional systems that were designed for simpler lifestyles of millions of years ago. Culprits might include overworking and generally competitive lives (e.g. working long hours to keep our jobs; women competing to be thin with computer-enhanced images in the media); segregating systems (e.g. women on their own trying to cope with young children); and exclusive tendencies (e.g. poorer people being unable to gain access to the benefits that wealthier others can afford, while being only too aware through the media just how much others have). And while marriage works well for many, we are not monogamous by nature. When relationships go wrong, we can feel trapped in them.

In just the past few years a number of books have appeared that explore this issue of how troublesome our innate needs (e.g. for love, sex, status and approval, friendships, a sense of belonging and community) can be in modern societies which do not always respect them. One consequence of this discrepancy is that our stress systems have become too easily triggered, are too intense for the level of actual threat, and stay turned on for too long.

Triggers

We want our emotions and moods to be triggered when they are needed – but not otherwise. If we vomited after every meal, got anxious whenever something new happened, or flew into a rage or got depressed every time things didn't go our way, then we could see that our responses were being too easily triggered. If this is the case we might need to become less sensitive to events that trigger our emotions and moods; that is, to desensitize ourselves. People who have food allergies often try to desensitize themselves in various ways, for example by gradual exposure to the substance to which they are allergic. The same principle applies to our emotions and feelings. Sometimes we need to make our emotions and moods less volatile by learning new ways of coping and re-interpreting some of the things that trigger negative feelings. If anxiety is a problem, you may need to follow a routine of gradual exposure to the things that make you anxious, rather than avoiding them entirely, so that over time you retrain your mind not to trigger anxiety so easily. This book will explore ways to do this for low moods too, by changing thinking patterns.

Intensity

Sometimes our responses to things are too intense. Too much fear in (potentially) friendly social situations can lead to excessive shyness and social anxiety. Too much guilt can lead to difficulties in being assertive. Too much anger can make loving relationships difficult. So one of the key issues in life is *how to manage our emotions*. Because evolution has designed us to have various emotions and moods, it does not follow that they will work adaptively in all situations. Again, changing the way we interpret and think about things can help us reduce the intensity of some of our feelings.

Duration

Sometimes a low mood or negative feelings may go on for too long. In fact, many of our negative emotions and bodily defensive responses are designed for short-term, not long-term use. For example, suppose you eat some bad food and get food poisoning. You may vomit and have diarrhoea. This is not pleasant, but it is an excellent defence against noxious substances and gets rid of them quickly. What happens, though, if this goes on for days? You become very sick, because you will start to dehydrate and lose important body vitamins and minerals. In fact, before the advent of modern medicine many people died from food poisoning because their vomiting and diarrhoea went on too long – they became weak and could not sustain themselves. So here is the paradox: evolution has designed a bodily defence system that can also kill you! The fact that on the whole this system does more good that harm should not lead us to underestimate how damaging it can be.

Or take stress. We saw earlier that short-term stress reactions were often helpful; but, like diarrhoea and vomiting, they can become very unhelpful. Indeed, chronic stress is bad for your heart, your immune system and your moods. So one of the key ideas to grasp is that evolution has not designed, and does not design, perfect systems. What this means is that we need to think about the factors that turn off negative feelings and low moods by becoming aware of factors that maintain them.

Recovery

This chapter has taken us around the houses a bit, but by now you will, I hope, have come to see that some aspects of depression, like our emotions, may have had adaptive functions. However, this does not mean that all depressions are adaptive. Far from it. In many cases where people cannot cope with the stress they are under, depression gets locked into a negative feedback cycle. They may be unable to get away from the stressful situation, or it may be that the way they think about themselves and their situation is making matters much worse; or both conditions may apply. People living like this can simply become exhausted. When this happens, we need to find ways that we can give our stress (and other) systems a chance to recover. One way is to take antidepressant drugs. Some people are reluctant to take medication, saying that they feel the drug is shielding them or making them less responsive to stress – as if the drug acts as a barrier. They see this negatively – but they shouldn't, because this may be exactly what is needed. If you have too much stomach acid, you may take an antacid to allow the system to settle down and cure itself. Or if we have a serious cut, we put a dressing on it so that it can heal. We don't keep picking at it, or leave it open to infection; we cover it and protect it. We don't worry about doing this, because we know we are giving the system some time to repair itself. When I did have some bad stomach pains and had an investigation in hospital it was discovered I had mild inflammation. It was very painful, but not serious. I took some medication; but my friendly doctor also advised me not to eat over-large meals or to eat late at night, not to drink too much alcohol, and not to smoke. In other words, I had to protect my stomach *and* change my lifestyle a bit.

In many cases of depression the principles are exactly the same. Drugs may be necessary to protect your stress systems and boost certain mood chemicals that may have been depleted. But there are also many things that you can learn to do that may help protect you in the future. One of these is to exert more control over *the way you think* about stressful situations, so that you don't unintentionally overstimulate your stress systems by losing perspective and focusing only on feelings of defeat, failure and inferiority. By changing how you think and some of your key beliefs, you may change your triggers for depression, reduce its intensity and find ways to come out of it, rather than thinking and behaving in ways that keep you in it. Learning ways to do this by changing the way you think is what this book is about.

Inner Compassion

In Parts II and III we will explore lots of ways in which you can try to bring your stress and depressing thoughts under control. For example, we will explore the value of writing things down to slow down your thinking, look at the evidence for some of your negative thoughts, and show you how to come up with alternatives for your negative thoughts. However, I am also going to stress the importance of developing *inner compassion*. The reasons for this are quite simple, and they relate to how our brains work. Basically, our brain is designed to respond to negative signals, such as being criticized, rejected, threatened or abused, by increasing stress and (if we can't defend ourselves) reducing our mood chemicals. On the other hand, in general the brain responds by *reducing* stress hormones and *increasing* mood chemicals when we receive signals of being loved, wanted, supported, approved and valued. Even our immune systems work better in supportive and kind environments compared to hostile and unfriendly ones.

Now, as we saw in Chapter 2, our thoughts can work in the same way. Remember how sexual fantasies can release sex hormones from the pituitary? So, very simply, if you are very critical and hostile to yourself and tell yourself nasty things about yourself (e.g. I'm no good, I'm inferior, I'm useless), this can act like a 'dominant' attacking a 'subordinate': it can only increase your stress and make you feel more subordinate and even worse. You might even agree, and submit to those negative, self-attacking thoughts! But just imagine what might happen in your brain if you learn to give yourself different types of signal. Suppose you start to empathize with your depression and focus on becoming more understanding, forgiving and supportive of yourself, especially when things go badly. This may not be easy, but by giving your brain different signals you will give it a chance to reduce the stress hormones and boost the mood chemicals – simply because of how the brain is designed. To put it most simply, we can learn to minimize the negative and maximize the positive. This is the road to good psychological health and well-being. Sure, it is not going to solve all your problems; but understanding how your brain works and the kind of signals that turn on stress (e.g. self-attacking, seeing self as inferior or useless) and reduce it (e.g. empathizing, self-supporting) at least gives you an insight into why treating yourself more kindly is likely to be *biologically* useful to you.

In this chapter I have tried to give you an outline of the complex interactions that take place as we become depressed. We can now see that far from this being 'our fault', changes in our thinking and feelings are partly a result of the way the brain has been put together – how it evolved. However, we have also noted that much depends on how we think about things – the kind of meanings we make. In the next chapter we will look at the psychological and social aspects of depression and see how these relate to some of the themes we have explored in the last two chapters.

Key Points

- Depression is a powerful state of mind that is related to biological processes. Your brain is in a different physical state when you are depressed from when you are not.

continued on next page

- Sometimes depression results from something that has been 'turned on' in us. Just as a painful state of grief can be turned on by the loss of a loved one, so too depression can be turned on by the problems we have in our lives and how we come to view them.
- There are aspects of depression that seem to relate to mechanisms in the brain that evolved long ago (e.g. for coping with loss of loved ones and/or coping with being subordinated and/or defeated).
- Depression therefore tends to focus our minds on certain kinds of thoughts – e.g. unlovability, inferiority, defeat or entrapment.
- Once depression starts, our thoughts can play a powerful role in whether the depressed state remains 'turned on' or comes back under our control.
- Self-attacking may activate more stress while self-supporting may reduce it.

4

Causes of Depression: Early Life, and Psychological and Social Aspects

When psychologists explore depression they focus on two key areas. The first is how we *give meaning* to events and feelings. To one person, a divorce is a tragedy; to another, a relief. To one person, feeling angry is empowering; to another, it's frightening. The second area is how we *cope* with life's difficulties. Some people are able to break problems down into manageable tasks, seek out help from others and plan ways to overcome the difficulty, whereas others feel overwhelmed, don't share their problems and hope they will just go away (see Chapter 2).

These two processes, how we give meaning to events and how we cope, are key to an approach to therapy called *cognitive therapy*. The Foreword to this book by Dr Le Fanu and the Introduction by Professor Peter Cooper outline this approach, and in later chapters we will explore it in a lot more detail. Cognitive therapists point out that, for example, if an apple falls on your head and you are depressed, you might think: 'That's typical, I can't even sit under a tree without something falling on me.' If you are in a positive frame of mind you might think: 'Oh, thank God that wasn't a coconut.' And if you are Isaac Newton you will be inspired to develop a theory of gravity and become world-famous.

Cognitive therapy helps us to see that there are many ways we *give meaning* to feelings and events, and that some meanings are more likely to increase depression than others. Even more importantly, by leaning how to challenge some of the negative meanings we automatically put on things, we may gain more control over our feelings and moods. This approach was developed independently by the psychiatrist Aaron Beck and by the psychologist Albert Ellis. Many self-help books on depression have been written using this approach, and it will also figure strongly in many of the suggestions for getting out of depression that appear in Parts II and III of this book.

The cognitive approach suggests that particular kinds of thinking go with particular kinds of problems. For example:

Problem	Thoughts
Panic	I am going to die from these symptoms of anxiety.
Social anxiety	I will do something that will make me look foolish/stupid and I'll be rejected or shamed.
Depression	I am a bad/weak/inadequate person and the future is hopeless.
Paranoia	People are out to get me.
Anger	Other people are bad/unkind, are treating me unfairly, or taking advantage, and deserve to be punished.

By focusing on the *thoughts* that are associated with certain types of problem, people can learn to see how much their depressed moods push them to see things negatively. Cognitive therapy then helps people to test the evidence for their thoughts and learn to generate alternatives. For example, we may see ourselves as powerless to do anything to solve our problems and feel totally defeated; we may see bad things as our own fault, caused by our personal inadequacies, or good things as simply luck. By learning how to test out the accuracy of these thoughts, think of alternatives and avoid damaging negative beliefs about the self (e.g. 'I am useless'), depressed people can feel better about themselves and their prospects, and are often better placed to work on their external problems.

So, being depressed often goes with *thinking* in certain ways (e.g. defeated, subordinate, inferior). However, this suggests another question. How did we get into thinking negatively in the first place?

Early Life and Core Beliefs

We saw in Chapter 2 that early life experiences can biologically sensitize people to certain forms of stress. According to the cognitive approach, when we are young we develop *basic* or *core beliefs* about ourselves, others and the world. Over time, these basic beliefs come to exert an important influence on our feelings and attitudes towards various things. For example, if children are consistently told that they are no good at sports, this is the view they are likely to develop about themselves. Consequently, they may tend to avoid sports, and because they avoid sports, they will, of course, never get better at them, thus confirming the idea that they are bad at sports. And when these children become adults, they may continue to avoid sports because, when they try to play, the feelings of looking silly or being no good can dominate their thinking. Thus early beliefs and experiences may have strong effects on people's behavior and feelings much later in life.

Core Beliefs

A *core belief* is something that you think is basic to you. So you might say, for example, 'When all is said and done I feel *this* about me,' or 'At heart I feel . . .', or 'Right in the centre of me I feel . . .' As we move on through this book, we will have much to say about core beliefs that you might hold about yourself. Now, when these beliefs are activated they can come along with powerful feelings and emotions. Cognitive therapists therefore sometimes call them 'hot beliefs', indicating their emotional power. We fail, and have a sinking feeling or sense of shamc. Our lover phones up and says he or she does not want to go out with us any more, and that 'hits' us, in the stomach maybe. It is usually the emotions and feclings that strike us first; only later do we recognize that these feelings are associated with core beliefs and ideas about ourselves. When the lover ends the relationship we wonder what we might have done wrong – why has s/he pulled out? Now, if you already have negative beliefs about yourself that come from your childhood (e.g. that you are not very lovable), you can see that the 'emotional hit' of losing the relationship will also activate these core beliefs about you, giving you another 'hit' (a deep sense of being unlovable).

Negative beliefs about ourselves or our abilities can become subdued or 'latent' rather than 'active'. But if some major life event happens – say, an important relationship breaks up – the early beliefs and ideas we developed in childhood may come back. So, in our grief over the loss of a valued relationship, we may explain the break-up by referring to those core beliefs about the self – for example, 'This relationship broke up because I am unlovable.' A negative belief/idea developed long ago influences the way we interpret events now; and because we are (now) interpreting information negatively, to fit with the belief of being, say, unlovable, the belief is maintained.

Let me give an example. Sally had a fairly neglectful upbringing. When she was still relatively young, her mother told her that she had got married when she became pregnant with Sally. Unfortunately, the marriage was unhappy and her mother would ponder on how things might have been different for her had she not got pregnant. She would often say, 'If it hadn't been for you, I would have done such and such.' Sally felt that her mother saw her as the reason she had not done more with her life. Generally, these comments were not said in anger but with regret and sadness. At times, Sally's mother had strongly hinted that she felt like leaving home. Sally had taken these 'hints' as serious threats of abandonment, and gradually developed certain beliefs and ideas: 'I am a nuisance to others. I stop people doing what they want to do. People don't really want me around. I must not do anything that might push them away. Others might leave me at any moment.' OF

Sally carried these basic beliefs inside her throughout her life. Whenever there were conflicts, she would feel anxious and think 'Maybe I'm being a nuisance' or 'I must let others do what they want to do.' If she ever felt that she was putting others out, or letting them down, she would feel very guilty. As a result, she found it difficult to assert herself (act in a dominant or confident way) and was constantly on the look-out for clues that she was being a burden to others. When an important long-term relationship with a boyfriend broke up, her automatic thoughts were: 'Well, I guess nobody really wants me. I am just a nuisance. I will never be loved for myself.'

It is important to note that these beliefs were not cold and rational, but highly charged with emotion and feelings. Can you get a feel of how Sally's life was constantly stressful because she never really felt secure in her relationships, but had to be on the look-out for threats? And can you see how, when bad things did happen, her thoughts and beliefs increased her stress levels rather than reducing them?

As you might guess, underneath this surface set of beliefs was another set. Here lay a high degree of anger. Having to give in to others all the time (in effect, subordinate herself to the needs of others) had led to feelings that this was unfair. After all, Sally hadn't asked to be born. Why should she have to keep doing what others wanted? Why was she so unlovable? But, of course, she thought that if she asserted herself, this would expose her to threats of abandonment and feeling a nuisance. So these beliefs and feelings had to be 'repressed' and avoided. Also she felt, since her mother had done her best for her, that she had no right to be angry with her mother. Even thinking about her anger towards her mother for threatening abandonment made Sally feel bad, like a traitor – and more stressed.

As you can see – and we will go over this many times – our thoughts can take us on a downward spiral into depression: as we become stressed and depressed, we have more negative thoughts; and as we have more negative thoughts, we become more depressed. Here is an overview of Sally's beliefs and feelings and how they affected her:

Early childhood experiences
- Mother said that had it not been for me she would have done more with her life.
- Worried that mother might leave one day.

Basic beliefs
- I am a nuisance to others.
- I stop people doing what they want to do.
- People don't really want me around.
- I must not do anything that could push them away.
- I must be to others what they want me to be.
- Expressing anger and/or asserting my needs could lead to rejection.

- I must be grateful for love.
- I am a bad/ungrateful person if I express my dissatisfactions.

Basic social behaviors
- Non-assertive.
- Avoids conflicts.
- Does not initiate things she wants to do.

Depression-triggering event
- Break-up of a relationship; loss of a valued person who blamed me for being rather boring.

Typical thoughts
- I am a nuisance to others.
- I can never get it right.
- It would be better if I weren't here.
- Relationships are just too difficult.
- I can't bear to be alone.

Symptoms
- Poor sleep and exhaustion.
- Constant thinking about loss and self-blame.
- Feelings of worthlessness.
- Loss of pleasure and capacity to enjoy things.
- Feeling that the future seems hopeless.
- Weight loss.
- Inner feelings of emptiness.
- Increased fear and general feelings of disorientation.

You may have noticed two things about Sally. First, there was a clear problem in her *attachment system*. She was very anxious about forming close relationships and felt vulnerable to being left and abandoned. That anxiety and fear provided the underlying stress. But the way she behaved and coped with this – in effect, her strategy to stay in contact with others – made her act like a subordinate and, at times, even a servant. Her relationships did not boost her self-esteem very much. Indeed, apart from making herself 'fit in with others', she felt that she had no power to hold on to good relationships. So when it came to asserting her own needs and opinions, she felt that she had neither the right to do so, nor any justification for doing so. As a result, her confidence was always dependent on being in a relationship. Without one, and a lot of reassurance, she felt empty and vulnerable, and often felt inferior and subordinate to others.

The Role of Early Traumas

One powerful way that some individuals learn their values and how to judge and rate themselves is through having very painful experiences in childhood. For example, if they have been sexually abused, they might come to feel that sex is bad, disgusting, dirty or dangerous – and that they themselves are in some way bad or dirty and their sexual feelings are dangerous. In effect, the trauma robs them of their sexual lives and feelings of goodness.

Sometimes parents are unable to cope with frustration, and when things get tense, they lash out at their children or call them names. This is intensely painful for the children, who find it difficult to recognize that their parents have a low tolerance for frustration. The children on the receiving end of this rage might blame themselves and think that they really are very bad. And sometimes parents are unable to give their children physical affection, perhaps because they don't know how or because they feel very awkward about it. One of the saddest things is that some parents still think that being physically affectionate towards their children, especially their sons, will turn the boys into sissies.

Affectionless Control

Research has suggested that many depressed people can look back and see that their early life was often rather barren of affection, and sometimes even very harsh. Parents may have demanded high standards or have been very controlling. This is called 'affectionless-control parenting'. Because most of us, as children, are unable to see our parents as flawed individuals with problems of their own, we tend to think that the way they treated us was our own fault – there was something about us that made them behave in the way they did. If they were very critical of us, we tend to carry on the tradition and be critical of ourselves. However, with understanding, insight and hard work, we can change these habits and learn to be compassionate towards ourselves.

Relationships and Social Needs

As we saw in the last chapter, a lack of positive experiences (e.g. love, affection, support and care) in human relationships can be depressing. One reason for this is that the brain needs certain levels of positive inputs to maintain reasonable levels of mood chemicals and low levels of stress. On the whole, human beings throughout the world tend to be happier in some situations and unhappy in others. For example:

Happy situations	*Unhappy situations*
Loved and wanted	Unloved and unwanted
Close to others	Abandoned
Accepted and belonging	Not accepted – rejected
Have friends	Do not have friends
Accepted member of a group	An outsider or ostracized
Have value to others	Have little value for others
Appreciated	Taken for granted
Attractive to self and others	Unattractive to self and others
Have status and respect	Losing status or forced into low status

Basically, the situations on the left-hand side of this list are associated with low stress hormone levels and tend to boost our mood chemicals. They are 'feel-good things', while those things on the right-hand side are associated with increased stress and dips in our mood chemicals. The reason for this is that the brain is wired up to want the 'feel-good' things. Those who were able to have these needs met – who were 'socially successful', in evolutionary terms – did better than those who did not. By 'better' we mean they survived better and left more offspring. So we are biologically inclined to try to achieve the things in the left-hand column and avoid the things in the right-hand column. Social success is wired into our emotions. The more our beliefs begin to shift towards the things in the right-hand column, the more threatened and unhappy we are likely to become.

Core Beliefs, Caring and Relating

As noted above, we can develop core or basic beliefs about ourselves – the beliefs that 'at my core I am . . . *this* or *that*'. Given how important relationships are to our feelings and moods, let's look at some of the beliefs that affect our social relationships.

Depressed people can have very negative ideas about their ability to gain support, help, affection and approval from others. These beliefs might include:

Beliefs about being a burden to others
- Nobody could care for me.
- My needs are a nuisance.
- I am a burden to others.
- It is pathetic for me to need love and reassurance.
- I can't survive on my own.
- I will always be alone.
- It is childish to need reassurance.
- A needy person is a weak person.
- A needy person is a greedy person.
- My needs are far too much for anyone to cope with.

These beliefs can make it difficult for us to reach out to others. As you can imagine, they will also increase stress and make developing positive relationships with others more difficult. Talking to friends about these feelings can be helpful, because in this way we are making attempts to reach out to others and 'owning' our needs. Indeed, knowing what our needs are, and being able to express them, is important for mental health, especially if we are successful in eliciting supportive signals from others.

We can, of course, also have beliefs *about others*. These cover two broad concerns: the refusal or inability of others to care, and views that we are entitled to be cared for but other aren't doing enough.

Beliefs that others are not available or will be angry
- Others are too busy to bother with me.
- They are not up to caring for me.
- They will punish me for needing.
- They don't understand.
- They will like me less for needing.
- They have too many problems of their own.

Beliefs demanding that others help which may push them away
- Others should give me what I want when I want it.
- My needs are more important than others'.
- If they don't give me what I want, they don't love me.
- Others are selfish if they do not attend to me.

Expressing our needs, being sensitive to others, and working in partnership with others can be hard work. This is why close attachments and other types of continuing relationships are not always easy, and take some negotiating. You can see that beliefs such as those listed above could get in the way of this process of working at relationships.

Subordination and Self-Sacrifice

If we are honest, we will acknowledge that sometimes we care for others to make ourselves feel good: 'I am a good person because I care so much.' As long as we *are* honest, and recognize that we are giving care to others to make ourselves feel good or better, fair enough. But if we deceive ourselves that our caring really is purely for the sake of the other person, with no strings attached, we can feel very let down when others do not return our care.

Sometimes, in order to feel good about ourselves, we try to turn ourselves into very caring individuals and then find that we feel swamped by the needs of others. We have, in effect, made a rod for our own backs. You may have a desperate wish to escape from the burdens of caring, but if you are habitually inclined towards self-sacrifice, this need to escape is not seen as a signal to pull back a bit and look after yourself more, but becomes a source of guilt and bad feeling. Key beliefs here are the following:

Beliefs for becoming a servant
- I must always put others first.
- To put my needs before theirs means I am a selfish person.
- I must be what the other person wants me to be.
- Self-sacrifice is good/lovable/nice.
- I need to be needed.
- If I give lots to others, they will give to me.

If you behave like a servant, others may well treat you like one. A caring–sharing relationship is difficult unless you are open and honest about your own needs. We all have social and emotional needs because we are human beings, but some people either become overly needy as adults or develop strong beliefs that their needs cannot be met, and/or that they are in some way weak or inadequate for having them.

Exploitation and Distrust

We are born with a sensitivity to cheating, because being cheated is a threat. Just think about how common it is for humans to feel angry at being cheated. Finding that your lover has been unfaithful, or that your friends have let you down, or that an important promise has not been kept – all these tend to activate strong negative feelings.

However, when we become depressed we can see deceptions almost everywhere because, under threat, the brain jumps to conclusions. When Jane returned to work after being off sick, her colleagues asked her how she was. But Jane thought, 'They are only asking this to make themselves feel better, not because they really care about me.' In effect, Jane was saying that her colleagues were actively trying to deceive her. When we are depressed, we become far more sensitive to the possibility that others are only pretending to be nice, that they are cheating us. And if we receive mild put-downs or people ignore us for whatever reason, we can read all kinds of things into that. This is because, when we are depressed, we are on the look-out for various kinds of social threat. Our basic beliefs can lead us to let these fears get out of hand.

Beliefs about exploitation
- People really only care about themselves.
- If people are nice to me it's because they want something.
- People act nice to make themselves feel or look good.
- People will use me until I am no further use to them.
- Others will exploit me if they know my weaknesses.

Status

As we saw in the last chapter, some of the issues in depression are about our social standing in the world. Do we see ourselves as equal to others or inferior? Do we feel defeated and losers, or winners? Do we feel we have the 'power' to exert some influence over our relationships, or do we feel other people have more power? Recent research has found that depressed people often feel that others have more power than they do. The following are examples of basic beliefs about our status.

Beliefs about inferiority and low status
- Compared to others I am inadequate, useless, worthless.
- I am not worth caring for.
- Others are more capable/powerful than I am.
- I am not attractive or talented enough for others to want to relate to me.
- I lack confidence to get what I want.

When Mary lost her lover to another woman, it was not so much the loss that upset her (she had had doubts about the relationship and had wondered whether she wanted it to continue). Instead, her distress was focused on the 'status thought': 'What does she have that I don't? Maybe my love-making wasn't so good. Maybe I'm less attractive than I thought.' It was these concerns with *why* she had lost out to another woman that made her feel most depressed.

Inferiority beliefs show themselves in our feelings of shame and inadequacy. When John got depressed and lost an important argument at work, he thought, 'I didn't put my point of view carefully enough. I'm inadequate. I'll never be able to win when it matters to me.' As he said later when he felt better, normally, although he would have been disappointed by the defeat, he had always lived by the motto: 'You win some, you lose some.' In this case, however, the disappointment and stress of losing had led him to start jumping to conclusions. Interestingly, at the time his love relationship was not going well, and this background stress could have elevated his stress hormone level and made it much easier for his brain to switch to feelings of defeat and inadequacy.

The Social Environment

Our ways of relating and beliefs about relationships can play an important role in depression. However, it is useful to note that the social environment can have a significant influence on these. For example, in some parts of the world women are not allowed out without covering their faces in a veil. In other places women can dress and behave as they please – go skateboarding in bikinis if they like. Some of us grew up believing that there is a God who can send us to hell if we are too sinful, while others of us think this is just sadistic nonsense. In some parts of the world one's children are likely to die before the age of five, while in other parts of the world infant mortality is relatively low. In some of our inner cities crime, drug problems, intimidation, pollution and poverty are the rule, while in the leafy suburbs these are rare. Some of us grow up with happy, doting parents; others with violent, abusive and alcoholic ones. We live in very different social worlds, and these social worlds shape the kind of stresses we will be under and the kinds of beliefs and values we hold about ourselves and others. There is no question at all that some social environments are breeding grounds of stress and depression. In our rush for economic prosperity we don't focus nearly enough attention on psychological health, and that some environments are *psychologically toxic*.

Not surprisingly, then, depressed people often have a mixture of problems, both internal (styles of thinking, negative feelings) and external. Social researchers George Brown and Tirrel Harris have found that in women external, social factors play a large role both in the onset of some depressions and in the recovery from them. They found that there are things that make us vulnerable to depression (vulnerability factors) and things that push us into it (provoking agents).

As we might expect from our look at evolutionary theory in Chapter 3, vulnerability to depression is related to having no close relationships with people in whom one can confide, feel close to and supported by. Low self-esteem – feeling inadequate, inferior, worthless, of low rank or status – is also a vulnerability factor. Importantly, some of our self-esteem comes from having roles that give us a sense of meaning, status and accomplishment, and from having friends who value our company. Some people think that being a parent and looking after children should be enough of a role to support our self-esteem, but the evidence suggests that this is not true. Although we may love our children, and they can give us many pleasures, we did not evolve to live enclosed in houses with restless, demanding young offspring – and frankly, they can tax us to our limits! Young children need a lot from us, but we cannot, on the whole, confide in them or turn to them for support and the emotional sharing of problems. Nor, on the whole, do children boost our self-esteem, at least not in the same way that adults can.

The straw that breaks the camel's back, or the event that actually *provokes* depression, is often some event that just overwhelms us. This may be finding out that our partner is having an affair, or the loss of a job that threatens us with major financial hardship, or the discovery that one of our children has a serious illness, or a personal failure of some kind. Events with long-term implications can take us that one step too far – and we fall over the edge and spiral down into depression. It is as if we suddenly become exhausted, feel out of control, defeated and trapped.

Social Roles

Social psychologists recognize that much of our self-esteem and stress come from our roles – as mother, father, worker, boss, lover, student, spouse, etc.; in other words, from what we do. Psychologists Lorna Champion and Mick Power, for example, have pointed out that our roles also give us a sense of self-esteem, status and some rank in society. Sadly, today bringing up children and being a 'home-maker' or 'housewife' are not seen as roles conferring much status, despite these being some of the most important and emotionally taxing activities that people can tackle.

A major concern with depression in young people is that they may lack clear roles, especially if there are few jobs available, and may not feel part of their communities. Feeling that we have something to offer to others and that we are appreciated and valued for what we do are important sources of self-esteem and social status. Jobs also give us some direct control over our lives, as well as allowing us to plan for the future and providing opportunities to interact with other people. Without jobs, we can feel unwanted by society, feel deprived of an identity, and find it difficult to make plans. We can also feel socially isolated.

Sometimes we invest a lot in a certain role, and then if that fails we go under with it. Consider Kath. She had always wanted to get married but had never met the right person. However, she had dedicated herself to nursing and this had become her life. Then, at the age of 54, she developed a serious illness, which meant that she had to take early retirement. Grieving for the one thing in her life that had given her meaning, she slipped into depression and gradually lost contact with her friends, especially those who were still working.

Many who come to therapy have, as part of their depression, problems in being able to find work or some other meaningful, status-boosting role outside the home. Sometimes they are too anxious to try, sometimes their partners won't let them, and sometimes it is simply too difficult. In addition, many current Western ways of life are beyond those that humans have evolved to cope with, and these unnatural lifestyles cause problems. We evolved to live in close-knit communities where children were not enclosed in small homes, but were mostly active out in the open, where friends and relatives could keep an eye on them. Young mothers were certainly not segregated from the working of the group as they are today. In my view, some of the high rates of depression are due to our abnormal social patterns and lifestyles.

One reason for exploring these social aspects of depression is to highlight that suffering from depression can arise from real social hardships and is not about being a bad or weak person. There may be things in your life that make depression more likely. Once you give up blaming yourself and feeling inadequate, you might begin to see how to make changes. It is also important to note, for example, that a life looking after children on your own does not necessarily lead to happiness. On the contrary, it has been shown that the arrival of children can lead to a reduction in happiness in the relationship of the parents. This is not to say, however, that children can't bring great pleasures. Indeed, some people become depressed when they lose this parenting role, as children 'fly the nest'.

Why are Women More at Risk from Depression?

It has already been noted that, in general, women are around two to three times more likely to suffer from depression than men. There are various theories about why this should be so.

Biology

This view holds that the higher rates of depression in women are due to differences in reproductive biology (e.g. the levels of certain hormones). It is also possible that there is something different about the female brain compared to the male brain, which increases the risk of depression. Recent research suggests that emotional information may be processed slightly differently in the brains of men and women – although whether this increases the risk of depression is unknown.

Psychology

This view holds that the higher rates of depression in women are due to differences in the way we are 'socialized' as we grow up. Women are brought up to be more accepting of subordinate positions, are schooled to be carers and, compared to men, encouraged to be less assertive or competitive. The incidence of sexual abuse is higher in women than in men. Also, the ways in which men and women recognize and cope with distressing life events may be different (e.g. women are more likely to focus on feelings and blame themselves if they have relationship problems). Women, then, are more in touch with their feelings than men, and more able to express sad and unhappy feelings; and they may also have a greater need for closeness. Women may brood more on unhappiness – although this can be because they are more socially isolated. Men, by contrast, are more likely to blame others for problems and are less able to recognize and express sad feelings ('big boys don't cry'); many see any acknowledgment of the need for affection and closeness as a sign of being weak. They are more likely to turn to drink or become aggressive if they have emotional problems.

Social Factors

This view holds that variations in the incidence of depression between the sexes are due to differences in social opportunities and gender roles. Women are more likely to occupy subordinate positions in society and the family, to be restricted to the home and to be subjected to male dominance, even abuse. Marriage particularly may not always be helpful for women if it maintains them in subordinate positions with reduced opportunities to socialize with others and to engage in meaningful social roles outside the home.

My own view is that the differences in rates in depression between the sexes and also between different communities are, on the whole, due to a mixture of these factors.

Overview

Our routes into depression are many. As noted in Chapter 2, there may be genetic factors at work, or an accumulation of stresses. As we saw in Chapter 3, all of us may have some capacity for depression related to our evolutionary history of coping with losses, being in subordinate positions and experiencing defeat; but we vary in terms of the timing, intensity and duration of the feelings that result. And, as this chapter has suggested, there can be differences between us in respect of our backgrounds or the kinds of environments that we live in that affect our propensity to become depressed.

There is, then, no single cause of depression. However, once we become depressed there are some typical things that happen, such as negative thinking and giving up positive behaviors. If we target these, we might go some way towards climbing out of depression and exerting control over it.

We are now at the end of our exploration of some of the causes of depression. In the next part of the book the focus will be on helping those who are depressed to cope. I will leave you with one key thought, to which we will return to throughout this book: namely, that *the way we think about things can itself be highly stressful*. If we are critical of ourselves, lose perspective on things, and focus only on the negatives, then this is going to make our depressions much worse. If you can learn to be less critical and more kindly to yourself, find ways to keep a sense of perspective and cope, even in dark times, then this just might give your stress system a chance to settle down and heal.

Key Points

- Depression is associated with negative thinking and reduced positive behaviors.
- Many of the things that make us feel good in life are associated with the quality of our relationships, and when we are depressed we often see our relationships negatively.
- Our early life can be one reason why we find relationships difficult and feel unable to obtain the kinds of relationships we want.
- Vulnerability to depression might arise because we carry a number of latent negative beliefs/ideas/views about ourselves (e.g. as unlovable or a failure). We often develop these in childhood.
- These basic beliefs can become activated again when negative events happen to us. As a result, we tend to explain or interpret the reasons for the negative events with our negative beliefs – e.g. 'This relationship broke up because of me – I am unlovable.'
- It is often our social roles that give us a sense of self-esteem, and not having a valued social role can be depressing.

continued on next page

- Social environments can do much to help or hinder our goals and pursuit of meaningful social roles.
- Depression is never about personal weakness or inadequacy, though we might think so. It is about how our systems have become overstressed and exhausted, leaving us feeling defeated.

PART II

Learning How to Cope

Part II lays out some self-help approaches that people suffering from depression have found useful. My advice would be to read through the whole section first – to give yourself an overview – then go back to the beginning and, step by step, work through the chapters that you feel are most appropriate to you, doing the exercises at the end of each one.

Be your own adviser: test out whether these ideas are helpful to you and decide which best suit you.

5

Initial Steps

There is really no 'one thing' that is depression. There are many types and many causes. Depression is not like having the flu or a cold. Instead, a diagnosis of depression can be applied to a varied array of people who suffer from multiple problems and difficulties in unique ways, and whose depression has detrimental effects on their confidence and energy level. For some people, depression is triggered by a major life event such as unemployment, housing problems, poverty or serious financial loss. For others, there seems to be a high genetic loading. Still others are sensitive to depression as a result of negative early life experiences, and for yet others, depression arises in the context of difficult family and close relationships or social isolation. And, of course, people can have one or many of these various difficulties. Not surprisingly, then, we will need a whole range of approaches and treatments to deal with depression. What is helpful for one person may not be to another.

In this section of the book, I will outline some of the approaches that you might be able to use for yourself, to help you cope with any difficulties you may be experiencing or at least feel less overwhelmed and pessimistic about them. Because it is the nature of depression to think negatively about ourselves and the future, it is possible that these symptoms of depression may be stopping you from taking steps which may offer solutions to some of life's problems.

Changing Your Behavior

When we are depressed, all the activities we have to perform each day can seem overwhelming. However, it is useful to try to organize them in such a way that they can be approached step by step. Take staying in bed. Now, if staying in bed helps you feel better, all well and good, but often in depression it does not. We simply use bed, not to rest and regenerate our energies, but to hide away from the world. Then we feel guilty and attack ourselves for not doing the things we have to do. Also, when you are lying in bed, you may tend to brood on your problems. Although bed can seem like a safe place to be, it can actually make you feel much worse in the long run. So the most important step is to try to get up and plan to do one positive thing each day. Remember, your brain is telling you that you can't do things and to give up trying. So you have to slowly convince that part of yourself that you *can* do things – bit by bit.

Occasionally, however, because depressed people often bully themselves out of bed with thoughts such as 'Get up, you lazy bum. How can you just lie there?', it can sometimes be useful to try the opposite tack. This is to learn to stay in bed for a while, at least one day a week and enjoy it – read the newspaper or listen to the radio and tell yourself how pleasant it is. To be able to lie in bed without feeling guilty can be helpful for some people. So when we talk about getting up to do things, this is not to 'bully you out of bed' but to encourage you to get up because lying there and brooding on problems may only make you feel worse.

Breaking Down Large Problems into Smaller Ones

Suppose you have to go shopping. Try not to think about all the hassles before you start. Instead, first look in your cupboards and make a list of what you need. When you've done this, give yourself some praise. After all, you are one step further ahead than you were before you made the list. Next, get your bags and other things together to go to the shops. On the way, focus on the fact that you are now well prepared for shopping. Again, try not to think about the hassle of getting around the shops. When in a shop, work your way slowly around until you have everything on your list.

If this all sounds a bit like following a recipe, then in a way it is. The key thing is to try to avoid being distracted by thoughts of 'It will all be too difficult and can't be done.' The evidence suggests that, when we are depressed, we lose the tendency to plan things in an ordered way and are easily overwhelmed. Challenging depression can mean deliberately planning activities step by step. I agree that this may seem a boring thing to have to do, but remember you are training your brain to think differently. If you have broken a leg, you would have to learn gradually how to put weight on it and walk again. Challenging depression step by step is simply the mental equivalent of this.

Planning Positive Activities

Often, when we feel depressed, we think we have to do all the boring things first. Now, sometimes, boring chores are unavoidable, but you should also plan to do some positive activities – simple rewards that give (or used to give) you pleasure. For example, if you like sitting in the garden with a book, going to visit a friend or taking a walk, plan to do these activities. Sometimes depressed people are very poor at including positive activities in their plans for the day. All their time is spent struggling to get on top of the boring chores of life. They may feel guilty going out and, say, leaving the washing up undone. But we need to have positive activities. If we don't, it is like drawing on a bank account without putting anything into it. The positive things you do can be seen as depositing money in your account. Each time you do something that gives you pleasure, no matter how small that pleasure is, think to yourself: that's a bit more in my positive account.

Coping with Boredom

Some depressions are related to boredom. The lives of some depressed people have become repetitive and boring. Sometimes this appears unavoidable. However, again the key issue here is to diagnose boredom and then take steps to challenge it. One of my patients had gradually slipped into a lifestyle that involved going to work, coming home, watching TV and going to bed, having given up meeting friends and planning activities with them. Slowly, step by step, he began to think of things he would like to do, and then tried to see if he could do at least some of them. One of the things was joining the local football club and getting involved as a social member. Another was joining a local charity group and helping with fundraising.

Some depressions are related to feeling socially or emotionally isolated, lonely and understimulated. The problems are social and environmental ones, and low moods may be a natural reaction to boredom and a lack of social stimulation.

Women who are trapped in the home with young children are particularly vulnerable to boredom. Again, the main thing here is for them to recognize that they are bored and begin to explore ways of getting out more and developing new contacts. They could perhaps contact mother-and-baby groups, and ask their friends about other activities. If social anxiety is a problem, people who are depressed like this could try to do a little more each day in making outside contacts and/or contact their family doctors to ask if there are any local groups who might be able to help them with social anxiety and getting out more.

Increasing Activity and Distraction

Sometimes, when people feel very depressed or uptight, they can also feel agitated. At these times, trying to relax does not work so well. The mind just won't settle down to it. Then they need to distract themselves with a physical activity. There are various options here. Anything that involves physical activity – digging the garden, jogging, aerobic exercises, decorating – can be helpful. Physical activity can be especially useful if you are tense with anger or frustration.

In depressed states of mind, we tend to ruminate on all the negatives in our lives and, at times, lose our perspective. If you find your mind swirling around a number of negative thoughts, try to find something to distract you. You have probably tracked through some of these thoughts over and over again. They don't take you anywhere except to feeling worse.

Now, your thoughts do affect the way your brain works. For example, suppose a group of non-depressed people decided to carry out this experiment. At eight o'clock each night, they would start to dwell on sexual thoughts and fantasies. What do you think would happen to their feelings and their bodies? What they may well find is that, when they make themselves dwell on these fantasies, their bodies begin to become sexually aroused as a result of special hormones released in the brain to prepare them for sex.

You are probably well aware that people's bodies can be changed (aroused) by the fantasies they engage in. But what you may not have considered is that depressing thoughts may also affect the types of arousal that take place in your body and the chemicals released in your brain. So, just as people might try to control their sexual thoughts by taking cold showers or otherwise distracting themselves to avoid getting too aroused when they don't want to be, so also with depression. Try to find ways of distracting yourself, to avoid feeding depressive feelings by dwelling on the negative. We will later explore how you can challenge some of these thoughts, but the first step is to recognize how thoughts themselves can have an effect on how our bodies (and brains) operate.

Creating 'Personal Space'

Occasionally there may be a problem in creating 'personal space' – that is, time to be spent on oneself. We can feel so overwhelmed by the needs of others (e.g. the family) that we allow no 'space' for ourselves. We become overstimulated and want to run away. If you find that you need time on your own, try to talk to those close to you and explain this. Make clear that this is not a rejection of them. It is, instead, a positive choice on your part to be more in touch with yourself.

Many people feel guilty if they feel a need to be alone doing the things that interest and are important to them, but it is important to try to negotiate these needs with loved ones. Most importantly, do not assume that there is anything wrong with you for wanting space or that there is anything necessarily wrong with your relationships. Relationships can become claustrophobic from time to time. If you know that there is space for you within your close relationships, this may help to reduce possible resentments and urges to run away.

Knowing Your Limits

Various patients of mine have become exhausted from overwork and then couldn't cope with the demands placed upon them. They noticed that they were failing and becoming overwhelmed, felt ashamed about their failings and became depressed. Now most depressed people are real battlers. Very rarely do I see depressed individuals who put their feet up, enjoying having time off, and who know their own limits. Sometimes this problem is related to perfectionism (see Chapter 18). A term that some professionals use is *burnout*, meaning that an individual has reached a state of depletion. Burnout can be a trigger for depression in some people. Whether you are a parent struggling to bring up children at home or someone trying to cope with too many tasks at work, try to acknowledge that you, like all the rest of us, have limits to the amount of work you can do.

Try to think of ways that you might try to replenish yourself, but most importantly, don't criticize yourself for feeling burned out – acknowledge it honestly and think through steps that might help. Are there enough positive things in your life? Can you do anything to increase them? Can you speak with others about your feelings and seek their help? Burnout can occur if we have not created enough personal space. For example, young doctors can become depressed because they have not been able (or the system had not allowed them) to create personal space and they can suffer from overwork and burnout.

All of us vary on this. Although some people may seem to be able to cope with anything and everything (and make us feel that we should be able to do so as well), this does not mean that we should. Limits are personal things and they vary from person to person and change from time to time and situation to situation.

Dealing with Sleep Difficulties

Sleep varies from person to person. My daughter and I have never been particularly good sleepers, whereas my son and wife can fall asleep almost anywhere. In addition, the ease of getting to sleep and a person's need for sleep change as people grow older, so our sleep patterns are personal to us. Don't worry about not getting enough sleep. Margaret Thatcher only slept for four hours a day! Sleep problems can take various forms. Some people find it difficult to fall asleep, others wake up after being asleep for just an hour or two, still others wake up in the early hours, and there are also those who sleep extremely lightly.

Think of sleep as another behavior that needs managing. A milky drink before bed may help. Make sure that your bed is comfortable and the room well ventilated. Plan for sleep. Don't do what I used to, which was to work late into the night and then find I couldn't sleep because my head was buzzing with the things I had just been working on. In planning for sleep, think about relaxing (and try to relax) half an hour to an hour before bedtime. Listen to relaxing music and/or do a relaxation exercise. If possible, read a book that takes you out of yourself (but not one that scares you or is particularly mentally involving). If appropriate, ask your partner for a soothing massage. Take gentle exercise during the day.

Among the things to avoid is alcohol. Having a drink (or two) may seem helpful but usually is not. It leads to disturbed sleep patterns, and you can wake early in the morning with mild (and, if you drink heavily, not so mild) withdrawal symptoms. Also don't catnap during the day. If I sleep for longer than fifteen minutes during the afternoon, this can really mess up my night's sleep. If you wake early, get up and avoid lying in bed, ruminating on your difficulties. Frankly, as a poor sleeper, if I wake early I tend to get up and work. Of course, at times this leaves me feeling tired, but I have come to accept this as my style. If your sleep pattern is very disturbed, you may find an antidepressant very helpful (see below). Some people have found that going without sleep for a whole night and not catnapping the next day can help lift mood. This, however, is best done under supervision. There are some good self-help books on the market for sleep problems.

Body Work

An important consideration is the state of one's body. Your body is like a garden, and to function well, it needs looking after. It can become exhausted and need pampering. Learn to care for your body and treat it with respect. Teach it how to relax, exercise it and feed it good things.

I would advise trying to find a sympathetic family doctor with whom you can have a frank and open discussion about your depression. In 1992 the Royal College of Psychiatrists in Britain mounted a 'Defeat Depression' campaign to increase the awareness and skill of family doctors in this area of psychological problems.

Very occasionally, depression can arise from a number of physical conditions. These include:

- problems with the thyroid gland
- anemia
- vitamin deficiency (e.g. B12)
- hormone problems
- stroke
- complications with other medications

So it is obviously a good idea to have these screened out as soon as possible. However, one should also recognize that the vast majority of depressions are not triggered by a physical condition.

Antidepressant Drugs

The next thing to consider is whether or not to take antidepressant drugs. Many people worry that these drugs are addictive, but they are not. They work in a very different way from the minor tranquillizers such as diazepam (Valium). For one thing, they take between two to six weeks to affect mood, although they may improve some of the symptoms (e.g. sleep disturbance) before this. Some people do not like the side-effects of these drugs – which include sleepiness, dry mouth and weight gain – although these usually pass after the first few weeks. There are a number of different types of antidepressants, and if one does not suit you, another one might, although most have some side-effects and work in similar ways. Any disadvantages have to be balanced against the beneficial effects that medication may have on your mood (see pages 363–8).

You should discuss these issues with your family doctor and consider the pros and cons of taking medication. However, if you are very depressed and have become exhausted by poor sleep, very withdrawn or lost interest in everything around you, one of the antidepressant drugs may be extremely helpful to get you started on the way up. In addition, there are some forms of depression that are extremely difficult to get out of without drugs.

Your doctor may also recommend that you see a psychiatrist. There is nothing shameful about this. Psychiatrists are medically trained, and although some may over-medicalize depression, their opinions can be useful. Be as open as possible about your depression and set out to get the best advice you can.

It is difficult to offer general advice here because so much depends on the type of depression you have, how severe it is and how long it has lasted. But whether you choose to take medication or not, there is now increasing evidence that working on thoughts and basic beliefs can help to alleviate many of the mild to moderate depressions and can help prevent relapses. There are also issues that drugs cannot address. After all, they can't retrain us, teach us how to manage our thoughts or solve social problems.

Seasonal Affective Disorder

Some depressions seem to come on as the longer days of summer shorten in autumn and winter. This is called 'seasonal affective disorder', or SAD, and is caused by a sensitivity to a lack of natural light arriving through the eyes to the pineal gland in the centre of the brain. One tell-tale sign, apart from the depression coming on at a certain time of year, is sleeping heavily (over ten hours in some cases) and finding it difficult to wake up in the morning.

If you suspect that your depression is related to seasonal changes, you may wish to talk to your family doctor about this. Some people find that exposure to bright light early in the morning can be very helpful, as can light boxes that give out bright rays of light at a particular wavelength; you must sit near them for up to two hours a day. At the back of this book, I give the addresses of societies dealing with seasonal affective disorder, which you can contact to find out more information about the nature of this condition and where you can buy light boxes.

Changing the Way You Treat Your Body

Eat a healthy diet   People who are depressed often eat very poor diets. Try to work out a balanced diet including fresh fruit and vegetables and a high percentage of carbohydrate (e.g. pasta, bread, potatoes). This is because these foods release their energy slowly and may help to boost certain chemicals in the brain that are depleted when we are depressed. You may wish to take advice on this. A good book is Dr Alan Stewart's *Tired All the Time* (for details, see 'Useful Books', p. 370). There is increasing evidence that weight loss itself can affect various brain chemicals. So consider if your depression came on or got worse as you lost weight. Some research has also shown that eating large amounts of sugar and other refined foods might increase irritability in some people, so try cutting out cakes and other sweet things. Some people like to take extra vitamins. The evidence for these helping depression is very unclear, but provided you are not doing yourself any harm (e.g. too much vitamin A can damage your liver), these may work as a placebo if nothing else – that is, you may become less depressed simply because you believe in the vitamins, not because they have actually had a direct effect on your brain chemistry. A sympathetic family doctor will advise you on this.

Take exercise   There is increasing evidence that, for the mild-to-moderate depressions, exercise can be very beneficial because it tends to boost the production of certain chemicals in the brain. A patient of mine, who had a bipolar illness (and was taking lithium and an antidepressant), found that, if he awoke in the morning feeling down, a vigorous swim in the local pool helped to lift his mood. When we become depressed, we tend to do less, and if you can encourage yourself to take exercise, this can be helpful. It may give you a sense of achievement – in addition to being good for you and boosting certain brain chemicals.

Reduce your alcohol intake   Alcohol can have a depressant effect, and it is usually helpful to reduce your intake, especially if you tend to drink to control your moods. Sometimes people use it to get to sleep; as we have seen, this can be detrimental. Alcohol is a bad way of managing stress and depression.

Stimulants and other drugs   If you are taking stimulants, try to get off them. This applies even to mild stimulants such as coffee. Occasionally, I've found that some of my depressed patients drink vast amounts of strong coffee – sometimes over ten cups a day. Many stimulants can have depressant and/or anxiety-increasing side-effects.

And if you are using illicit drugs, try to get off them as they will not be doing your body any good. Some cannabis smokers lose motivation and become depressed and apathetic with this drug, and if there is an underlying sensitivity, it can also lead to mild paranoia. In fact, abuse of all drugs needs to be considered here, including painkillers. If you are taking a lot of painkillers, you should see your family doctor and plan to reduce your intake.

Tranquillizers   Taking the odd tranquillizer from time to time can be helpful. However, if you have been using tranquillizers for a long time, you should think about getting off them. You must not try to come off them too quickly, but rather reduce your intake slowly. It is important to obtain medical advice from your family doctor, who might refer you to a psychiatric nurse or psychologist. There are also self-help groups and books to help with tranquillizer withdrawal.

Learning to Relax

Sometimes this is easier said than done. However, there are a variety of books on relaxation and self-help tapes on the market, as well as classes and groups. Explore these and see if you can find one that suits you.

There are some key elements in relaxation. Here is a quick guide.

Breathing   First, learn how to control your breathing.

- Sit comfortably in a chair, or lie down, and focus on inhaling and exhaling. The key thing is rhythm.
- Inhale by slowly taking the air down into your lungs (try to feel the air going down to your diaphragm), hold the breath for a couple of seconds and then exhale slowly.
- Try breathing in and out, counting slowly: IN (*one, two, three, four*), HOLD (*one, two*) and OUT (*one, two, three, four*).
- When you have found the rhythm that suits you and is comfortable, focus on the words 'in' and 'out'. In your mind say, 'In–Out, In–Out, In–Out' – in line with your breathing.

Don't strain but try to breathe reasonably deeply and slowly and make the rhythm as comfortable and as easy as possible. Once you feel happy with the basic rhythm, consider the fact that you are attempting to slow your body down and bring it to a state of relaxation. Each time you exhale, say in your mind 'RELAX' – or, if you prefer, 'CALM'. Imagine that each time you breathe out, your body is relaxing, letting go of its tension and becoming heavier, floppier (like a rag doll) and warmer.

Muscular relaxation   Once you are comfortable with this style of breathing, you can focus more on your body. There are a number of ways of doing this. First, you can focus on one part of your body at a time. As you breathe in, slightly tense one part and then, as you breathe out, focus on releasing the tension and relaxing.

- Let's start with your feet. As you breathe in, tense your feet and feel the tension. Now, as you breathe out, say 'Relax' and let go of the tension in your feet. Repeat.
- Now move on to the calves of your legs and do the same thing. As you breathe in, tense your calf muscles and feel the tension. Now as you breathe out, say 'Relax' and let go of the tension in your calves. Repeat.

Note how the muscles feel different when tense and when you let the tension go. Imagine them becoming warm and heavy. Using the same method, focus on one muscle group at a time, moving up gradually to the muscles in your thighs, lower back, stomach, chest, neck and shoulders, arms and hands, and face. When tensing your face, screw it up a little and then let go. When you have been through all the major muscle groups, focus on your whole body, allowing it to become heavier and more relaxed as you breathe in and out.

Repeat this for a while until you are familiar with the technique and what it feels like to relax. Each session should last about ten minutes or so – longer if you prefer. You can perform these techniques at any time of the day or night – you may find them particularly helpful just before bedtime. You can also use relaxation techniques when you are sitting watching the television or on a bus or in a meeting. The idea is to bring your body under more control and teach it how to relax. It is not just something you can do when you are alone or sitting comfortably, but something you can learn to do at any time throughout the day.

Next, try to use your relaxation techniques while you are walking around.

- Stand up straight but not rigid.
- As you walk around, focus on your breathing.
- Breathe in gently and reasonably deeply (but do not strain).
- As you breathe out, focus on the word 'Relax'.
- Notice how your body feels. Explore it for tension and try to relax any part that feels tense. Let your body go loose and heavy. How do your shoulders feel? Are they tense? If so, let them drop and go heavy. What about other muscles – e.g. those in your neck or forehead?
- Make a conscious effort to relax your body.
- Learn to attend to your body and get to know when you are holding tension in it. Like most things in life, this will take practice.

A key aspect of relaxation is to re-focus your attention away from your negative thoughts. The more you can concentrate on relaxing, the less your mind will dwell on other matters, and this can help to reduce depressing stress.

Other Relaxation Techniques

Some people find they can deepen their relaxation by *creative visualization* – that is, bringing pleasant images to mind. For example, when listening to the sound of your breathing in and out, see if imagining the sea coming in and out deepens your relaxation. Focus on the smell of the sea, and how gently it laps against the shore in rhythm with your breathing. With each exhalation, your tension is ebbing out of you, taken away on the tide. Other people prefer images of a cool garden or woods, or being by a river, or watching a hot-air balloon sail up into a clear sky, or even snuggling up next to a warm fire. Each of these images is personal to the person visualizing. Think of images that tend to be associated with relaxation for you. In your mind, create a place of peace and healing and return to it when you relax.

Once you have the basic relaxation techniques, you might experiment with different approaches and see which one suits you. Some people find it helpful to listen to relaxing music. Meditation, too, can be beneficial. This can be done alone or in a group. Not only might such a group teach you some useful ways of relaxing, but it will bring you into contact with others and give you a focus for a shared activity.

Key Points

- There are many forms and causes of depression.
- Because of these differences we need to have a variety of different approaches to depression.
- It can be helpful to plan activities step by step. Break problems or tasks down into simple steps and follow them one at a time.
- Try to include some positive activities in your life. At times, you may need to increase your social contacts, at other times reduce them (i.e. create personal space). Much of this is about working out your own needs.
- The type of thoughts we have can affect the way our brains work. Sometimes, certain thoughts can be controlled via distraction.
- Don't assume that you have become an inexhaustible supplier of good works. No one can be. Learn to work out your limits. If you think that there are very few things that you aren't able to cope with, the chances are that you are not working within your own limits.
- Finally, treatment often needs to be aimed at how our bodies are working. It may require us to take seriously the possibility of using an antidepressant to help us get going again. We may need to change our life styles (e.g., take more exercise, improve our diets, cut out the coffee, learn how to relax, distract ourselves).

Exercises

- Make a list of the points in this chapter that you think are relevant to you.
- Clarify in your mind:
  (a) How are you treating your body?
  (b) How are you organizing your activities? Can you plan to do things step by step?
- Make a list of the positive things you would like to include in your life. These can be quite simple – e.g. I would like to see my friends more, go to the movies more, have more time to myself. Consider ways that might make some of these things happen.

6

Thoughts and Feelings

In this chapter we are going to explore how our thoughts and feelings are often linked together, and how together they can push you down into depression. Let's begin with a hypothetical situation. Suppose you are standing in a crowded train and someone steps back onto your foot. It's quite painful. Your first thought might be: 'Clumsy idiot!' and your feelings are of irritation or anger. However, if the person turns around and you see that he or she is carrying a white stick, indicating blindness, not only might your thoughts change (i.e. it was not clumsiness) but so will your feelings. You might feel sorry for the other person, and even guilty for having felt so angry and for not realizing the situation.

The point is that, when an event happens to us, we must decide what the event means before we can respond to it emotionally. Change the meaning and the emotions change. Now one way of capturing this is to distinguish the event from the meanings we give to it and the emotions and other reactions that we may have to it. We can explore this by using three columns:

A	B	C
Event	**Meanings**	**Consequences**
Triggering event	Beliefs and key thoughts Interpretations	Emotions Behavior Physical reactions

Suppose a good friend or lover promises to phone you at 11 pm and asks you to wait in for the call, but then the time comes and goes and there is no phone call. What are the various possibilities for the consequences – what might you feel? Well, you could feel many things: anxiety, anger, sadness or even relief. And you would be absolutely right to say that it all depends on what you think the reason is for the person not phoning. That's the point. We can see this below using the three columns.

A	B	C
No phone call	Something has happened to him/her – e.g. an accident.	Anxiety
	He/she went to a party and forgot about me.	Anger
	He/she doesn't care enough to remember.	Sad
	He/she will phone tomorrow so I can just go to bed now.	Calm/relief

Automatic Thoughts

As we have already seen, jumping to conclusions is a very common response when we feel threatened in some way. In the above example, the negative emotions indicate that the lack of a phone call from the friend/lover is taken as some kind of threat. Jumping to the conclusion that, for example, your friend/lover has had an accident is called an 'automatic thought'. You can't know what has happened or the reasons why he or she did not phone until you have the *evidence*. So all other thoughts are guesses or theories. None the less, you may feel anxious or worried. Now, as the term implies, automatic thoughts are those interpretations/ideas/thoughts that seem to come automatically to mind; they are our 'pop-up thoughts'. They are immediate, consciously available thoughts that require little or no effort and can seem plausible. They are not arrived at through much in the way of reflective reasoning.

Let's consider these thoughts a little more, this time using the example of anger over the lack of a phone call. The first thing to note is that you probably don't often think in words like, 'Oh, I think my friend/lover has gone to a party and has forgotten to ring and left me waiting in for the call.' More likely, you have flashes of pictures in your mind. Can you answer these questions: Is he/she having a good time? Is he/she talking with other people? Is there music playing? Is it classical or disco music? Now, I would imagine that you can answer these questions fairly easily. This is because we often create images in our thoughts.

Sometimes automatic thoughts are difficult to catch because they happen so fast. Had I not asked you about the party, those thoughts might have gone relatively unnoticed or been only semi-conscious, but when I drew your attention to them, you may have become aware that you had had them. So, sometimes, when we feel a change of emotion, we have to focus on our thoughts and what is actually going through our minds.

It is common for automatic thoughts to occur in images, day-dreams and fantasies. As in the example above, we may construct scenarios of seeing the friend/lover in some particular place (e.g. the party) and imagine him/her having a good time, laughing, drinking and so on. We may also enter into a kind of discussion with ourselves as a result of our automatic thoughts and fantasies. For example, having decided that the friend/lover is out having a good time while you are waiting for his/her call, you may start to rehearse in your mind an argument or what you intend to say the next time your friend/lover does phone. You might even rehearse something that you know that, in reality, you would not carry out due to fear of being rejected/disliked or because of moral concerns.

Sometimes we may not be fully aware that we are constructing such scenes in our heads but experience only emotions and feel-ings. For example, when the phone does not ring, you may find yourself becoming more sad or irritated, but your awareness of your thinking processes may be hazy. Sometimes we just let the scenes in our minds run on, as if there is some 'inner director' in our heads feeding our minds various ideas and pictures that are full of meaning. Hence, we may need to train ourselves to sharpen the focus of our automatic thoughts and make them more easily known, recognized and challenged. We may need to use active imagination – that is, to allow ourselves to tune into the thoughts so that we can examine and deal with them more easily.

One Thought Leads to Another

You may have noticed something important in the examples given above – one thought leads to another. Humans are highly creative in their thinking and we are usually not happy with just one or two thoughts. At times, especially when we are heading into a depressive spiral, our thoughts spin down into catastrophes. For example, let's consider how someone heading into a depressive spiral might think about the friend/lover who didn't phone. The sequence of thoughts might go like this.

He/she hasn't phoned.
This is because he/she has forgotten about me.
Maybe he/she had better or more fun things to do.
If he/she cared about me, he/she would have phoned.
Therefore, he/she doesn't really care.
I don't ever seem to be able to find someone who cares about me.
What's wrong with me?
Maybe I am just too boring and unattractive.
I'll never have a good, long-lasting relationship.
I'll always end up abandoned.
Life is completely pointless and empty.

This cascade of thoughts can be so rapid that we hardly notice it. But rather than just being disappointed or slightly irritated by the phone not ringing, we end up feeling much more depressed because our thoughts lead us to the conclusion that we are boring, not cared for, are going to be abandoned or are being used by others. When we enter into depression, we often experience such rapid cascades of thoughts like those above. When we are depressed, our thoughts can literally run away with us and take us to the worse possible scenarios. And this can happen very quickly – sometimes within seconds.

Downward Spirals and Emotional Amplifiers

Usually thoughts like these provide feedback for each other. For example, when we are depressed we often don't feel like doing much; when we don't achieve much, we tell ourselves how useless we are; and when we tell ourselves how useless we are, we feel more depressed.

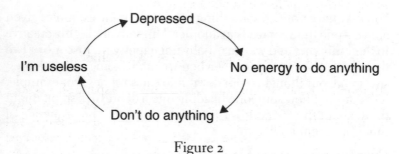

Figure 2

Now, you can probably see that, if you are caught up in this type of spiral, it will be very difficult to get out of it, unless you take steps to stop it. These thoughts might be called *emotional amplifiers* because, as they go around and around, they become more intense. There is nothing in the spiral that dampens them down. So you need to build in *emotional dampeners* – ways to break the cycle. You may also see that there are some key links in this spiral that you could challenge. You could do just a little bit of some activity and then give yourself a lot of praise for doing something even though you are depressed. You could learn to praise your efforts rather than the results. The problem here is that, when we are depressed, we often discount the small positive things we do. Unless we make big strides of progress, we tend to be dissatisfied.

Another way that you might break the circle is to say, 'Even though I'm not achieving much right now, this doesn't make me a worthless human being. There is more to me than just my uses or achievements.' Now, if you are depressed, don't be surprised if these arguments don't impress you. You can be expected to discount them – after all, you feel depressed and that's what we all do when we are depressed. We stick rigidly to what we think and the way we see things – we are not easily persuaded by rational arguments, especially from someone else. We can also become pretty arrogant and believe that only we know the truth – and thus ignore other people's point of view about us. We say that they don't understand, or can't really know – we do all kinds of things to ensure that we are correct in our negative views and others are wrong. I will explore ways to challenge these ideas shortly.

Thoughts About Feelings and Behavior

Although it is often situations and events that spark off negative thoughts, this is not always so. Sometimes, we can have inner feelings such as anger and then have thoughts about those. For example, you might think it is bad to have intense feelings of anger. Or you might have sexual feelings about someone and feel very guilty because you tell yourself that such feelings and fantasies are bad. Or you might feel anxious about something and then think that you are stupid or weak for feeling anxious. You may just wake up feeling tired and think, 'Oh, God, another bloody day! How am I going to get through it?'

We may also have negative thoughts about what we have done or failed to do. We may dwell on our actions and start to judge ourselves negatively. For example, because we are anxious, we might not go to a party or some other function to which we have been invited. We might then think that we have behaved badly and let other people down. We become preoccupied with guilt.

Because he suffered from social anxiety, Colin did not go to a friend's leaving party at work. He had the following thoughts:

I should have gone.
I've let my friend down.
He will be angry that I didn't go and will lose interest in me.
Others will wonder what's the matter with me.
I have missed out on a good time again.
I'm useless in social situations.
I'm pathetic to get anxious.

The more that these thoughts took hold, the more anxious and depressed he became.

And sometimes it is what we feel within our bodies that generates negative thoughts. For example, people who have panic attacks may notice that, when they become anxious, their heart rate goes up. This leads to the thought: 'There must be something wrong with my heart for it to beat like this.' They then focus attention on their heart rate, and because they are thinking that there is something wrong with their heart, they become more anxious. And, of course, as they become more anxious, their heart rate goes up even further. Even though the heart is basically a pump and is designed to increase and decrease its beating as circumstances require, the idea that an increased heart rate signals an oncoming heart attack produces an intense anxiety spiral.

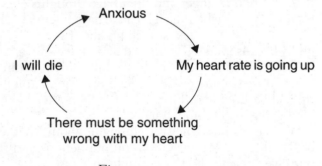

Figure 3

Hence we can see that we can have negative thoughts about ourselves, others and the future, all of which can increase our depression, and that these can be sparked off by events, our inner feelings, things we notice in our bodies or past actions.

Writing Down Your Thoughts

In Monitoring and Challenging Your Thoughts (see p. 348), I give an example of a form that can be used to write down automatic thoughts. This is similar to the one we used with the phone call example on page 85. However, in this form you will see that, in the first column, various things can spark off negative thoughts and lead to various negative evaluations and conclusions. You can include events such as people criticizing you or things not working out as you would like (like not receiving the phone call). We can also make negative evaluations of our *feelings* (e.g. I am a bad person for feeling angry; it is wrong to feel sexual towards someone else who is not my partner), our *behavior* (I should not have acted like that; I am a bad person for losing control) or our *bodies* (when my heart rate goes up, this means there is something wrong with it and I might die). Then you can fill in the other two columns as before – that is, the beliefs and key thoughts of the 'triggering' event and its consequences.

The key thing is to choose what you want to focus on, then write down the thoughts that go through your mind. If you habitually write these down, you will get better at identifying them. Writing thoughts down helps to clarify them and allows you to concentrate on them, thus avoiding having them slip in and out of your mind in a rather chaotic fashion. A good way to start is to try to notice how your moods and feelings change. Try to remember what might have been happening to you at the time they changed – for instance, a criticism, or something that did not work out as you wanted it to, or something you hadn't done or thought you ought to do. Next, write down the thoughts associated with these situations.

Another useful way to begin is, if you notice a change in your feelings, or even if you notice that you are feeling something that you can identify as anxiety, depression or sadness, ask the question: 'If my feelings could speak, what would they say to me?'

You will notice that there is a fourth column for writing down alternative thoughts. Some worked examples are given on pp. 348–54. As you go through this book, I hope that you will get better at not only identifying what goes through your mind and noting your own depressive spirals (and emotional amplifiers), but that you will also be able to challenge some of your more negative thoughts and not let that 'better safe than sorry' and 'assume the worst' type of thinking run away with you. If you find such a challenge difficult – don't worry. It takes time and practice. We are going to work on it in later chapters.

How to Identify Your Thoughts

Sometimes it is difficult to know what we are thinking, so how can you help yourself work out what is going on in your mind? Well, one way is to ask yourself some questions. For example, let's suppose that you tried to do something and it did not turn out right. You feel disappointed and your mood takes a dip. You could then ask yourself:

Question	Possible Answer
What do I think are the implications of this event?	I won't be able to achieve what I want to achieve.
What does that lead me to think/believe?	I tend to fail at most things I try to do.
What conclusions am I drawing from this situation?	I am not going to succeed in what I want to achieve.

You can also ask questions about what you think others will think or how others will react.

What do I think they will think about my failure?	They will think I'm not capable of much.

Another set of questions asks you to think about the conclusions that you might be drawing about yourself as a person. Ask yourself:

What does this say about me?	If I fail at this, it means I am inadequate.
What do I think this means for my future?	I will never get anything right.

In general, there are three basic types of question to ask yourself. These are:

1 Questions about how you see yourself as a person.
2 Questions about how you think others see you.
3 Questions about implications, including for the future.

So then, if we take our example of 'trying to do something that does not go well,' we might have a set of thoughts that are something like this:

- I have not succeeded in this task.
- Failing at this means I am an inadequate person.
- Other people will think I am not capable of much.
- I am not going to succeed in anything I want to achieve.

These thoughts might not have been obvious before we asked ourselves the questions. Moreover, taking the time to consider these questions allowed us to focus on our thoughts. By asking certain questions, we can get some insight into what we think about certain situations and events.

Like many things in life, doing this will take practice and it may seem odd at first, but after a while, you might notice that there are some repeating themes in how you think. For example, in depression, we often make negative conclusions about the future, about what others will think about us and what we think about ourselves.

Basic Beliefs and Attitudes

You may well ask: Where do these negative thoughts come from? One answer is that they are generated by the state of depression itself. But it is also often the case that automatic thoughts are generated from the various attitudes and basic beliefs we have about ourselves, others and life in general, and these predate the depression. They include such beliefs as:

- If people make mistakes, they are inadequate.
- People who show strong anger are unlovable.
- You can never be happy if you do not have a conflict-free, close relationship.
- If you have strong arguments with someone close to you, they don't love you.
- If your parents did not love you or treated you badly, you are unlovable.
- Sex is dirty.

There are many types of attitudes and basic negative beliefs like these that tend to lead to negative conclusions. In my own case, I was bad at English and I developed the negative belief: 'Being poor at English equals being stupid.' When I was depressed, this belief seemed very true to me – and I therefore felt not very bright or able. When I noticed poor spelling in my work, or I was criticized for my poor English, I would have a particularly uncomfortable 'sinking feeling'. It was only later that I realized that this belief ('I am stupid') was untrue and that I only applied it to myself and not to others. But that's the way with basic beliefs – we often don't realize that we have them. It is how our feelings react to certain situations that tells us that we should be alert to the possibility that we may have some basic negative beliefs that need identifying and changing.

As a rule of thumb, negative automatic thoughts are triggered by situations at specific points in time. They may often include basic negative beliefs, but these are also key ideas we have all the time – like our basic views about life. Have another look at Sally, who we discussed in Chapter 4. Here are her basic beliefs again.

- I am a nuisance to others.
- I stop people doing what they want to do.
- People don't really want me around.
- I must not do anything that could push them away.
- I must be to others what they want me to be.
- Expressing anger and/or asserting my needs could lead to rejection.
- I must be grateful for love.
- I am a bad/ungrateful person if I express my dissatisfactions.

Although these thoughts and beliefs were not active all the time, it did not take much to trigger them.

Dwelling on Thoughts

There is a difference between thoughts that are indeed automatic and thoughts that we dwell on. Automatic thoughts are those that are related to fast reactions and come with emotions and feelings. For example, someone jumps out in front of your car and you immediately go into a stomach-churning panic associated with the thought, 'I might hit them.' Someone phones you up and says your lover is sleeping with someone else, and again this 'hits you' almost immediately. In these examples, personal meanings are made extremely rapidly. In the case of the phone call, you might reflect on what was said and then decide that the information is not true and that someone is trying to stir up trouble between you and your lover. In other words, you backtrack and start to 'undo' your first emotional reaction. Alternatively, you might assume the information is true and start to dwell on it.

When we dwell on something, we turn an idea or set of beliefs over and over in our minds. A common situation is to lie in bed and worry, your mind focusing on a particular train of thoughts. This is not the same as having an immediate reaction to something and then pulling back and seeking out the evidence. When we dwell on things, we are allowing ourselves to think along a certain path for many minutes or even hours. When we respond rapidly and emotionally to something, we may need to stop ourselves and focus on what we are thinking. When we dwell on something, we are more clear about what we are thinking. The important thing here is to recognize that dwelling on negative thoughts can have the effect of making negative feelings become more entrenched.

Depression involves not just automatic thoughts and immediate reactions to situations, but what is called 'ruminating' – that is, dwelling on the same negative thoughts. This type of thinking is the most important to recognize and interrupt. You could try distracting yourself. Or you could try asking yourself: Where are my thoughts taking me? Is this helpful? Am I going over old ground and will only end up feeling worse? If this is the case, writing your thoughts down – rather than allowing them to go around and around in your mind – can be one way to interrupt them. Or you could say to yourself, 'I know where these thoughts are leading, and if I let them go on, my mood will go down.' Once thoughts are written down, they may be easier to dispute and challenge.

By now, you will probably be aware of the kinds of things you dwell on. These may be thoughts of inadequacy, injustice and unfairness, revenge, loss, and/or negative predictions of the future – in fact, just the kinds of thoughts that everyone has from time to time. Try to identify the things that you usually find yourself dwelling on and try to become more aware of any common 'themes' in your thoughts. If you find it difficult to recognize when your mind is dwelling on things, you can leave notes to yourself around the house that remind you to check on what you are thinking. Or you could carry a stone (or some other small object) in your pocket so that, each time you feel it there, this will be a signal to check on your thoughts. If you have been dwelling on certain things, gently remind yourself that you can break off from these thoughts. Indeed, do whatever works for you to stop yourself from dwelling on and indoctrinating yourself with negative thoughts.

Of course, this is not to say that we should never have sad, anxious or negative thoughts and feelings or that we should always try to distract ourselves from things that are painful. In fact, some of these can help us to develop solutions to problems or to work through painful feelings such as grief. Rather, the thoughts and feelings you should avoid are those that lead to downward spirals and do not serve any purpose other than to increase depression.

Key Points

- When things happen to us, we often have various thoughts about what the event means to us. These are our interpretations.
- These thoughts can be automatic and just pop into the mind.
- One automatic thought can lead to another and spiral us down into deeper, more depressed feelings.
- We can have negative thoughts not only about particular situations but also about our inner feelings, fantasies and past actions.
- Our thoughts may be difficult to pin down, but if we ask ourselves certain types of questions, they might become clearer.
- We may ruminate and dwell on these thoughts and ideas, and so spiral down into deeper, more depressed feelings.

continued on next page

- We often need to train ourselves to become more aware of our automatic thoughts and the themes we tend to dwell on.
- One way to begin to gain more awareness of your thinking is to make a habit of writing down your thoughts.
- Some of our negative automatic thoughts are triggered because we have underlying basic negative beliefs. Until we recognize our automatic thoughts, we may not be aware of these basic beliefs that could be guiding our lives.

Exercises

- Think about and try writing down your thoughts. At first, you might use a notebook that you keep handy. Draw up three columns that allow you to separate out triggering events, beliefs and key thoughts, and feelings. Look up Monitoring and Challenging Your Thoughts (pp. 348–54) to explore some worked examples.
- Write down whatever comes into your mind – even if, at first, it does not make much sense.
- Start to consider your thoughts when your mood changes. Learn to 'catch' your thoughts. Give yourself time and space to focus on them.
- To gain more insight into your thoughts, ask yourself some questions. These can include:
  1 Questions about how you see yourself as a person.
  2 Questions about how you think others see you.
  3 Questions about implications, including for the future.
- Make copies of the Thought Monitoring and Challenging form on p. 384, familiarize yourself with it, and try using it.
- As you become better at catching and noting your thoughts, work on the fourth column – to challenge your thoughts. To help you do this, read the next few chapters.

continued on next page

- Watch out for negative thoughts such as 'This can't work for me.' Instead, say to yourself: 'Maybe this won't help, but what have I got to lose from trying?'

7

Challenging Negative Thoughts and Feelings

In the last few chapters we noted that, when we become depressed and feel so low and tired, our thoughts tend to take us downward. They rarely encourage us or offer uplifts – just when we need them. If anything, our thoughts are rather bullying and critical. In this chapter, we are going to explore ways of breaking out of the downward spiral. Look at the fourth column of the Thought Monitoring and Challenging form on p. 351. We are now going to learn about how to use this – how to challenge and dispute negative thoughts. In the last part of the chapter I will explore with you how to make your own thought forms to suit your needs.

To challenge our negative thinking styles that can increase our stress we need to start by looking at things from different angles. Just as when we want to buy something – say, a house or a car – we like to have some alternatives to choose from, so too with our thoughts; we need to try generating alternatives. Now, the voice of depression is often a bully and it tends to block out alternatives. Depression is like the car manufacturer Henry Ford, who once said, 'You can have any color you like as long as it's black.' Depression likes us to believe that what it says is the way things really are; it can be terribly arrogant in this respect, and it too usually chooses black. Depression is very keen to tell us what we can't do, what we shouldn't do and how bad things are. But it is a primitive part of our brains speaking, and there are two basic orientations that we can take that will help to control it: insisting on rational questioning and alternatives, and developing basic compassion.

99

Rational Minds to the Rescue

To help control the spiral downwards into depression, we need to encourage our *rational* minds to do more work. As we noted in Chapter 2, high stress tends to push this rational part of us to one side. Under stress, we automatically look at the negatives. But first, a word of caution. Although learning to think in a different way can be extremely helpful in overcoming depression, this is not all there is to change. Sometimes depressed people need to form relationships with others who can help them grieve, remember things they have forgotten or face things they can't face alone, or even help them mature. Sometimes people become so depressed that they will benefit from medication to kick-start the system and/or help with sleep. But when thoughts are stacked against you, gaining more insight and control over them can be a tremendous help. One way of doing this is to be more rational about them. So let's look at the functions and qualities of the rational mind – since we want to recruit it to help you.

- The rational mind likes to look at the evidence. It is a scientist or detective and treats ideas and thoughts as theories that can be proved incorrect. The rational mind does not settle for simple answers; like a Sherlock Holmes, it observes carefully and wants to know as much as possible before coming to a decision.
- The rational mind likes to have several alternatives to choose from. It does not like to have few choices because it tends to assume that there is always more than one way of seeing things.
- The rational mind likes to test things and run experiments.
- The rational mind does not like being overly influenced by emotional appeal or hasty conclusions.
- The rational mind knows that knowledge develops slowly. Things become more complex as we know more, and this is a source of fascination and deepening understanding.
- The rational mind knows that sometimes we learn most from trial and error – that, in fact, we often learn more from our errors than we do from our successes.
- The rational mind will attempt (if given the chance) to weigh up the advantages and disadvantages of a particular view or course of action.

- The rational mind likes to take a long-term view of things and recognizes that we often get to where we are going step by step. It realizes that it is our long-term interests that are important, regardless of short-term setbacks or benefits.

So the 'rational approach' is one side of ourselves that we need to cultivate. However, the rational mind works best at combating depression when it has a friend. This friend and ally we can call the *compassionate mind*. Thus, we need to develop a compassionate/friendly rationality – not a cold impersonal one.

The Compassionate Mind

We have evolved the capacity to care for other people, animals and things. For example, parents know that if their children are hurt, rationalizing with them is often not enough. The children will usually need a cuddle and a bit of tender loving care. We recognize that other people often need looking after and caring for, and we have evolved the capacity to do this within our brains. We can *empathize* with others – feel happy with them and sad for them – and often want to help them. However, in depression we often lose this inner capability. We often fail to look after or nurture ourselves, and we may not even recognize that we need to become more inwardly caring.

Now, we saw in Chapter 2 that the kinds of thoughts you have act like signals to the brain, and that the thoughts/signals you give yourself affect how your mood chemicals work. Recall how, if we form sexual images in our minds, we can (through our fantasies alone) get ourselves aroused and 'hot'. And if we suddenly think of negative things, this can activate our stress hormones – our blood pressure might go up, for example. The principle with developing 'inner warmth' is exactly the same. The brain is tuned to respond to support, help, affection and love. These signals are good for your immune system and boost mood chemicals. If our brains were not so sensitive to these signals, then none of these things would matter much to us. But we have evolved in such a way that they do.

When we get depressed, these positive caring signals go down. We become more self-critical and generally negative. We reduce our boosting signals/thoughts: for example, we don't give ourselves much praise by thinking things like 'I think I look nice in this,' or 'I think that was a job well done'; and we also reduce our caring/compassionate signals/thoughts. When times are hard we *do not* take an understanding, warm and compassionate approach with thoughts like 'Well, this has been hard for me and I am bound to feel sad and disappointed about it.' Instead, we are more likely to become angry or feel hopeless, rather than compassionately understanding and supportive.

To heal often means we have to learn (1) to give our brains some boosting signals via focusing on things that we are OK or good at, and (2) to reactivate the caring–healing part of ourselves that depression has knocked out. We need to learn to be more warm, encouraging and supportive rather than harsh and bullying. So we need to harness and develop the compassionate side of ourselves – the compassionate mindset, or 'compassionate mind' for short

The compassionate mind, like the rational mind, has certain qualities:

- The compassionate mind has empathy and sympathy for those who are in pain and hurting.
- The compassionate mind is concerned with growth and helping people reach their potential.
- The compassionate mind is concerned with supporting, healing and listening to what we and others need.
- The compassionate mind listens and enquires about problems in a kind and friendly way.
- The compassionate mind is quick to forgive and slow to condemn.
- The compassionate mind does not attack but seeks to bring healing, repair and reunion.
- The compassionate mind recognizes that life can be painful and that we are all imperfect beings.
- The compassionate mind does not treat ourselves or others simply as objects with a market value. Self-worth and self-acceptance are not things that can be earned; they are not conditional or based on fulfilling contracts.

We can learn to train our thoughts to be warm and friendly and cultivate the qualities of the compassionate mind. For some of us, especially those who have not received much in the way of warmth and kindness when young, this can be a most difficult but important step.

Bonds, Tasks and Goals

When people seek therapy, they want to find a compassionate therapist who will try (1) to understand and not condemn them; (2) to show warmth and friendliness; and (3) to help them see things in a different way, and to mature and grow. In seeking these things, people are showing an inner wisdom – recognition of what heals.

When therapists are trained, they are often taught to focus on three things: the bonds and relationships between patient and therapist; the tasks that need to be undertaken; and the goals and aims of the therapy. In helping yourself to get out of depression, you can take the same approach.

Bonds

The bonds here refer to your inner relationship with yourself. The idea is that you may need to shift from a bullying and hostile relationship with yourself to a more compassionate, helpful, friendly and accepting one. This is not always easy, and you may have to work hard at it. Here are some pointers.

- If you are monitoring your thoughts and can detect that you are being overly critical or defeatist, imagine what you would say to people you cared for (e.g. friends or family). Imagine how you would encourage them to try out different things or to keep going. Write down what you might say. Concentrate on the tone of your voice, your manner, whether you might put an arm around them. Note how you might accept their crying or fear and how you can understand their pain. Recognize how, when someone else is in pain, you do not want to bully or ridicule them and kick them when they are down. Now, the basic attitude and approach you have towards caring and helping someone else is what you are trying to develop for yourself.

Come up with a motto such as 'Caring and forgiveness heals; bullying, criticizing and attacking hurts' or 'I intend to relate to my inner healer/helper rather than my inner bully.'

- Imagine a caring, helpful person reaching out to you, perhaps someone who is both compassionate and rational – the father or mother you would like to have had. Sometimes depressed people, when they are struggling to challenge their negative views, prefer to imagine what their compassionate helper would think and advise. And remember: your inner helper has no limit to his/her patience.

Tasks

Often, as we move forward out of depression, there are various tasks that we can set for ourselves on our step-by-step journey. The following are examples:

- Learn to tune into and monitor more accurately your thoughts and feelings.
- Write your thoughts down.
- Try recording ideas that are good challenges to your negative thoughts on a tape. When you feel down, play them to yourself.
- Learn to be honest with yourself.
- Learn how to take big problems and break them down into smaller ones.
- Set yourself small pieces of homework to complete.
- Learn to be more assertive or less self-attacking.

Goals

These goals are the things you want to achieve. At first, depressed people usually just want to feel better. But this large goal needs to be broken down into smaller ones. These smaller goals might be:

- To do a little more each day.
- To be more assertive with some other person.
- To spend more time on something you enjoy.

It can be useful to set yourself a couple of goals at the beginning of each day or week. Start by setting small ones – the smaller, the better. Then think about the tasks involved to achieve these goals and how you might maximize your chances of success. If things are difficult or you don't reach your goals, ask yourself some questions.

- Were the goals too ambitious?
- Could I have broken them down further?
- Did I run into unexpected problems?
- Did I put enough effort into achieving them?
- In my heart of hearts, did I think that achieving them wouldn't really help?
- If I failed, am I being compassionate with myself?

Some Ways of Challenging Negative Thoughts

Getting the Evidence

When we jump to conclusions, we usually don't do much in the way of gathering evidence. We'd make very poor scientists or detectives. So we often need to strongly encourage ourselves to do this, and train ourselves to collect evidence. When we have a negative idea about ourselves, others, our future or the world, we need to ask: 'Do I have enough evidence for this conclusion?'

Anne thought that she had ruined a dinner party by overcooking the meal. She was clearly disappointed about the food, but in fact, there was no evidence that the whole evening had been messed up or that the guests had not enjoyed her party. So how might we help Anne not to dwell on the overcooked meal, but instead to focus on what was good about the evening? One way is to take a thought like 'I've messed up the whole evening with my overcooked meal' and dispute it. The kinds of thoughts that might go into the fourth column of the Thought Monitoring and Challenging form (p. 351) could be both rational and compassionate:

Rational mind
- Where is the evidence that the whole evening was messed up?

Compassionate/friendly mind
- This is very harsh isn't it?
- How does being so critical help you?

- Did your guests seem unhappy?
- Do you think they will come again?

- Ask people if they enjoyed it and see what they say.

- What's one overcooked meal between friends?
- You wouldn't judge your friends so harshly. What would you say to them?
- To overcook is human. Forgive yourself and let's plan the next party.

Getting the evidence is important when it comes to putting effort into things. When we give up on something too quickly, it is often because we have jumped to the conclusion that we could not do it. We focus too much on the bits of information that point to a negative conclusion and ignore the bits of information that point to a more positive one.

Thinking about Alternatives

Related to getting better evidence on the basis of which to make decisions is the need to learn how to generate alternatives. When we are depressed, it is quite difficult to do this. But we can begin by looking at the evidence that does not support a particular idea or belief.

Jane and Terry had an argument over money. Because the argument got rather heated, Jane concluded that Terry no longer loved her. If Jane had read this book, she might handle things differently by writing out her reasons for such a belief and considering alternatives, in the following way.

We had the argument because:

Negative ideas	Alternatives
He doesn't care about me.	He's worried about money, too.
He said hurtful things.	He's prone to say hurtful things when he loses his temper. And, if I'm honest, so do I. Well, I think them even if I don't say them.

- He's stressed out at the moment – we both are because he might lose his job.
- It's difficult to be very understanding when you're stressed out.
- If we weren't so worried about money, we probably wouldn't have gone at each other like that.
- Our argument is more evidence of stress than of not being cared for.

Another way that Jane could have done this would be to write two columns, of evidence for and evidence against. The main idea here is that, whenever you come up with evidence that points one way, try thinking about the evidence that points the other way. Don't allow yourself to settle for only one view.

When Jane went through some alternative reasons for the hurtful things that had been said, she still felt unhappy about the conflicts in her relationship with Terry. However, she recognized that there were a number of factors related to the argument and not just the idea that she was not loved. When the heat had gone out of the situation, she decided to talk to Terry about this. At first, he said that he thought that she didn't really understand how he felt and how difficult things were for him – in other words, it was not that he did not love Jane but that he felt misunderstood by her. Although they then got into something of a competition over who was the less understanding, eventually they talked about the fact that the shortage of money was the common problem. They agreed that both of them were under stress because of that, and that they needed to join together against the common problem rather than venting their anger at each other. This would have been difficult to achieve if Jane had hung on to the idea that Terry's anger was evidence of his not loving her. In fact, both of them tended to interpret arguments as evidence of a lack of love.

Of course, it may well be that, when you are angry, the person you are arguing with is not your best-loved person *at that moment*; but this does not mean that you do not love them, nor does it mean that they don't love you. And we all need to watch out for the terrible 'must': 'I must be loved all the time' or 'In a love relationship we must never be angry with each other.'

Sometimes, however, the evidence points in the other direction – that there may not be much caring in a relationship. Karen had been going out with Tim for about eighteen months. He tended to be demanding and rough sexually. At times, he would come to her flat drunk, and often he broke their dates. Increasingly depressed, Karen made excuse after excuse for him.

Positive ideas	*Alternatives*
• He'd change if we were married.	• I saw his last girlfriend last month and she said that he was the same with her and that I was welcome to him. All accounts I have read suggest that, on the whole, people don't change that much after marriage.
• This is typical of all men.	• I know many other men who are not like this.
• When he's down, he always likes to talk to me.	• There is more to a relationship than just supporting people when they are down. I might be being used here.
• He is often nice and takes me out sometimes.	• Even Hitler was nice at times. It's really what I feel about it overall that counts.

Doing this was difficult for Karen, but when she began to look at alternatives to her idea that Tim did care for her, unfortunately the evidence was that he did not – or at least, not in the way that she wanted.

Generating alternatives means that we get more than one point of view. Sometimes we don't want to think about the alternatives because they lead to painful decisions. In Karen's case, she had a deeper belief that, if she gave up this relationship, she might not find another. It was this belief that had stopped her looking at alternative thoughts about whether Tim cared or not, and really focusing on the evidence. When she did look hard at the evidence, she realized that, on the whole, this was not a good or supportive relationship to be in. There was more pain than gain.

When she tried to use her compassionate mind by focusing on how she might talk to a friend, Karen came up with these ideas:

I know I'm worried about being on my own. But I can learn to face this possibility. I might be more miserable if I stay in than if I get out. Even if I get out of this relationship, this doesn't mean that I'll give up trying to find a better one. I can think about the qualities I could bring to a relationship and not just focus on my bad points. I'm honest and very loyal. I try to consider other people's feelings. Of course, no one's perfect but I deserve better. In my heart, I know this. It has just seemed too frightening to end it. But then again, I have survived on my own before, and rather than hoping that a relationship with a man will make my life great, I can start to work on relationships with other people who can give me some pleasure and closeness. Ending this relationship doesn't make me unlovable.

Karen both wrote this down and spoke these ideas on to a tape when she wasn't feeling too depressed. She was then able to read and listen to them whenever she felt down. She was encouraged to feel kind and compassionate when she offered herself these alternative ideas and words of advice. This helped her to stop sinking into depression and face up to getting out of the relationship.

One typical response at this stage might be: 'Well, okay, I can generate alternative views; but I don't really believe them. I'm just trying to fool myself.' If this is what you think, consider that this is typical of depression – it always thinks it knows what's real and accurate. At this stage, the act of generating alternatives and avoiding concentrating on single ideas is the important first step.

Advantages and Disadvantages

By now, you will have got the idea that writing things down can be very helpful, enabling you to clarify, focus and concentrate. It helps to stop ideas and thoughts swirling around in your mind without any focus. It is especially important to do this because, like physical exercise which helps you build up your muscles and get fit, you often need to put effort into building up your skills in challenging negative thoughts.

Writing things down can also help you to clarify conflicts and dilemmas. In this case you can write down two columns: advantages (pros or gains) and disadvantages (cons or losses) of making a change. Kevin was in two minds about moving house, so he wrote out the pros and cons:

Advantages	*Disadvantages*
• Nicer district.	• Further to travel to work.
• Bigger house with more space for the family.	• Unfamiliar. I like my old house.
• Bigger garden that I could enjoy and relax in.	• Might not have the time to maintain it.
• Good investment.	• More expensive.

Kevin's next task was to weigh each pro and con. He did this with his family, with he and his wife putting arguments both for and against. Through discussion, it became clear that it was the unfamiliarity of a new house and district that was the biggest hurdle. Kevin realized that he did not like to leave the familiar. Once this was clarified in his mind, he was able to challenge this view and accept that while it might take him time to adjust to a new home, in the long term it would be a good decision to move.

Sometimes we can feel very blocked in changing our basic views of ourselves or ways of doing things. There always seems to be a cost. In therapy, Karen realized that, if things went wrong in relationships, she tended to blame herself. Although she readily acknowledged that giving up doing this would be helpful, she found it difficult to do. So she wrote down the pros and cons of giving up self-blame to try to discover why.

Advantages		*Disadvantages*
I would feel better	*but*	I would become more angry with others.
		I would become like my mother who always blamed others, and whom I disliked.

| I would take more risks | *but* | I would provoke others to be angry or reject me. |
| I would not feel inferior | *but* | I might not see my faults, and might become arrogant. |

By writing these thoughts down, it became clear that, for Karen, there were a number of unrecognized disadvantages to changing – not least the fear of becoming the kind of person she did not like. Now, of course, no one would change if they saw that as the possible result. So Karen needed to consider the evidence for the disadvantages that she had identified. What evidence was there that not taking the blame for everything would make her arrogant? Aren't there many people who do not blame themselves but are also not arrogant?

In therapy, people often see many disadvantages to changing. Of course, they don't want to be depressed – but getting out of depression may appear to involve rather difficult things. They have to try to identify what these might be. What would change involve? What might be the fear in that? Not every advantage of change has a countering 'but'; still, it is useful to think of such possibilities. People can continue to resist change if the perceived disadvantages and fears associated with change are not explored. Once they can see more clearly what is blocking them, they may be better placed to start challenging some of those blocks.

Sometimes advantages and disadvantages are not seen. For example, someone who feels a need to be in an intimate relationship to be happy can become dependent and tend to stay in unsupportive relationships – as in Karen's case. Someone who, by contrast, feels a need to be strong and independent might suffer the disadvantage of being unable to ask others for help.

You can do these written exercises on pros and cons many times, and can carry them out quite slowly, allowing time for self-reflection and/or discussion with others along the way.

Designing Experiments

It is useful to challenge depressive ideas by setting experiments: that is, testing things out and rehearsing new skills. This is likely to help you to gather evidence for and against your thoughts and beliefs. A useful motto here is 'challenging but not overwhelming'. Remember – try to design your experiments to take you forward step by step, rather than rushing into something that has a high risk of failure. Don't worry if the steps seem too small. As they say, a journey of a thousand miles begins with a single step.

If your experiment doesn't work out, try to find out why. Was there anything about it that was a success? Were you attempting too much? Were your expectations too high? Did your negative thoughts overwhelm you? Did you really put the effort into it that you needed to?

Charlie was very prone to dismissing his own work as inadequate. In therapy, we had worked out some ways that he could challenge and dispute his negative thoughts. These were written down on a card for him to look at. He decided that he was going to experiment with using the card to combat his negative thoughts when they came up. However, he would only occasionally get out the card and read the more rational/compassionate thoughts that were written down. And when he did read them, he would not really put much effort into thinking seriously about these alternative thoughts. He was very casual about it and looked at the words without thinking through their meaning. In the back of his mind, he thought, 'This approach can't work.' So he had stacked the experiment against himself before he had begun.

Now, of course, challenging negative thoughts won't work by magic. It does take some effort to try to dispute them. So in this case, although the experiment seemed like a failure, it actually produced useful evidence, namely that Charlie constantly had the idea in his mind that this approach could not work; and it was this that undermined his efforts. He had to learn to use his compassionate mind to tell himself in a friendly, supportive way:

> *Look, I know this is hard, and yes, it is a shit being depressed, but let's not stack things against yourself. Let's give it a fair go. After all, what have you got to lose? If you were helping a friend, you'd know how tough it is but you'd also try to encourage them to give it a go. Let's go through this step by step.*

Getting out of depression takes effort, and this is especially true if you are trying to help yourself. It is the same with getting physically fit. It would be no good putting on your trainers and running to the garden gate and back – you have to push yourself more than that. Now, some people find this tough going, and it may be that they need some extra help from professionals. There's no point in berating yourself if you've tried your best and have found it just too hard. On the other hand, if you design an experiment for yourself, try to put all the effort you can into it. For example, when you consider alternative thoughts, make sure that you really *consider* them, rather than just 'looking at the words'. Allow yourself to dwell on how you would feel if you accepted these alternatives.

Writing Things Down: Why This Is So Important

Many people think that if they have understood the principles of the approach we are outlining here, then they do not need to spend time writing things down. It can seem like a pointless and long-winded way of doing things. Or you might feel you don't write that well, or can't spell. That does not matter – as long as you can read your own writing. There are important reasons why you should write things down – especially to begin with – and not just try to challenge the thoughts in your head.

- *Writing down is slowing down*. The first reason is that writing slows your thinking down and helps you to focus. It helps to stop those half-formed but emotionally powerful thoughts whizzing around out of control.
- *Attention*. Writing things down helps concentrate your attention and enables you to stand back a little. Seeing the words coming on to the page helps you to distance yourself from the thoughts, as you have to focus on the process of writing.
- *Catching thoughts*. By slowing down and focusing you may discover all kinds of thoughts 'lurking in the background'. In other words, having felt something, you stop and say, 'Now, how can I explain this to myself? How can account for what I feel? What am I thinking?' This can help you to pinpoint and identify your thoughts. The more you slow your thinking down, especially by writing, the more likely you are to 'catch' the key thoughts and meanings that are associated with what you are feeling.

- *Clarity.* Writing down is an excellent means of gaining clarity. When you have written your thoughts down, you have a pre-served record of them in front of you; something you can look over calmly to see how negative your thoughts really are.
- *Gaining a perspective.* Seeing your thoughts written out in front of you may well help you see that your depression is pushing you to be overly negative and losing perspective. This is much more difficult to see if you just try to challenge your thoughts in your head, because it is hard to gain the distance that is achieved by writing them down.

This is not to say that challenging your thoughts in your head, without writing them down, is no use – it is. But we have to prac-tise our skills bit by bit, and writing down is a really good way to make it as easy as possible for you to identify and focus on the negative thoughts you are trying to change.

Thought Forms

If you are a person who reads self-help books you may have dis-covered that different books suggest different types of forms to use for writing down your thoughts. Melanie Fennell, for example, in her excellent book in this series on *Overcoming Low Self-Esteem*, offers many types of form to write out your thoughts.

In dealing with depression, my advice is: keep it simple. Use whatever kind of form suits you, rather than struggling with any-thing that you find too complex – provided it does the job, of course. The most basic thought-challenging form is simply a page divided into two columns. You write your negative thoughts in the left-hand column, and challenge them in the right-hand column. These negative thoughts might be triggered by an event, or might just come on as your mood dips. The key point is catching what these thoughts are and offering a challenge to them.

Here is an example.

Negative thoughts	Challenging thoughts
Here I am just lying in bed again.	I have to admit I am not
Can't see the point of getting up.	feeling too good right now.
Things are bound to go wrong.	Even though it will be a

Nothing is worth doing anyway – I won't enjoy it.	struggle, if I can make myself get up and move around a bit this often helps. I can sit down and make an activity plan. If I can achieve a couple of things I'll feel better. Sure, I don't enjoy things much because I am depressed – the trick is doing things to overcome depression. I know I can enjoy things when I am not depressed
Degree of belief: 70%	Degree of belief: 40%

Rate Your Belief

You will see that at the bottom of each column in this example there is a figure for 'degree of belief' – that is, *how much* do you believe what you have written down? Some people find that if they rate how much they believe something this can be helpful to seeing that beliefs are not black and white, all or nothing. Also, as time passes and you start to feel better you'll be able to look back and see how the strength of your beliefs has changed with your recovery.

Make Up Your Own Column Headings

You can make up your own column headings for different tasks. For example, sometimes it can be useful to write down in two columns the evidence for a belief and the evidence against it, or the advantages and disadvantages of a particular belief. Or you might prefer to label the two columns 'what my negative and/or self-attacking part says' and 'what my rational and compassionate part says'. For all these variations you can use the two-column format and simply change the headings to suit.

Adding More Columns

In the thought forms given in the appendix to this book (pages 351/

354) you will see other columns. In addition to the two noted above, we also have a column for writing down any critical *events* that might have triggered your negative thoughts and a column for describing negative *feelings*. This helps to give you a more complete picture; it will help your progress if you can be clear on what kinds of things tend to trigger your change of mood, arouse negative thoughts and feelings, or what those emotions and feelings actually are.

Rate Change

It is often useful to rate the change in the strength of your beliefs and in your emotions after you have been through the exercise. For that, we might add a third column to the simple two-column form. Here is the same example we used above, with the third column added on.

Negative thoughts	Challenging thoughts	How I feel now compared to before
Here I am just lying in bed again. Can't see the point of getting up. Things are bound to go wrong. Nothing is worth doing anyway – I won't enjoy it.	I have to admit I am not feeling too good right now. Even though it will be a struggle, if I can make myself get up and move around a bit this often helps . . . (etc.)	Yes, I can see that this might be helpful and a way forward. I feel maybe 5% less depressed by challenging my negative thoughts

You might actually carry out your plan to get up and out of bed, move about and do something in your 'plan for the day'. If so, then you might rate how you feel having done this, compared to how you were feeling before you started. Note the difference. You could even compare how you feel now with how you might feel if you had not done anything at all but stayed in bed. The point here is that the more you, yourself, see the value in these kinds of exercises the more you are likely to have a go.

Adapting the Basic Idea to Suit Yourself

Once you have got the basic idea of the importance of writing things down and slowing your thinking down, you are prepared to start working on your thoughts, feelings, and moods. However, the exact framework you choose to do this should be something you decide for yourself: it's important that you are happy with the form you use. Also, different forms will be useful for working on different things. I have started you off here with a fairly basic thought-recording form; now it's up to you to tailor it to suit you. Experiment with these forms and try out designs of your own. But always keep in mind the basic point of all this: that is, to help you stop hitting your brain with lots of negatives, to get a better perspective on things and start giving your brain a boost and some warmth.

Questions to Put to Yourself as Challenges

Thought forms are a useful framework; but of course we have to know *how* to actually challenge our negative thoughts. We have already looked at some ideas for doing this, and as we go through this book we will discuss many more. Sometimes the best route for a challenge is through logical suggestions; sometimes it is better to use more compassionate ones. Below is a short selection of useful challenges to get you started, divided into three groups: some based on rationality and logic; and some based on compassion; and some based on a problem-solving approach which looks for ways to think about life's problems and tackle them.

Rational and Logical Questions

- What is the evidence that may support my belief and what is the evidence that may not support it?
- How would I typically see this if I were not depressed? To what degree therefore is this way of thinking reflecting my mood state rather than some 'truth'?
- What alternatives might there be to this view?
- What other explanations may there be for this event?
- What kind of thoughts would help me cope with this at the moment?

- How might I see this event in three or six months' time?
- What are the advantages and disadvantages of thinking about this difficulty in this way?
- What are the advantages and disadvantages of changing the way I think?
- If I overcame my depression, how might I look at this situation?
- What might I learn from changing negative thoughts?

Compassionate Questions

- If I had a friend who felt like this, how would I help them see this differently?
- How would a kindly person who was helping me with this sound?
- How would I like someone who cared about me to help me see this differently?
- If my thoughts were sympathetic, warm and compassionate, what would they be and how would I feel?

Problem-solving

- How could I break this problem down into smaller chunks?
- Is there one bit of this problem I can tackle?
- How could I generate a step-by-step approach to this problem?
- Can I think of anyone who might help me?
- Can I ask them for their help and support?

Generating Warmth

To generate warmth using thought records, start by writing down various of the challenges to your negative thoughts that seem helpful to you. Suppose that you have the kind of thoughts noted above and you lie in bed a lot. Now, you could challenge yourself with: 'Come on, get out of bed, you lazy sod. You will only feel worse in there. For goodness' sake make yourself a plan and stop feeling sorry for yourself' – etc. You will note here that the tone of the challenge is impatient and rather aggressive, even though you are trying to stop putting negative signals into your head. So, having written out your alternative and challenging thoughts, make sure they are not aggressive or bullying. Develop supportive ones, then read them through and try to express them in your mind with as much warmth as you can. If the words you have written down do not sound encouraging, but instead rather hectoring and harsh, try again to express the challenge in less hostile terms. This may not be easy for you, but persevere: go over your challenging thoughts a number of times, and each time you read them or re-write them, try to *really feel* a certain warmth, understanding and encouragement coming through.

Key Points

- To combat depression, we can call on different parts and abilities of ourselves: our rational minds and our compassionate/friendly minds.
- We can learn that there may be evidence for a negative belief but also evidence against it, which we often overlook.
- Generating alternatives involves trying to think about an issue, belief or problem from as many different angles as possible.
- By focusing on a situation or possibility for change, we can try to identify the key advantages and disadvantages. Once a block to change has been noted, we can try to challenge that block.
- We can do experiments to gain more information or more evidence and try things out. These experiments should have a chance of success. To do this, we might have to break large problems down into smaller ones.

Exercises

- Write down your negative thoughts about a particular situation. Now look at them carefully.
- As you think about challenging and disputing these ideas, try to take a rational/compassionate approach. If you have

continued on next page

---

negative thoughts, try thinking about what you might say to a friend who is in a similar situation. You might also consider how you think when you are not depressed.

- To begin challenging negative thoughts, focus on two things:
  1 Explore the evidence for (the things that support your idea or belief) and against (the things that do not support your idea or belief).
  2 Practise generating alternatives to your negative thoughts and beliefs. Even if you do not have much faith in these alternatives at first, the act of trying to generate them is an important first step.
- Take a specific difficulty that you might have and consider the pros and cons of changing your situation. Not only focus on the advantages but also try to spot some of the disadvantages that might be stopping you from changing.

8

Styles of Negative Thinking

This chapter explores the types of thoughts you may have when you are depressed. If you can gain insight into the fact that some of your thoughts tend to lack perspective or balance, you will be in a better position to challenge them.

As we become depressed, the way we think changes. Negative thoughts, interpretations and memories become much easier to bring to mind and dwell on. There is a shift to what is called a *negative thinking bias*. As we have seen, there are two possible reasons why this happens. First, our brains tend to go for 'better safe than sorry' thinking in situations of stress and emotional arousal. We lose flexibility in our thinking, choosing to seek certainty and assuming the worst. This is a basic design feature of the brain, and without care and effort to keep our thoughts on a rational, more flexible track, it can be quite easy to lose perspective. The second reason is that negative beliefs and personal judgments (such as being unlovable, a failure or inadequate) developed in childhood may become activated by negative life-events. The latter may include the break-up of a relationship, difficulties in a relationship that lead to increased conflicts, or major disappointments of some kind. The events trigger negative beliefs from the memory, and these begin to impose their meaning on situations. A typical spiral is outlined in Figure 4 (overleaf).

As our thinking takes on a downward spiral, we start to look for evidence that confirms or fits the negative belief. We may start to remember other failures, and the feelings begin to spread out like a dark tide rolling in to cover the sands of our positive abilities. Such thoughts tend to lock in the depression, deepen it and make it more difficult to recover from (see also page 25).

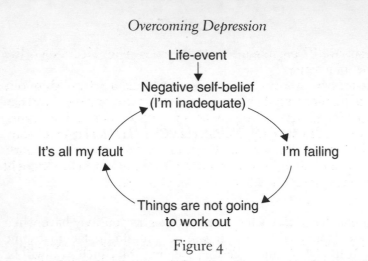

Figure 4

Certain *styles* of depressive thinking are fairly common. To challenge them, we have to (a) recognize them and (b) make an effort to bring our rational and compassionate minds to the problem. Let's begin with jumping to conclusions, which as I have previously suggested is often a key to other negative thoughts.

Jumping to Conclusions

If we feel vulnerable to abandonment, or have the basic belief, 'I can never be happy without a close relationship,' it is natural that, at times, we may jump to the conclusion that others are about to leave us. This will often impel us to try to cling on to these relationships, unable to face up to our fear of being abandoned.

Our primitive mind tells us that we could not possibly cope with being alone. Now that might have been true if we were still living in the wild – being abandoned is a serious threat, especially to the young – but it is not true today. Of course, being abandoned might be terribly painful and we might feel very sad, but we could cope if we allowed ourselves to look at the evidence and plan contingencies, such as eliciting help from friends, or reminding ourselves that, before we had a relationship with this person, we had coped on our own, or that many people suffer the break-up of relationships and survive. There might even be advantages from learning to live alone for a while.

If you have a fear of rejection or of losing a relationship, one way of helping might be to write down that fear and see if you can dispute it and think of ways of coping with a break-up if it occurs. Of course, the break-up will be painful – you can't protect yourself from that – but you can teach yourself to cope with it better. Here we are using the second and forth columns from the 'thought form' presented in the appendix, on page 384.

Negative thought	Disputes and ways of coping
If I were to stand up for myself I might be rejected.	First, do I have evidence that I will be rejected or that this relationship will end? What is the evidence for and against this idea and fear?
	But let's suppose the worst for a moment. How can I learn to face this?
	It would be painful, but I can't be held hostage to these feelings.
	I can face this risk and take steps to deal with it. These steps might include talking to friends and seeking their support, and planning and allowing myself to think about living on my own.
	Relationships do break up, and there is nothing different about me if this happens.
	A break-up does not mean that I am unlovable. It just means that this particular relationship has not worked out.
	Maybe the time has come to see how I might cope on my own and overcome this fear of abandonment. The benefit of this might be that I will see that I am a person in my own right.

> So I might be jumping to conclusions
> in two ways: (1) by assuming that the
> break-up is about to happen when it is
> not; and (2) by assuming that I could
> not cope with the pain of it if it did.

Another form of jumping to conclusions is 'mind reading'. We automatically assume that people do not like us because they do not give sufficient cues of approval of liking us. In 'mind reading' we believe that we can intuitively know what others think.

Now, it is useful to know who your friends are and to be sensitive to being deceived by others. If we were not, we might put a lot of work into relationships but, when the chips are down, not get much back. However, as we start to spiral into depression, we become more sensitive to being deceived, being used or taken advantage of, because these are threats. We might start to think that people do not really care for us, that they are only pretending – they are unreliable allies and friends. We may also recall times from the past when we felt uncared for.

We can challenge these thoughts by considering the following:

It is only natural for people to look after themselves, and maybe they are not caring for me as much as I would like. But this does not mean that they don't like me at all. Perhaps there are aspects of me that they don't like: come to think of it, there are aspects I don't like about them. But who said that I have to like everything about them or they have to like everything about me? We are only human, after all, and people will let each other down from time to time. That's life.

Another challenge might be 'let's look at the evidence':

The other person might be having a bad day and does not understand how I feel. Is it possible that I am reading a slight or put-down into their actions when none was intended? Are there alternative explanations for their actions other than they don't like me? If, after careful consideration, I decide that they are exploiting me or really don't give a damn, then maybe I'd be better off without them, or at least expecting less from them.

Predicting the Future

We often need to be able to predict the future, at least to a degree. We need to have some idea about what threats, opportunities and blocks lie ahead to know whether to put effort into things or not. How much energy/effort our brains devote to securing goals depends a great deal on whether we have an optimistic or a pessimistic view of the future. It may be highly disadvantageous to put in a lot of effort when the chances of success appear slim. The problem is that, as we become depressed, the brain veers too much to the conclusion that nothing will work, and continuously signals: 'Times are hard.' Depression says: 'You can put a lot of effort into this but not get much in return. Close down and wait for better times.' So getting out of depression may involve both patience and a preparedness to think that the brain is being overly pessimistic about the future.

One way to tackle this is to recognize that feeling overwhelmed can be a natural consequence of the situation we are in. However, this does not mean that nothing can work. It might be possible to break problems down into smaller bits. For example, when Dan had to do a project for his degree, he felt overwhelmed by it and was sure he was not up to it. But eventually he was able to challenge these thoughts with: 'Let's break the problem down. First, I'll talk to my adviser, then get the relevant material and read as much as I can. Then I'll draw up a plan of what to include.' In a way, this is like mountain climbing: if you are frightened of heights, go one step at a time, and don't look down or up.

Sometimes we need to learn when to bow out gracefully. However, as a rule of thumb, if you give up too quickly, before trying out various plans to cope, and thus lack good evidence that nothing can be done, this might be because you have become overwhelmed.

Becoming Active

Predicting that things won't work out, that things will be too difficult or that nothing can help or work, are reasons why we tend to do less, fail to put effort into things and become inactive. It is very important to challenge this view. Sometimes the key to success is to keep going even when things don't look promising. Suppose your inactivity is about carrying out some of the advice suggested in this book. Here are some challenges to this view.

Negative thought	*Disputes and ways of coping*
Nothing I do will work out.	Do I really have enough evidence to say this or is this just how I feel about it?
	I feel like this because I am depressed and therefore it is natural to feel like this.
	What have I got to lose by trying? If I put effort into this and it doesn't work out, I'll certainly be no worse off and might have gained something.
	Am I defeating myself before I start?
	If I try, at least I'll know I made the effort even if things don't work out.
	I can go one step at a time. If I break my problems down into smaller ones, they may not seem so overwhelming. I don't have to try to do too much at once.
	I will probably feel better if I try to do something rather than nothing.
	I can praise myself for effort.

The trick in overcoming inactivity is to try to start with something 'do-able'.

Emotional Reasoning

Strong feelings and emotions start us thinking in certain ways, and this can happen despite the fact that we know it is irrational. The problem is that, at times, we may not try to get our more rational minds to overrule our feelings. Given the strength of these we may take the view: 'I feel it, therefore it must be true.'

Feelings are very unreliable sources of truth. For example, at the times of the Crusades, many Europeans 'felt' that God wanted them to kill Muslims – and they did. Throughout the ages, humans have done some terrible things because their feelings dictated it. So, as a general rule, if you are depressed, don't trust your feelings – especially if they are highly critical and hostile to you. Here are some typical 'I feel it therefore it must be true' ideas.

Situation	I feel it, therefore it must be true
Going to a party	I feel frightened, therefore this situation is dangerous and threatening.
Feeling anxious	I feel as if I will have a heart attack, therefore I will.
Being accused of a minor fault	I feel guilty, therefore I am guilty and a bad person.
Losing your temper and shouting	I feel terrible when I get angry, therefore anger is terrible and I am bad and rejectable.
Wanting to cry	I feel that, if I start crying, the flood gates will open and I will never stop; therefore I must stop myself from crying.
Feeling self-conscious when I cry	I feel ashamed when I cry, therefore crying is shameful and a sign of weakness.
Making a mistake	I feel stupid, therefore I am stupid.

No matter how much you feel a failure or unlovable or stupid or any other thing, this does not make it true. The strength of your feelings does not reflect reality. So you can challenge and dispute these types of emotional reasoning with:

> *I may make mistakes or even behave stupidly, but this does not make me stupid. I am a mosaic of possibilities and potentials that can't be so easily judged, no matter what I feel at any one*

moment. After all, I could learn to be different. I may feel now that I will never get better, but again, this does not make it a fact. I may feel that I will never stop crying, but everyone stops in the end. Crying is a sign of hurt and the need to heal, not of weakness.

In their right place, feelings are enormously valuable, and indeed, they give vitality to life. But when we use feelings to do the work of our rational minds, we are liable to get into trouble. The strength of our feelings is not a good guide to reality or accuracy. Perhaps you could give some thought to how your rational/compassionate self might dispute the thoughts and ideas in the list above. This, of course, does not mean that you cannot be intuitive, but make sure you get the evidence to back up your intuitions.

'I Must'

Feelings come into the picture in another way. As we become depressed, and sometimes before, we can believe that we *must* do certain things or *must* live in a certain way or *must* have certain things. For example, if you say, 'I would like to have a fortune, otherwise I will never be happy,' then you're in trouble. There is nothing new in this idea. For many centuries, Buddhists have suggested that the source of all suffering is derived from our wanting and attachments to things in the world, from our *cravings*.

We express our cravings in many ways and over many things. 'I *must* be loved all the time. I *must* never fail. I *must* prove that I am always in control. I *must*, I *must*, I *must* . . .' Nine times out of ten we don't realize that we are doing this to ourselves – but the strength of our feelings can be a guide. We can also '*must*' others like this: 'Others *must* always be nice to me. Others *must* never lie to me or let me down' and so on. Violence and frustration can be linked to the 'musts'. For example, some violent males believe that women *must* obey them and not strongly argue with them, and they *must* provide sex more or less whenever the man wants it. When we get into strong 'musts', we also get into strong tendencies to obey the dictates of our 'musts' – and, at times, force others to obey them.

Use the strength of your feelings to test whether there are some 'musts' around – and then challenge them. And, of course, our 'musts' are not either/or – in other words, the strength of the 'must' varies. Typical 'musts' are: 'I *must* be loved to be happy,' 'I *must* achieve things to be loved,' 'Others *must* understand how I feel.' The key here is to try to turn your 'musts' into preferences – for example, 'I would prefer to be loved and in a close relationship, but I can still be happy if I am not,' or 'I would very much like others to understand how I feel, but if they don't, this would be disappointing but not the end of the world.'

If you find the rational approach a bit cold for you, try thinking about what the Buddha said: 'Our cravings are the source of our unhappiness.' By gaining control over our cravings, we are gaining control over our more primitive emotional minds. Whatever your own particular 'musts', try to identify them and turn them into preferences. Try to recognize that reducing the strength of your cravings can set you free, or at least freer. And remember that there is often an irony in our 'musts'. For example, at times we can be so needing of success and so fearful of failure that we may withdraw and not try at all. If you go to a party and feel that 'everyone *must* like you,' the chances are that you'll be so anxious that you won't enjoy it and even may not go. And if you do go, you may be so defensive that others won't have a chance to get to know you.

Disbelieving and Discounting the Positive in Personal Efforts

If we have been threatened or experienced a major setback, we may need a lot of reassurance before trying again. Now this makes good evolutionary sense. It is adaptive to be wary and cautious. We even have a saying for it: 'Once bitten, twice shy.'

The problem is that this same process can apply in depression in an unhelpful way. If we have experienced a failure or setback, we may think we need to have a major success before we can reassure ourselves that we are back on track. Small successes may not be enough to convince us. However, getting out of depression often depends on small steps, not giant leaps. Typical automatic thoughts that can undermine this step-by-step approach are:

- I used to do so much more when I was not depressed. Managing to do this one small thing today seems so insignificant.
- Other people could take things like this in their stride. Because it is such an effort for me, this proves that I am not making any headway.
- Anyone could do that.
- Small steps are all right for some people, but I want giant leaps and nothing else will do.

Now, remember what we have said about depression. In depression, your brain is working differently. Perhaps the levels of some of your brain chemicals have got a little on the low side. Perhaps you are exhausted. Therefore, you have to compare like with like. Other people may accomplish more – and so might you if you were not depressed – but you are. So, given the way your brain is and the effort 'you have to make,' you are really doing a lot if you achieve one small step. Think about it this way. If you had broken your leg and were learning to walk again, being able to go a few paces might be real progress. Depressed people often wish that they could show their injuries to others, but unfortunately that is not possible. But this does not mean that there is nothing physically different in your brain and body when you are depressed than when you are not.

If you can do things when you find them difficult to do, surely that is worth even more praise than being able to do them when they are easy to accomplish. So we can learn to praise and appreciate our *efforts*, rather than the results.

Also remember that, even if other people can do more than you, this does not mean you have to be the same. I know many good psychologists who accomplish far more than I do, and I can value them rather than think I have to be exactly like them or reach the same standards.

Dwelling on the Negative

Not only do we dismiss the positives, but in depression, there is a tendency to notice and dwell and brood on the negative. It is as if we are wearing dark glasses. We see the flaws rather than the good in things. One way to challenge this is to say, 'Okay, I accept that I am very good at spotting flaws, but can I become equally good at seeing what is good in things – for example, in myself and other people?'

Put time aside to think about yourself and others and only look for what is good, helpful or useful. Another approach is to look at the alternatives and evidence for the idea that something is all bad – what can you come up with that challenges the 'all bad' view? Now, this exercise should not involve only looking on the bright side and discounting genuine problems and difficulties. Rather, it is designed to introduce more balance into your thinking, to get that part of your brain that controls positive feelings to do some work.

Disbelieving the Positive from Others

Another area where we disbelieve the positive is when others are approving of us. To quote Groucho Marx, 'I don't want to belong to any club that will accept me as a member.' Even being accepted is turned into a negative. Here are some other examples.

When Steve was paid a compliment at work by his boss, he thought, 'He's just saying that to get me to work harder. He's not satisfied with me.' When Ella was asked how she had been feeling when she returned to work after being ill, she concluded, 'They are just asking what's expected. They don't really care, but I guess *they'll* feel better if they ask.' When Peter passed a nice comment on how Maureen looked, she thought, 'He's just saying that to cheer me up. Maybe he wants sex.' Paul sent in a report at work, even though he knew there were one or two areas where it was weak. When he got approving feedback, he thought, 'Deceived them again. They obviously didn't read it very carefully. No one takes much notice of my work.'

Rather than allowing himself to keep on thinking so negatively, Paul was encouraged to ask his boss about his report, especially the shaky areas. He did not get the response he expected. His boss said, 'Yes, we knew those areas were unclear in your report, but then the whole area is unclear. In any case, some of the other things you said gave us some new ideas on how to approach the project.' So Paul got some evidence about the report rather than continuing to rely on his own feelings about it.

From an evolutionary point of view, the part of us that is on the lookout for deceptions can become overactive, and we become very sensitive to the possibility of being deceived. Moreover, fear of deception works both ways. On the one hand, we can think that others are deceiving us with their supportive words and on the other, we can think that, if we do get praise, we have deceived *them*. Because deceptions are really threats, when we become depressed we can become very sensitive to them. But again we can challenge these ideas. For example:

> *Even if people are mildly deceptive, does this matter? What harm can they do? I don't have to insist that people are always completely straight. And life being life, some people are more deceptive than others. But I can live with that.*

Generally, if people offer you praise and you find yourself discounting or dismissing it, try to make note of that and work out why. Are they deceiving you or do you think you have deceived them? Do you think you don't deserve praise? Are you discounting the positives, and if you are, what use is that to you? Think of the advantages of accepting praise, rather than automatically dismissing it.

All-or-Nothing

All-or-nothing thinking (sometimes also called either/or, polarized or black-and-white thinking) is typical of the extreme forms of thought that can arise when we are threatened. We need quick answers, not indeterminacy. Mistakes, if we still lived in the wild, could be costly. Animals often need to jump to conclusions (e.g., whether to run from a sound in the bushes), and it is easier to jump to conclusions if the choices are clear – all or nothing. All-or-nothing thinking helps us to be certain and make quick decisions.

The problem here is that all-or-nothing thinking can lead us seriously astray. We do not take the time or effort to consider the evidence of alternatives thoroughly. Here are some typical all-or-nothing thoughts:

- My efforts are either a success or they are an abject failure.
- I am/other people are either all good or all bad.
- There is right and there is wrong, and nothing in between.
- If I'm not perfect, I'm a failure.
- You're either a real man or you're a wimp.
- If you're not with us, you're against us.
- If it doesn't go exactly as I planned or hoped, it is a fiasco.
- If you don't always show me that you love me, you don't love me at all.

All-or-nothing thinking is common for two reasons. First, we feel threatened by *uncertainty*. Indeed, some people can feel very threatened by this and must know for sure how to act and what is right, and they may try to create the certainty they need by all-or-nothing thinking. Sometimes we may think that people who 'know their own minds' and can be clear on key issues are strong, and we admire them and try to be like them. But watch out. Hitler knew his own mind and was a very good example of an all-or-nothing thinker. Some apparently strong people may actually be quite rigid. Indeed, I have found that some depressed people admire those they see as strong individuals, but when you really explore this with them, they discover that the people they are admiring and trying to be like are neither strong nor compassionate. They are rather shallow, rigid, all-or-nothing thinkers who are always ready to give their opinions.

There is nothing wrong with sitting on the fence for a while and seeing things as grey areas. Even though we may eventually have to come off the fence, at least we have given ourselves space to weigh up the evidence and let our rational minds do some work.

The other common reason why we go in for all-or-nothing thinking has to do with *frustration* and *disappointment* (see Chapter 17). Here is Anne again, whom we met in the last chapter. During her dinner party, she was so focused on making her guests comfortable that she forgot the meal and it overcooked. She concluded: 'I messed up the whole evening. I can't even cook a simple meal. Everyone will now know how inadequate I am.' It was her disappointment/frustration and feelings of threat – of being seen to be no good – that led to her all-or-nothing thinking: 'The whole evening was messed up.' Again this is not that uncommon. How often have we thrown down our tools because we can't get something to go right?

But what was the evidence that the whole evening was messed up? I asked Anne some questions about this (Anne's responses are given in the brackets):

- Did people talk to each other? (Yes)
- Did they chat and laugh? (Yes)
- Was the atmosphere relaxed or tense? (Relaxed)
- Did people throw up after eating your food? (No)
- Did they say they enjoyed it? (Yes)

As Anne later reflected, the food *had* been a disappointment, but this failure had done no more than dent her pride a little. Maybe if she hadn't been so depressed and anxious, she might have seen the funny side of it and cracked a joke. And, if she were honest with herself (she said), her guests might not have realized that the food was overcooked, for only she had known what she had intended to achieve.

So getting out of all-or-nothing thinking and our tendency to make extreme judgments of good/bad or success/failure can be very important in recovering from depression. The state of depression itself can reduce our tolerance of frustration and push us into all-or-nothing thinking, so we have to be aware of this and be careful not to let it get the better of us.

Overgeneralization

If one thing goes wrong, we think that everything is going to go wrong. Our sense of failure can grow until we believe that everything we have ever done was a failure or faked. When we overgeneralize like this, we see one setback or defeat as a neverending pattern of defeats. Nothing will work; it will always be this way.

- A student received a bad mark and concluded, 'I will never make it. My work is never good enough.'
- A friend had told Sue that she would come to her party, but

then she forgot the date. Sue thought, 'This is typical of how people always treat me. No one ever cares.'

- Dan broke up with his girlfriend and thought, 'I will never be as happy again as I was with her. I will always be miserable without her.'

Let's explore some typical challenges/disputes to overgeneralization.

Negative thought	*Disputes and ways of coping*
Things will never work out for me.	'Never' and 'always' are big words. True, I feel really upset and frustrated now, but overgeneralizing is typical when I feel upset.
	I have thought like this before and things did work out – at least to a degree.
	Let me focus on what I can do and the things that might go okay, rather than just blanking out everything.
	Predicting the future is a chancy business.
	Maybe I can learn how to make things go better. I don't have to load the dice against myself.
	If a friend had a setback, I would not speak to him/her like this. Maybe I can learn to speak to myself as I might to a friend.

Egocentric Thinking

In this situation, we have difficulty in believing that others have a different point of view from our own. The way we see things must be the way they see things – e.g. 'I think I'm a failure, thus so must they.'

But there is another way we can be egocentric in our thinking. This is when we insist that others obey the same rules for living and have the same values as we do. Janet was very keen on birthdays and always remembered them. But her husband Eddie did not think in these terms; he liked to give small presents as surprises, out of the blue. One year, he forgot to buy a present for Janet's birthday. She thought, 'He knows how important birthdays are to me. I would never have forgotten his, so how could he forget mine? If he loved me, he would not have forgotten.' But the fact was Eddie did not really know how important birthdays were to Janet because she had never told him. He was simply supposed to think the same way as Janet.

In therapy together with Janet, Eddie was surprised at how upset she had been and pointed out that he did bring small surprise presents, which showed that he was thinking about her. He also mentioned to her – for the first time – that she rarely gave gifts except at birthdays, and to his way of thinking, this meant that she only thought about giving him something or surprising him once a year!

So people often have different views, and because of this, it is often unhelpful to assume that others think as we do – often they don't. All of us have different life experiences and personalities, and our views and values differ, too. These differences can be a source of growth or conflict. It is because we are all different that there is such a rich and varied range of human beings. Unfortunately, at times we may downgrade people if they don't think or behave like us. On the bookstands today, you will find many books that address the fact that men and women tend to think differently about relationships and want different things out of them. This need not be a problem if we are upfront about our needs and wants and openly negotiate with our partners. It becomes a problem when we are not clear with them about our wants or we try to force other people to think as we do.

Key Points

- The way we think about things can lead us further into depression rather than out of it.

continued on next page

- When we are depressed, our brains change in such a way that we become very sensitive to various kinds of harm, threats and losses. Now it is (or was) adaptive for the brain to go for a 'better safe than sorry' type of thinking and to expect the worst when under threat. In these situations, control over our feelings is given more to the primitive emotional brain and less control is given to the rational brain (see Chapters 2 and 3).
- We should try to focus on our negative thoughts and recognize them for what they are.
- There are some typical types of thoughts that are encountered in depression. These include jumping to (negative) conclusions, 'I must', dismissing the positives, all-or-nothing thinking and overgeneralizing. All of these can be successfully challenged.

Exercises

- Review the different types of thinking outlined in this chapter. Identify which ones seem to apply to you (see pp. 355–6 for a quick overview of typical types of negative thinking).
- As you monitor your thoughts, ask yourself which of these depressing styles of thinking you might be using. The more practice you get at identifying and challenging them, the better.
- If you have written down your thoughts, try to spot which kind of depressive style each thought is an example of – for instance, is it an example of jumping to conclusions, or emotional reasoning, or all-or-nothing thinking?
- Use your rational/compassionate mind to remind you of which kind of thought you are using and how to challenge it. Do you have enough evidence? Are you trying to force a certainty when none exists? Are you disbelieving the positives?

continued on next page

- Try to check with yourself to see if these styles of thoughts are going through your mind. Identify them as they happen and try disputing them.
- Consider how you might help someone you like dispute, say, all-or-nothing thinking or jumping to conclusions. Learn to be gentle with yourself rather than harsh and critical, and see things in grey rather than insisting on black and white.
- Try to focus on what you can do rather than what you can't. Have the motto: 'The secret of success is the ability to fail.' (See Chapter 18 for further discussion of this motto.)
- Ask 'How am I looking after myself? Do my thoughts help me care for myself?' Slowly build on your insights.

9

Self-Bullying and How to Challenge It

Thoughts and feelings about yourself as a person usually become very negative in depression. I say 'usually' because this is not always the case. For example, I recall a patient who became depressed when new people moved in next door, and played loud music into the early hours. She tried to get the authorities to stop them, but although they were very sympathetic, they were not much help. Slowly she slipped into depression, feeling her whole life was being ruined and there was nothing she could do. However, she did not think her depression was her fault or that she was in any way inadequate, worthless, weak or bad. Her depression was focused on a loss of control over a very difficult situation.

Sometimes depression can be triggered by conflicts and splits in families or other important relationships. The depressed person may feel very defeated and trapped by these relationships but not to blame for them. Sometimes depressed people feel bad about being depressed and the effects this is having on them and others around them, but they do not feel that they are bad or inadequate as people; they blame the depression.

Nevertheless, many depressed people have a very poor relationship with themselves, and certainly depression does nothing to improve what they feel about themselves. A poor relationship with yourself can predate a depression or develop with it. So in this chapter we will explore the typical styles of 'self-thinking' that depressed people engage in and consider how these thoughts can be challenged. All the styles discussed here can be seen as types of self-bullying. As you will see, we can bully ourselves in many different ways.

Self-Blaming

Blaming occurs when we try to seek the reasons for or causes of things – why did such and such a thing happen? When we are depressed, we often feel a great sense of responsibility for negative events and so blame ourselves. The reasons for this are complex. Sometimes we self-blame because as children we were taught to. Whenever things went wrong in the family, we tended to get the blame. Even young children who are sexually abused can be told that they are to blame for it – which, of course, is absurd. Sadly, adults in looking for someone to blame can simply pick on those least able to defend themselves.

Sylvia was a harsh self-blamer. Her mother had frequently blamed her for making her life a constant misery; over time, this got through to Sylvia and she began to blame herself whenever other people close to her had difficulties. Yet when Sylvia looked at the evidence, she realized that her mother's life was unhappy for a number of reasons, including a difficult marriage and money worries. However, Sylvia as a child could not see this wider perspective but believed what her mother told her.

When people are depressed, their self-blaming can be total. When bad things happen or conflicts arise, they may see them as completely their fault. This is called *personalization* – the tendency to assume responsibility for things that are either not our fault or only partly so. However, most life events are a combination of various circumstances. When we are depressed, it is often helpful to stand back and think of as many reasons as possible about why something happened the way it did. We can learn to consider alternative explanations rather than just blame ourselves.

Sheila's husband had an affair for which she blamed herself. Her thinking was: 'If I had been more attentive, he would not have had an affair. If I had been more sexually alluring, he would not have had an affair. If I had been more interesting as a person and less focused on the children, he would not have had an affair.' All her thoughts were focused on herself. However, she could have had alternative thoughts. For example, she could have thought: 'He could have taken more responsibility for the children, then I wouldn't have felt so overloaded. He could have spent more time

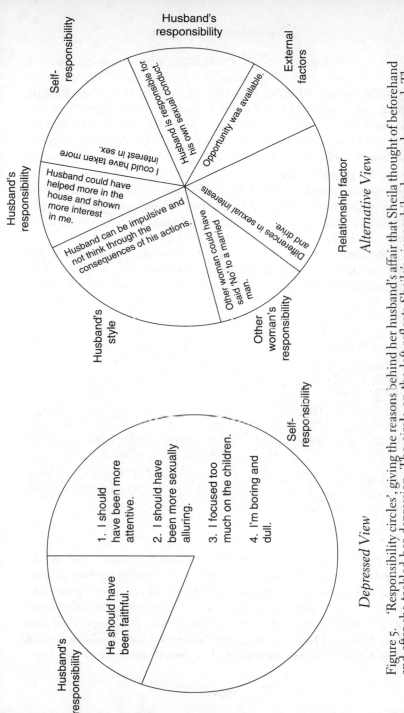

Depressed View

Husband's responsibility

He should have been faithful.

Self-responsibility

1. I should have been more attentive.
2. I should have been more sexually alluring.
3. I focused too much on the children.
4. I'm boring and dull.

Alternative View

Self-responsibility

I could have taken more interest in sex.

Husband's responsibility

Husband is responsible for his own sexual conduct.

Husband's responsibility

Husband could have helped more in the house and shown more interest in me.

Husband's style

Husband can be impulsive and not think through the consequences of his actions.

External factors

Opportunity was available.

Relationship factor

Differences in sexual interests and drive.

Other woman's responsibility

Other woman could have said 'No' to a married man.

Figure 5. 'Responsibility circles', giving the reasons behind her husband's affair that Sheila thought of beforehand and after she tackled her depression. The circle on the left reflects Sheila's views while she was depressed. The circle on the right show how her views changed after she considered the evidence and generated alternatives.

at home. If he had been more attentive in his lovemaking, I might have felt more sexually inclined. Even if he felt attracted to another woman, he did not have to act on it. The other woman could have realized he was married and not encouraged him.'

One can then write down these various alternatives side by side and rate them in terms of *percentage of truth*. Or one might draw a circle and for each reason allocate a slice of the circle. The size of each slice represents the percentage of truth. In Figure 5 on page 141 you can see how this worked for Sheila. The two circles represent a depressed view and a more balanced view. Note how some situations often have many causes. Sheila's more balanced, 'alternative view' circle seemed more true to her once she had considered it.

The same basic principle can apply when we blame others. We may simply blame them without considering the complexity of the issue, and label them as bad, weak and so forth.

Self-Blame and Control

One reason we might self-blame is that, paradoxically, it might offer hope. For example, if a certain event is our fault, we have a chance of changing things in the future. We have (potential) control over it and so don't have to face the possibility that, maybe, we actually don't have much control. In depression, it is sometimes important to exert more control over our lives, but it is also important to know our limits and what we cannot control. Sheila had to face the fact that she could not control her husband's sexual conduct. It was his responsibility, not hers. We have to be careful that, in self-blaming, we are not trying to give ourselves more control (and power) than we actually have (or had).

Avoiding Conflict

Another reason for self-blame is that it may be more comfortable to blame ourselves than to blame others. It may be that self-blame keeps the peace and stops us from having to challenge others. If, when we were children, our parents told us that they hit us because we were bad in some way, we might have accepted their view and rarely argued. This attitude can be carried on into adulthood. The other person always seems blameless, beyond rebuke.

Sometimes we recognize that we are not totally blameless in something, but when it comes to arguing our case, the part that is our responsibility gets blown out of proportion. We become overfocused on it and feel that we have not got a leg to stand on. However, most things in life have many causes, and the idea here is to try to avoid all-or-nothing thinking. By all means, accept your share of responsibility – none of us is an angel – but don't overdo it. Healing comes from forgiving yourself and others.

Expecting Punishment

Sometimes when bad things happen, depressed people feel that they are being punished for being bad in some way. It is as if we believe that good things will only happen if we are good and only bad things will happen if we are bad, so if bad things do happen, this must be because we have been or simply are bad. When Kate lost a child to sudden infant death syndrome, she felt that God was punishing her for having had an abortion some years earlier. The sense of being punished can be quite strong in depression, and quite often, if this is explored, it turns out to relate to a person's own guilt or shame about something in the past. For instance, Richard's parents had given him strong messages that masturbation was bad. But when he began doing it when he was twelve, he enjoyed it – but also felt terribly guilty. For many years, he carried the belief that he was bad for having enjoyed masturbating and sooner or later he was going to be punished for it. When bad things happened to him, he would think that these were 'part of his punishment'.

To come to terms with these feelings we usually have to admit to the things we feel guilty about and then learn how to forgive ourselves for them. It can be difficult to come to terms with the fact that the principles of 'justice' and 'punishment' are human creations. There is no justice in those who starve to death from droughts in Africa. Good and bad things can happen to people whether or not they behave well or badly.

Self-Criticism

Related to self-blame is self-criticism. At times, we can blame ourselves for things but also accept that this was unfortunate and that we can forgive (i.e. be compassionate with) ourselves. However, when we are depressed, we often give much more power to the internal (self-critical) bully who can have a fine time commenting on and criticizing everything we do.

Some people believe that self-criticism is the only way to make them do things. For example, a person might say, 'If I didn't kick myself, I'd never do anything.' They use their self-bullying part to drive them on – sometimes in rather sadistic-masochistic ways. Such a person may believe that threats and punishments are the best ways to get things done. In some cases, this view goes back to childhood. Parents may have said things like, 'If I didn't always get on at you, you wouldn't do anything' or 'Punishment is the only thing that works with you.' They may also have been poor at paying attention to and praising good conduct and rather more attentive of and quick to punish bad conduct. As a result, the child becomes good at self-criticism and self-punishment but poor at self-rewarding and valuing.

In depression, however, self-criticism can get out of hand. The internal bully/critic becomes so forceful that we can feel totally beaten down by it. Then, when we are disappointed about things or find out that our conduct has fallen short of our ideal in some way, we can become angry and frustrated and launch savage attacks on ourselves.

It–Me

Self-criticism can lead to an 'it–me problem': 'I only accept "me" if I do "it" well.' The 'it' can be anything you happen to judge as important. For example, if you are a student, the 'it' may be passing exams. You might say to yourself: 'I'll only accept myself if I pass my exams and I'll hate myself if I don't.' Or the 'it' might be coping with housework or a job: 'I'm only a good and worthwhile *person* if I do these *things* well.' Success leads to self-acceptance, but failure leads to self-dislike and self-attacking.

This kind of thinking means: 'I am only as good as my last performance.' But how much does success or failure actually change us? Do you (as a person) really become good if you succeed and become bad (as a person) if you fail? Whether we succeed or fail, we have not gained or lost any brain cells; we have not grown an extra arm; our hair, eyes and taste in music have not changed. The essence of our being has not changed. Of course, we may lose things that have importance to us if we fail. We may feel terribly disappointed or grieve for what is lost and what we can't have. But the point is that these will be more difficult to cope with if our disappointment becomes an attack on ourselves and we label ourselves rather than our actions as 'failures'.

So it can be helpful to learn that succeeding and failing may feel good and bad – and we can be disappointed by failing – but this does not make us good and bad *people*. If we place too much emphasis on our actions rather than on feeling good about our inner selves, we are at risk of becoming *addicted* to a need always to succeed. We may only feel good if we do succeed. Every failure hurts us so badly because we think that it turns us totally bad inside.

These are not new concepts. In Buddhist and other spiritual traditions, there has long been the idea that we suffer because we become too attached to external successes or failures. They say, 'Be in the world but not of the world.' These approaches can help us recognize that, if we devalue ourselves rather than become disappointed in our actions, we are digging away at the very foundations of our being. Or consider it this way. Your inner being, yourself, is like the inside of a house. Failures and disappointments are like storms that can swirl around it. If a storm blows up, it is preferable to close the doors and windows and protect the inner house rather than throwing open all the windows and doors and letting the storm rip through it.

The key challenge to this problem is to separate *self*-rating and judgments from *behavior* rating and judgments. It may be true that your behavior falls short of what you would like, but this does not change the complexity and essence of you as a *person*. We can be disappointed in our behavior or at what happens to us, but as human beings, we do not have to rate ourselves in such all-or-nothing terms as 'good' or 'bad', 'worthwhile' or 'worthless'. If we do that, we are giving away our humanity and turning ourselves into objects with a market value – we literally dehumanize ourselves. We are saying, 'I can be treated like a car, soap powder or some other "thing".' 'If I perform well, I deserve to be valued. If I don't perform well, I am worthless junk.' But we are not things or objects. We are living, feeling, highly complex beings, and to judge ourselves as if we are just objects carries great risks.

Self-Attack

Recent research has suggested that depression is much more likely if a person's weak/bad, hopeless sense of self is triggered than if self-critical thoughts alone are activated. It seems that, rather than the self-criticism itself, it is the person's response to self-criticism that is associated with depression. When self-criticism becomes hostile and activates basic beliefs and self-labels (e.g. of being weak, bad, inadequate, hopeless, etc.), then depression really takes root.

We all have a tendency to be self-critical. However, when we become angry, frustrated and aggressive with ourselves and start bullying and labelling ourselves as worthless, bad or weak, we are more likely to slip deeper into depression. In a way, we become enemies to ourselves; we lose our capacity for inner compassion. It is as if the self becomes trapped in certain ways of feeling and then (because of emotional reasoning) over-identifies with these feelings. We think our feelings are true reflections of ourselves. For example, 'I *feel* stupid/worthless, therefore I *am* stupid/worthless.'

The main challenges here are to all-or-nothing thinking and emotional reasoning:

- To sum up a person (e.g. myself) in simple terms of good/bad, worthwhile/worthless is all-or-nothing thinking. It is preferable for me to think that there are some things I can do okay and some things I don't do as well as I would like.
- Because I feel stupid and worthless does not make it true.
- The idea of worth can be applied to objects such as cars or soap powder but not to people.
- I don't have to treat myself as an object, whose only value is what I achieve or do.
- If I say 'worthless' is just one of a number of possible feelings that I, as a human being, can have about myself, I can put these negative feelings in perspective.

- If I over-identify with the feelings of worthlessness, I am more likely to get depressed.

Self-Hatred

At the extreme, some depressions involve not just self-criticism and self-attack, but also self-hatred. This is not just a sense of disappointment in the self; the self is treated like a hated enemy. Whereas self-criticism often comes from disappointment and a desire to do better, self-hatred is not focused on the need to do better. It is focused on a desire to destroy and get rid of.

Sometimes with self-hatred are feelings of *self-disgust*. Now, disgust is an interesting feeling and usually involves the desire to get rid of or expel the thing we are disgusted by. In self-hatred, part of us may judge ourselves to be disgusting, bad or evil. When we have these feelings, there may be a strong desire to attack ourselves in quite a savage way – not just because we are disappointed and feel let down, but because we really have come to hate parts of ourselves.

Kate would become overpowered by feelings of anxiety and worthlessness. When things did not work out right, or she got into conflicts with others, she'd feel intense rage. But even while she was having these feelings, she was also having thoughts and feelings of intense hatred towards herself. Her internal bully was really sadistic. She had thoughts like: 'You are a pathetic creature. A whining, useless piece of shit.' Frequently the labels people use when they hate themselves are those that invite feelings of disgust (e.g. 'shit'). Kate had been sexually abused, and at times she hated her genitals and wanted to 'take a knife to them'. In extreme cases, self-hatred can lead to serious self-harming.

Sonia had not been sexually abused but hated the shape of her face and was constantly seeking out plastic surgeons. It is not uncommon for self-hatred to be directed at the body, although this is not always so. It is also often related to shame.

It is important to try to work out what you actually feel about yourself, and see if your bullying, self-critical side has become more than critical and has turned to self-dislike or self-hatred. Even though you may be disappointed in yourself and the state you are in, can you still maintain a reasonably friendly relationship with your inner self? If your internal bully is getting out of hand, you may want to try the following challenges. Using your compassionate mind, and in as warm and friendly a way as you can muster, say:

- My self-hatred is highly destructive.
- Am I a person who values hatred?
- If I don't value hatred and can see how destructive it is, maybe I can learn to get more control over this part of myself.
- What value does my self-hatred serve?
- I know perfectly well that, if I cared for someone, I would not treat them with hatred.
- Am I engaging in all-or-nothing thinking here? Am I discounting my positives?
- Am I as bad as Hitler? No? Then maybe I need to get my hatred into perspective.
- Maybe I need to be tougher with this internal bully and not let it get away with what I am allowing at the moment.
- After all, my self-hating or self-disliking does me no good. It just beats me down.
- Maybe I have learned to hate myself because of the way others have treated me. If I attack myself, I am only repeating what they did to me.

The tough part in all this is that you will need to be absolutely honest with yourself and decide whether or not you want hatred to live in you. Only when you decide that you do not, can you train yourself to become its master rather than allowing it to master you. However, if you are secretly on the side of self-hatred and think it reasonable and acceptable to hate yourself, this will be very difficult to do, and it will be hard to open yourself to compassion and healing. For some people, this is a most soul-searching journey. But as one patient said to me:

The hard part was realizing that, whatever had happened in the past and whatever rage and hatred I carried from those years, the key turning point had to be my decision that I had had enough of my hatred. Only then could I start to take the steps to find the way out.

And, of course, it is not just with depression that coming to terms with and conquering hatred can be helpful. Many of our problems of living together in the world today could be helped if we worked on this. We all have the potential to hate – there is nothing abnormal about you if you feel it. The primary question is: how much life will we give it?

Hatred often comes from hurt – we hate what hurts us or causes us pain. So rather than focus on hatred, it is useful to focus on what the pain and hurt is about. Also, of course, if you discover that there are elements of self-hatred in your depression, don't turn this insight into another attack. Say instead:

> *I am glad I have discovered my hatred. I can now set about learning to be compassionate and test the rationality of my self-hatred. Maybe I am engaging in all-or-nothing thinking or emotional reasoning. When I feel hatred I can recognize it as a symptom of hurt.*

Social Comparisons

Some of our negative self-attacking thoughts arise when we look at others and compare ourselves disparagingly with them. In fact, humans are constantly comparing themselves with others: 'Is mine bigger than yours?' and so on. Even animals use this 'social comparison' to work out which individuals to challenge and which to avoid, whom they can beat and who they are likely to be beaten by. Our brains are set up to socially compare and it can be very difficult to avoid doing it.

Social comparison provides us with much important information. It can be used to make decisions such as 'Am I like others or not like them?', 'Am I one of them or not?', 'Am I an insider or an outsider?', 'Am I better [brighter, stronger, more attractive, more competent] than others, less so, or about the same?' Even a failure can feel better if a social comparison turns out to be positive. Imagine that you fail at an important task – e.g. an exam or driving test. You feel down about your failure. Then you phone your friends and find out that they failed, too. The chances are that you will feel some relief. You will know that it was not just you, so you are not inferior to your friends.

When we are depressed, we tend to compare ourselves with others in negative ways. And for these comparisons, we pick individuals who are indeed (we think) much better than us in some way. In other words, we don't compare ourselves with Mr or Ms Average but with someone we think is doing really well. Jane, a mother of two who devoted herself to their care, had a number of friends who went out to work even though they, too, had children. Jane thought, 'I'm not as competent as them because I don't go out to work, and I have to struggle just to keep the home going.' When I asked her if she had other friends with children who did not have outside employment, she agreed that most of her friends didn't. However, it was not them she compared herself with but the few who did have jobs.

Diane felt really depressed after the birth of her child. She thought that her reaction was different from that of all her friends and therefore there was something wrong with her to feel this way. As a result, she never told anyone but suffered in silence. Then there was Bill, who was a keen tennis player. He was average for his club, but because he would compare himself with the top players, he constantly felt inferior if his performance did not match theirs.

Depressed people tend to discount comparisons with those who would give them good feelings about their abilities and only compare themselves with those who would tend to leave them feeling bad about their performance. In other words, they tend to choose the wrong targets for comparison. Instead of thinking that they are better than XYZ, they focus on how far short they are from ABC. Now, ideally we would not socially compare at all, but set our own standards and live by our own internal feelings. But research suggests this can be difficult, especially for people who have low self-esteem. So if you do compare yourself with others, it is useful to ensure that you don't make these comparisons in ways that leave you feeling depressed and inferior.

Social comparison is rife in relationships between brothers and sisters and other family members. If you have children, you will know that they are always trying to work out if you (as the parent) prefer one of their brothers or sisters. How often have you heard: 'But you let Ken or Sue stay up and watch television – why can't you let me?' 'You said it was all right for Ken or Sue to go and see their friends – why can't you let me go?' Sometimes depressed people have many unresolved problems about these early relationships. They may feel that they have always lived in the shadow of a sibling – were less bright, less attractive and so forth. Jim went to university and did well, but his brother Tom was a more practical person and not cut out for the academic life. However, instead of being happy with himself, Tom constantly compared himself with Jim and felt a failure. He would say, 'Why couldn't I have been the bright one?'

These kinds of problems relate to envy, which can be very destructive if it gets turned against oneself. For example, you might envy those who win prizes or make a lot of money, but if you start to tell yourself that you failed and feel cheated unless you get those things, too, you will run into trouble. In the example above, Tom was very focused on an idea that life had been unfair to him.

Social comparison is one reason why people who seem to have quite prestigious positions in society can become depressed. Some time ago, I worked with a doctor who had done quite well during his training yet, when be became qualified, found the work stressful. He thought that he was doing much worse than his colleagues. Compared with them, he did not feel confident or on a par. So again, the targets of our social comparisons – those with whom we choose to compare ourselves – are important.

Although it can be very difficult if not impossible to avoid making social comparisons, there are some things that we can do to challenge the negative thoughts that arise from them.

- Choose a target to compare yourself with who is most like you. In other words, avoid comparing yourself with those who are clearly a lot better in certain ways.
- When non-depressed people compare themselves with others and find that they don't do so well, they usually discount the comparisons. Depressed people, however, do not discount such comparisons but dwell on them. So if a comparison turns out badly, consider the reasons and evidence why this comparison may not be an appropriate one for you.
- If certain comparisons are making you unhappy, write out the advantages and disadvantages of making such comparisons. If a

comparison benefits you, avoid looking down on others. But if it just leaves you feeling bad and frustrated (and you look down on yourself), there are more disadvantages than advantages.

- If you do compare and feel down, avoid self-attacking. Try to remember that, in all things, there are those who are better at doing certain things or have more, but this does not make you a failure or inadequate because you can't do these things or don't have as much.

- Try to think of your life as your own unique journey, with its own unique ups and downs and challenges. Although you might want to live the life of someone else, this is not possible. Focus on you as yourself rather than you as compared with others.

- Focus on what you can do rather than on what others seem to do better. Don't disqualify the positives in your own performance.

- If you are depressed, try to avoid labelling yourself as inadequate because you think others don't get depressed. Sadly many people do get depressed and anxious.

The Inner Bully

All these negative, self-directed thoughts are *forms of bullying*, so I shall refer to them as the 'inner bully'. The inner bully observes the self and passes judgments ranging from mild criticism to hatred. Where it comes from is unclear, but often it arises from early childhood (see also Chapter 17). If you ask people who their inner bully most sounds like, it is sometimes one or both of their parents. It tends to spring to life in situations of frustration and disappointment with ourselves – when we don't do certain things or fail to reach certain standards.

As I have already pointed out, some people think that, if they did not bully themselves and goad themselves into action, they would never get anything done. But we can see that, if the inner bully gets too much out of control, it can do great internal damage. Consider Anne and the overcooked meal again (page 133). When she did not cook the food well enough, she told herself that she had messed up the whole evening and that she was a failure. But note how destructive her thoughts are. Suppose you said such things to a friend. Would you say, 'You've messed up the whole evening with your poor cooking. You're a failure'? Your friend would be very upset if you did – and would probably never invite you back. But this is the kind of thing depressed people say to themselves constantly.

The inner bully (or internal critic) sets up a self-defeating spiral, shown in Figure 6. So the bully – your internal self-attacks – actually causes many of the problems (e.g. doing less) that it attacks you for. It's as if, after I knock you down, I then hit you because you have gone down. It is very important to see this spiral, for we shall meet it many more times on the journey ahead.

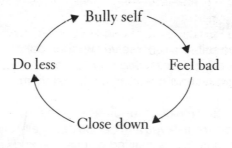

Figure 6

When faced with an inner bully, it is always worth saying something like:

Look, I'm not nearly as lazy/bad/inadequate as I think I am. To be frank, it is my bully hitting me so hard that makes me depressed. This causes most of my problems. I kick myself when I'm down. If I'm really as keen on success as I say I am, the best way to treat myself is with kindness and support when things are not going well. If I feel confident, I am likely to do far more than if I am full of fear, anger and disappointment.

The next thing is to plan out actions so that you can learn to praise your success rather than attack your disappointments. Suppose your inner bully is berating you because you have not worked hard enough on something. You can say:

I am depressed right now, so it's natural not to have my normal drive. Even though I can't do everything I used to, I can still do some things. I can praise myself for what I do rather than attacking myself for what I don't do. There is no way I'm going to bully myself out of depression. All I do is what I am able to do. I can go step by step. By praising my steps, no matter how small they may seem to be, I am moving forward.

And if you fancy a bit of rebellion, you might say to your chores: 'To hell with it. They can wait. I'm going to do something that I want to today!'

Key Points

- We often self-attack ourselves without really realizing what we are doing. Our feelings and moods seem to carry us along into certain styles of thinking and evaluating ourselves.
- If we are to climb out of depression, we may have to take a good look at ourselves and decide if our self-criticism, anger and self-hatred are justified or useful – and what we can do to heal them.
- The hard part can be helping ourselves to focus on the need for inner healing. Once we have, we can then start to focus on what we need to do to be healed. Often the first step is to sort out our relationships with ourselves.

Exercises

- Review the styles of self-bullying thinking covered by this chapter (see also pp. 357–8).
- Try to consider which of these styles (if any) apply to you in general. Get to know the typical ways you bully yourself.

continued on next page

- If something happens and you feel bad about yourself, ask yourself: 'What am I saying about myself? What does this mean about me?' Write down these thoughts.
- Consider in what ways you might be using: all-or-nothing thinking, emotional reasoning, disbelieving positives (see pp. 355–9).
- Using your 'thought form', focus on the fourth column (see pp. 351–54). Use your rational/compassionate mind to generate alternative views about yourself. Look through the examples given in this and other chapters to dispute your negative self-directed thoughts.
- Consider how you might help someone you like stop self-attacking and bullying themselves, and then apply this to yourself. Learn to be gentle with yourself. Imagine a really caring person advising you. What would he or she say? Look at the evidence and think of alternatives. Ask yourself: How am I looking after myself with these thoughts/feelings? Do my thoughts help me to care for or look after myself?' In this way slowly build up your insights.

10

Calling Ourselves Names: How Negative Labels Affect Us

The last chapter focused on thoughts and feelings against the self. Here we consider other types of self-evaluations: how we come to experience ourselves and label that experience. These labels are not necessarily hostile to ourselves but can still play a major role in depression.

Self-Labelling

Most of us have had the experience of feeling bad, inadequate and useless at times. These feelings usually arise when we are disappointed by our actions, have failed at something or have been criticized by others. As we grow up, our parents, teachers, siblings and peers label us in various ways and occasionally call us things that are hurtful. We may be told that we are a nuisance, bad, unlovable, stupid. Or perhaps overprotective parents say that we are not able to make our own decisions or cannot cope by ourselves. Over time, we develop various ways of thinking about ourselves as being certain kinds of people – that is, we come to label and describe ourselves in various ways.

For example, suppose you wrote a letter to a pen friend – how would you describe yourself? Now supposing you were writing for a job – how would you describe yourself? If you were writing to a dating agency, how would you describe yourself? And finally, if you were writing to a priest or someone similar to confess something and seek forgiveness, how would you then describe yourself? If you wrote each of those letters, the chances are that each one would say different things about you.

This is because we as humans are very complex and have many different qualities. But when we become depressed, the richness, variety and vitality of our potential selves drain away and we start thinking of ourselves in rather simple terms, or labels. The labels might be triggered by life events. For instance, you might be rejected by someone you love and then label yourself as unlovable. Or you might fail at some important task and then label yourself as a failure. Negative *labels* are often sparked off by negative *feelings*, which in turn may be strong echoes from the past.

Suppose you were rejected by a lover you were very keen on, and you started to think that you were unlovable. If you are becoming depressed, this is what might happen. When you go into work the next day, the rejection is on your mind. You go down to see a colleague, but she/he is too busy to chat to you and seems to have her/his own problems. Now you start to think, 'Maybe my friend is not so keen on me after all. Actually, maybe we aren't as close as I thought.' Can you see what is happening here? This internal feeling and label of unlovability are now being used to judge other relationships and situations. So the point is that internal labels – the way you think and feel about yourself as a person – can influence many of your perceptions.

Self-labelling is essentially a form of name-calling. In depression, we come to experience ourselves as if that label (e.g. weak, inadequate, worthless, bad) sums up the whole truth about us. Our whole self becomes identified with the label.

The judgments, labels and feelings that we have about ourselves when we are depressed tend to be the same the world over. Whether we live in China, the United States or Europe, depression often speaks with the same voice. The following are some of the words depressed people typically use to describe themselves:

bad	inadequate	outsider	unlovable
empty	incompetent	rejectable	useless
failure	inferior	small	victim
fake	loser	ugly	weak
hopeless	nuisance	unattractive	worthless

To challenge self-labels requires us, first, to recognize that we are thinking of (and experiencing) ourselves in single-word descriptions.

We can try to stand back from the depression and see that it tends to come up with these harsh judgments over and over again. However, we can train our minds to realize that this is only one of many possible sets of judgments. There are others, such as: honest, hardworking, carer, helper, lover, old, young, lover of rock music, gardener. Our depressed negative judgments, which seem so certain and 'all or nothing', can also be examined for their accuracy and challenged. Although depression tends to push us towards certain types of extreme judgments, it is helpful to think that these are only parts of ourselves. Like a piano, we can have and play different notes, and we are far more complex than our depression would have us believe.

Challenges to self-labels can include the following:

- As a human being, I am a complex person. I am the product of many millions of years of evolution, with an immensely complex genetic code and billions of brain cells in my head. I am also the product of many years of development, with a personal history. I can operate in many different states of mind and in different roles. Therefore to judge my whole self, my being and my essence, in single negative terms is taking all-or-nothing thinking to the grossest of extremes.
- When I am depressed, it is natural and understandable that I tend to feel bad and inadequate, but this does not *make* me bad or inadequate. To believe it did would be a form of emotional reasoning. I might feel worthless but this does not make it true.
- Although I tend to focus on negative labels when I am depressed, I can try to balance out these with other ideas about myself. For example, I can also tell myself that I am honest, hardworking and caring – at least sometimes. I can consider alternative labels and inner experiences.
- I can check to see if my thinking has become rather one-sided. Am I discounting the positives in my life, relying too much on my mood to tell me how things really are, overgeneralizing and thinking in extreme ways?
- How do I see myself when I'm not depressed? Okay, maybe not as good a person as I might like, but certainly not as I do now.
- Although depression likes simplistic answers to complex problems

and tends to see things in black and white, good and bad, I don't have to accept this view but can try challenging it.

Having explored the issue of self-labelling and how, at times, we can use very simplistic and crude labels to judge ourselves, we can now consider some typical labels and how to challenge them.

The Empty Self

In some depressions, people can see themselves as empty. Depression tends to knock out many of our positive emotions, and it is not uncommon to find that people lose feelings of affection for those around them. Hence they feel emotionally dead, drained and exhausted. As one patient told me, 'I am just an empty shell.'

An important challenge may be to recognize that this can be a natural symptom of depression. It can knock out your capacity to feel. Thus, it is not you, as a person, who *cannot feel*; rather, you are *in a mental state of not feeling*. As soon as your mood lifts, you will feel again. Try not to attack yourself for your loss of feelings, even though it can be desperately sad and disappointing. Indeed, if you focus on the sadness of it, rather than the badness, you might find that you want to cry, and crying might be the first glimmerings of a return of feelings.

In some depressions, the experience of emptiness is not linked to negative things about the person but the absence of positive things. Paula explained this feeling to me: 'I've never felt bad about myself really. I think I'm not a bad person on the whole, but I just feel that I'm a "wallpaper person".' She felt neither lovable nor unlovable; she just didn't feel anything strongly about herself one way or another. She revealed a history of emotional neglect by her parents. They had not been unkind to her in an aggressive way but were simply not interested in her. With no one in her life who she felt valued her, she had been left with feelings of emptiness and drifting through life. When Paula looked at the advantages and disadvantages of this idea of being a 'wallpaper person', she discovered that, although it gave her a feeling of emptiness, it was also serving a useful purpose: it protected her from taking any risks. She had a motto: 'Nothing ventured, nothing lost.'

Beginning to work towards overcoming this feeling of emptiness often requires a number of things.

- A preparedness to take risks and learn how to cope with failure, disappointment and possible rejection.
- A willingness to explore the possibility that emptiness may, in some way, be protecting you from other fears (e.g. of failure, and taking risks).
- A recognition that emptiness is a form of emotional reasoning – e.g. 'I feel empty therefore I am,' which, of course, does not make it true.

To start to challenge the idea of inner emptiness, let's be clear that you do have preferences, desires, wants and wishes. The pattern of your preferences make you a unique person. Now, if you do have preferences, wishes and wants, you can't be empty or just wallpaper. For a start, you probably want to feel different from how you do now. So that must mean that you desire to achieve a certain state of mind – i.e. non-depressed.

Let's begin by looking at your preferences. What kinds of films do you prefer and what kinds of films do you tend to avoid? What kind of music do you like and what leaves you cold? What kind of food do you like and what makes you feel sick? Would you prefer to eat a piping-hot baked potato or a raw snake or a cockroach? So you do have preferences! What kinds of people do you like and feel comfortable with? Which season do you like best? What kinds of clothes do you prefer? If you say that you have no preferences, try wearing a salmon pink top with fluorescent green trousers that don't fit!

People who feel empty need to awaken something inside themselves. It is as if that 'thing' is asleep. Think about what would happen if it did wake up and you started working on and developing your preferences. Since this means not only thinking about your preferences but also acting on them, this might lead to some anxiety. If so, try to write down your anxious thoughts and challenge them – see if your fears are exaggerated. How could you take steps to overcome your anxieties?

Okay, so you admit that, however mild they might be, you do have preferences. Therefore, you are not completely empty: your situation is not all-or-nothing. But then you might say, 'Yes, but I don't have any qualities that another person might find attractive.' If this is what you think, then your feelings of emptiness may possibly be more related to loneliness. Or it may be that it is a problem of confidence. Have you shared your preferences with others? If not, what stops you? What would it take to turn to someone you know and say, 'I'd like to do this or that. Would you?' If you find that you have thoughts of 'But they may not want to, or they might think that I was being silly or too demanding,' the problem is less one of emptiness and more one of confidence.

It may also be that you are being unrealistic. Do you want to be attractive to some people or to everyone you meet? Are you too focused on social comparison (see pp. 149–52)? Do you believe that, because your parents didn't seem that interested in you, nobody will ever be?

The challenges for this kind of emptiness might include:

- Telling myself I'm empty is a form of emotional reasoning.
- I can learn to focus on my preferences and start to share these with others.
- Emptiness is not a black-and-white issue, not all-or-nothing.
- I may be discounting the positives in my life and saying that some things about myself don't count. If so, what would they be?
- I might be self-labelling here and not appreciating that all human beings are highly complex.
- Maybe it is not so much that I am empty but that I am lonely and I have difficulties in reaching out to others.
- Maybe it is a problem with confidence. If I felt more confident in expressing myself, would I feel empty?
- Am I attacking myself by saying that nobody could be interested in me without giving them much of a chance? If so, how could I give them a chance?

The Nuisance

Nearly all of us humans want the approval of others. This often means that we want to be seen as having things (e.g. talents and abilities) to offer others. And it may be easier to care for others than to be cared for. One problem that can arise is that, when we have needs that can only be met by sharing our difficulties with other people, we feel that we are being a nuisance and may not deserve to be cared for. People can be riddled with guilt and shame about needing help. In their early life, their needs may not have been taken seriously. One patient of mine – whose motto was: 'A problem shared is a problem doubled' – was constantly monitoring the possibility that she was a burden to others. This led to guilt and feeling worse, which, of course, increased her need to be cared for and loved.

The fear of being a nuisance is a sad one. It often means that these people have difficulty in being fully open about their needs and asking others for help. Instead, they tend to 'beat about the bush' when it comes to their own needs and feelings, and send conflicting messages to others. Sometimes patients come to therapy but feel awkward, and instead of getting down to the business of trying to sort out what they feel and why, they constantly worry about burdening me. I try to explore this fear of being a nuisance quite early on. Sometimes it relates to shame, sometimes to a fear that I won't be able to cope with their needs because these are too great and complex. At other times it relates to trust: they think that, while I will be nice to them on the surface, secretly I will be thinking that they are time-wasters, that I will deceive them about my true feelings.

Some challenges to these thoughts might include:

- All humans have a need for help from time to time.
- Am I labelling and criticizing myself for having these needs rather than facing up to them and understanding what they are?
- What does my compassionate/rational mind say about that?
- What is the evidence that others won't help me if I ask them?
- Am I predicting a rejection before it comes?
- Am I choosing to ask people for help who I know in advance are not very caring or would have difficulty understanding my feelings?
- Am I saying that all my needs must be met before I can be helped and therefore am thinking in all-or-nothing terms? Are

some of my needs more important than others? Can I work on a few specific problems or needs at a time?

- Can I break my needs down into smaller needs, rather than feeling overwhelmed by such large ones?
- Can I learn to be more assertive and clear about my specific needs? Would that help me?

There is another aspect that can be useful to consider. Sometimes we know that we are in need of healing or help and that we have to reach out to others, but we don't know what for or what exactly our needs are. That takes some thought. But if you do become clearer on these issues, consider: 'What will you do to help yourself if you do find someone who can meet some of your needs?' This is quite an important question. Of course, you might feel happier with some of your needs having been met, but how will this change you? How will you use these met needs for personal growth?

Sharon was afraid to ask her husband to spend more time with her and to be more affectionate. She thought that this would interfere with his work and that she was simply being a nuisance to him. However, as she explored these needs and considered how she would be different if they were satisfied, she realized that she actually needed his support and approval to boost her own self-confidence and then she would be more able to go and look for work. By thinking what she would do if some of her needs were met – that is, how this would change her – she recognized two things: first, that there were things she could do for herself to help boost her own confidence (e.g. not criticizing herself and learning to be more assertive); and second, she recognized that she could be clearer with her husband about the fact that she wanted him to help her gain confidence to go looking for work.

Let me make one final point about being open about our needs in our close relationships. Sharon also realized that seeking more affection from her husband might not be a burden but would actually strengthen the relationship, and this was something she could test. On reflection, she saw that her husband may well benefit from talking more about his feelings and needs, too. She was able to see that her needs could be joint needs. When she spoke to her husband about this, at first he did not really understand. But she stuck to her guns, and later he, too, came to see that he had been so focused on work that he had become lonely in himself and felt their relationship was drifting. Moreover, he admitted that he knew that Sharon had felt down but was not sure what to do because she only spoke about her feelings in a general way, not the problems that lay behind her feelings – how she was bored and lonely in the house and she wanted to get out and find a job. Also, in order not to burden her when she felt down, he had stopped sharing his own problems with her.

So sometimes our needs may seem very personal to us and we may feel that we are being a burden to others, but sometimes we are actually feeling things about the quality of our relationships. If we worry too much about burdening our nearest and dearest, we will all end up not sharing our problems – everyone keeps things to themselves and the emotional quality of the relationship suffers.

Fakery

Related to emptiness but different from it is the feeling that one is a fake. Now, from an evolutionary point of view, deception and fakery have been very important behaviors for both animals and humans. Quite a lot of animal behavior depends on fakery and bluff, often preventing serious conflict. It is also important to note that children have to learn how to lie. The ability to lie and fake things is actually an important social skill. Sometimes it is better to be slightly less straight or at least diplomatic with people rather than risk hurting their feelings. Those who insist on being 100 percent honest, believing that genuineness is the most important human quality, can actually be real pains. By being honest, they usually mean having the right to be as critical as they want; they don't think about the other person's feelings, but only their own need to be honest. However, the moment someone is as direct with them, they get really upset. At times, we do need to cover our true thoughts and feelings – too much honesty is not always helpful.

The psychoanalyst Carl Jung argued that we all have a 'persona', or mask, that we wear to make ourselves acceptable to others. We simply would not be able to cope with raw feelings all the time. We need to obey certain social rules and be reasonably polite. However, as in most things, a well-functioning persona is a question of balance (not all-or-nothing). If we back off too much from being honest with people and feel that they are taking advantage of us, we can feel intense inner resentment.

When we become depressed, however, we can feel as if everything we have ever done has been a pretence or a fake, or simply the result of luck. Depressed people begin to devalue their previous or current successes. The reasons for this vary. Sometimes these individuals are perfectionists and think less of things that they feel are not up to standard. They know that there are flaws in their actions or achievements but become overly focused on them. They think that they were pretending to be more competent, more good or better in some way than they now feel is reasonable. When one patient – who held an exalted position in the academic world and had won a prestigious prize – became depressed, he felt that he had fooled everyone and that all his writings were false – of little value.

We may also start to worry about whether the feelings we had for others in the past were genuine – or were we just fooling ourselves? However, depression is the worst possible time to start making these kinds of decisions. This is because depression reduces the capacity for positive feelings, and we often become less affectionate. In addition, feeling that we are deceiving others can lead to guilt, which we then try to cover up (see Chapter 14).

When Brenda became depressed, she became preoccupied with having fooled Nick into marrying her and that she was now faking love for him. When she came to see me, we had a conversation that, boiled down to its essentials, went something like this:

PAUL. When you got married, did you think that you were faking your love for Nick?

BRENDA. No, I wouldn't put it like that. I was, to be honest, more unsure about him and more worried than I let on, but we got on okay and I thought it would work.

PAUL. Marriage can be a scary time. So maybe you had mixed feelings and were unsure of what to make of those feelings.

BRENDA. Yeah, I guess so. It was a big step to get married and I was worried about whether I was making the right decision.

PAUL. Do you think that being understandably worried about making the right decision means that you were being deceptive?

BRENDA. I'm not sure.

PAUL. Okay, well, let's put it this way. If you are being deceptive with Nick, is it possible that this is because you are confused in your mind and not sure what you really feel about him?

BRENDA. Oh, yes, all my feelings seem confused right now.

PAUL. Okay, well, let's see this problem as one of confusion rather than one of deliberate deception. Sure, right now you may not feel a lot of love for Nick, but we aren't sure why that is. Maybe there are things you are resentful about, or maybe there are other reasons, but if we work through these, step by step, we might get a clearer picture of what you feel. The problem is, if you just attack yourself for feeling that you are deceiving Nick, then you will feel guilty and find it more difficult to sort out your feelings.

This gradually made sense to Brenda. It turned out that, because she had not been passionately in love with Nick from the start, she felt in her heart that she had deceived him and this made her feel terribly guilty. To overcome her guilt, she would do things in the relationship that she did not want to do (e.g. sex, going out), but she also felt resentful for giving in. She felt rather used by Nick. Slowly Brenda began to see that her main feelings were actually anger and resentment. Once she stopped feeling guilty for having deceived Nick and faking love, she could move on to sort out the genuine problems in the relationship. To do this, she also had to recognize that love is complex and not at all like the movies make out. Brenda discounted the positive in her life by only focusing on her negative feelings and on the times she felt confused about her feelings for Nick rather than on the times she enjoyed being with him.

Sometimes people feel that they have no choice but to fake things. For instance, they may feel that they have to fake love in order to hold together a relationship or a family or, as in the following example, a career. Mike faked a liking for his boss who, he thought, could sack him if he did not make a good impression. But he came to hate himself for being (as he saw it) weak. However, he could have looked at it differently. He could have said, 'I understand that I need to hold on to this job and I don't have that much power to do this other than creating a good impression and getting on with my boss. Actually, I am a very skilled social operator.' This is not to say that it's okay to fake – that's a personal decision. Rather, we need to be honest about it, understand the reasons for it and avoid attacking ourselves for it. If we want to reduce the degree to which we fake things with others, we need to learn how to be more self-confident, compassionate with ourselves and others, and assertive. That will be hard to do if we are attacking and running ourselves down.

The fear of being a fake is not only associated with guilt (as it was for Brenda) but carries the fear of being found out. Some people live in constant fear that, because they are living a pretend life, they will be found out, ridiculed and shunned.

Some challenges of fakery might be:

- It may be true that I may have been lucky in some things, but this cannot account for everything I have achieved. I must have some talent even if it is not as great as I would like.
- Sometimes I fake things because I am confused and/or frightened. It would be better to work on this confusion and fear rather than simply attack myself for the fakery and pretence.
- Faking or not faking is rarely all-or-nothing. There are degrees of faking.
- If I say, 'Everything I have done is a fake,' this is an over-generalization.
- If, since I feel like a fake, I believe I am a fake, this is emotional reasoning. I need to focus on the evidence for and against.
- Feeling like a fake is often a symptom of depression. My depression may not be giving me an accurate view of things or myself.
- If faking is upsetting me, it would be better for me to understand my reasons for it. I might then be in a better position to change. If I attack myself for faking, I will feel much worse and need to fake more, not less. Let's try to be compassionate here and see what lies behind these feelings.

Fakery and deception are more commonly experienced in depression than is often recognized. And the question of fakery and deception often goes to the heart of many social dilemmas. We can feel intensely guilty when we know that we are not being fully honest and genuine. Or we can feel very vulnerable when we are not confident of our behavior or performance and think others might spot the flaws and regard us as fakes. The problem is that, in many situations, there is often no one genuine feeling but many. If you have a row with your partner today, this does not mean that all the other good times you had together were fake. If you are depressed, this does not mean that the other times when you felt good or achieved things were a pretence. It means that you can feel different things at different times and when in different states of mind.

Key Points

- We often experience ourselves as if we could be summed up in single words (weak, empty, inadequate, unlovable, fake, etc).
- The labels may vary from person to person, but most of them imply a negative rather than positive judgment of ourselves.
- When negative feelings and labels about ourselves become central to the way we experience ourselves, they can influence much of what we feel and think.
- It is helpful to try to challenge these labels.

Exercises

- Look at the labels that appeared on page 157 and see if you think that any of these apply to you. If not, maybe there are others that might apply. Examine whether you tend to sum yourself up in single words.
- Think about when you first started to think of yourself in

continued on next page

168

this way. Is it the depression speaking or was it others who told you these things (labelled you)? If it is the depression, don't believe it. If it is others, think about what was happening at the time. How did it benefit them to label you in this way? Did it stop them having to blame themselves? Were you simply an easy target? If so, tell yourself: 'The time has come to give up the labels that others have given me. I wish to become my own person.' Allow yourself to think of giving up these labels – you don't need or want them. What effort would that take? What would the advantages and disadvantages be? What would stop you doing this?

- Begin to use your compassionate/rational mind to challenge these single labels. For example:

Label says   *Compassionate/rational mind says*

I am a failure   This label comes from feeling depressed, and when I am depressed, I tend to think in a lot of negative ways.
                  For example, I tend to discount the positives in my life and indulge in emotional reasoning.
                  Sure, right now I feel bad – but let's not turn that bad feeling into an attack on the whole of me.
                  What evidence is there against this label? Am I being all-or-nothing here?
                  If I was helping a friend in a similar situation, what would I say to him or her?
                  What would someone who cared for me say? How might they help me look at my other qualities? What could I do to stop myself from saying, 'Their views don't count'?

continued on next page

> Am I comparing myself disparagingly with others?

Try to work out other challenges that might help you. Be aware that you might tend to undermine your challenges. Ask yourself: 'What have I got to lose by going with these challenges for a while and seeing if they help?' Remember, in depression we are usually very good at focusing on the negatives. Negative beliefs from childhood and stress hormones both incline us to focus on the negative (see Chapter 2). The task now is to develop the ability to look for the positives. Also recall that the more you practise attending to the positives, the better this will be for your mood and reduce stressful signals (see Chapters 2 and 3).

11

Further Methods to Challenge Negative Thoughts

The last few chapters focused on various ideas on how to identify and challenge depressing thoughts and feelings: monitoring your thoughts; developing clarity by writing them down; learning to spot depressive thinking styles (e.g. overgeneralization, all-or-nothing thinking, self-attacking); challenging these thoughts by considering the evidence for and against; and looking for alternatives. This chapter explores some other options for challenging depressive thoughts and feelings. I would suggest that you try some of the exercises in the previous chapters first (so that you have some experience of identifying your thoughts and challenging them) before you try the ideas here.

Using Flash Cards

Flash cards can be used as reminders of the sorts of useful things that you tell yourself when you are feeling depressed. To make a flash card, get a blank postcard or a similarly sized piece of paper. On one side, write down one of your most typical negative thoughts; then, on the other side, write down some key challenges to this. Repeat this exercise for all the negative thoughts you usually have.

For example, suppose that you have the constant thought: 'I will never get better.' On a day when you don't feel quite so bad, write out this thought on one side of a card. Now, on the other side, write down what you imagine you might say to a friend or how you imagine someone who cares for you might speak to you. Remember, try to consider these ideas not with a cold mind but with as much warmth and friendliness as you can muster – as if someone who cares about you is encouraging you to make your journey out of depression. Here are some ideas:

- It is natural and normal to feel like this because I am depressed.
- This is typical of my depression – it always looks on the dark side.
- Because I feel like this it does not make it true or a fact. The evidence is that people do recover from depression.
- Although I (understandably) want to feel really well right away, I might be trying to achieve too much. Maybe I could aim for just a little improvement and work with that, step by step.
- Focusing on the idea 'I will never get better' will make me feel worse. It would therefore be preferable to focus on what I can do rather than what I can't.
- It would be a good idea to distract myself from dwelling on these thoughts by listening to music or the radio, by taking myself out for a walk or by doing some gardening.
- If I learn to go step by step, I might learn to get more control over my depression. Let's really give it a go and see how far we can get.

When you look at these ideas, how do they seem? Running through your mind are there ways of discounting them – as is typical in depression? Are you thinking 'yes but', or 'this might be okay for others but not me'? If you are having these thoughts, remember – this is the depression speaking. What have you got to lose by trying? How might you challenge these dismissive thoughts?

Let's try another typical negative thought that involves self-labelling: 'I am a bad, weak or inadequate person for being depressed. I never thought it would happen to me.' Your flash card might list some of the following:

- There is nothing bad, weak or abnormal about me because I am depressed. Up to one in five people could have times when they feel like me – at least to a degree.
- Many people in high places (film stars and politicians) have suffered from depression. Depression can't be about weakness if all these people can get depressed, too.
- There is a lot of evidence against depression being about weakness or badness. Winston Churchill got depressed and he was hardly a weak person.

- I would not speak to friends like this. I would try to understand and encourage them. Labelling them (and me) bad or weak does no good at all. It is just another form of bullying.
- When I get depressed, I focus on all my bad points. I need to focus on what I have done and can do.
- I'm better off not dwelling on depressing ideas. I can try to distract myself right now.

You can carry your flash cards with you (in a pocket or handbag) and take them out to give you a boost and help you focus on controlling negative thoughts. Some people have also found that pinning them up in particular places around the house can be beneficial. For example, a woman I know who wanted to lose weight and had trouble controlling her snacking put a card on her refrigerator. It read:

> So you feel like a snack right now? But think about this. Do you really need it? Would you feel better if you resisted the urge? Have a cup of tea instead. Hold on and you will be pleased with yourself tomorrow.

By reading this every time she was tempted to snack, she gained just that little bit of extra control.

Preparing Yourself for Stressful Situations

If you know that you have something stressful coming up, you can prepare for it in advance. You can use flash cards as reminders for coping. For example, suppose you are going to have people over for a meal. One response might be: 'Oh God, it's too much. I'll never cope.' You could write down some key coping thoughts before the event:

- Maybe it won't be as bad as I think. Let's get the evidence.
- I can break down what I have to do into small steps. Each small step might be 'do-able'.
- I can try to avoid filling my head with 'can't do' thoughts even though I don't feel like doing it.
- I can develop a plan of action. I can rehearse the relaxation skills while I'm doing it, keep a check on my body and try to control any tension. Concentrate on what I'm doing. If I start to

criticize myself, I'll say, 'Look, I'm doing okay, not great maybe but okay.'

- When the guests arrive, I can give them drinks and ask them about themselves. People like to be asked things about themselves; the focus does not have to be on me.
- If I feel tense during the meal, I can work on my relaxation. I can get up, go to the kitchen, or go outside for some air. I am not trapped here. I am free to go where I want – it's my house.
- I can try imagining it going off reasonably well rather than only imagining it going badly. The aim is to show myself that I can cope and this is all I want to do right now. I will avoid all-or-nothing thinking (i.e. it has to be great or it's a failure).
- Each step of the way, I will focus on doing okay and try to avoid telling myself negative things. I can do my best to keep my inner helper with me and praise myself for any small success.

The aim of this kind of work is to help you to prepare for things that you might find difficult. The more you try focusing on coping, the easier it may get.

If Emotions Could Speak

Some depressed people say that they do not have clear thoughts going through their minds, only feelings. I remember once driving to work feeling rather down. At first, I could not focus on anything in particular, so I used the technique of 'If my feelings could speak, what would they say?' I tried to get my 'down' feeling to tell me what was wrong. As I followed this idea, I found that I could begin to identify what my 'down' feeling was about. It said, rather out of the blue. 'Your life is going nowhere. You're getting old now and your chances have gone.' As I followed this thought, I recognized that it had been triggered by playing cricket. Through my thirties, I had been too involved with work to play the game, which I had enjoyed in my youth, but had taken it up again in my mid-forties. Although I'd been a reasonable player when at university, I was not now. Compared to the younger players, I was a lumbering oldie with a poor eye for the ball. I suddenly realized that I was grieving for a lost youth! When we allow our feelings to speak freely, they can take us to some strange places.

So if you can't identify thoughts but you can identify feelings, say to yourself, 'If my feelings could speak, what would they say?' Speak out loud the things that come into your mind; let the ideas flow. As you allow your thoughts to flow, be aware of them but avoid trying to direct them anywhere. Just see what comes up, what passes through your mind when you focus on the feelings. Be prepared to draw a blank sometimes or for thoughts not to make much sense. The idea here is to allow yourself to go on your own journey of guided discovery.

Joe felt angry but said he did not have any particular thoughts. I invited him to sit back in his chair, close his eyes, focus on that part of his body that seemed to hold his anger and just let thoughts go through his mind. I said: 'Okay, Joe, feel the anger in your body, go into it. Now, if your anger could speak, what would it say?' Joe found his mind coming up with: 'Why do people treat me so badly?' and 'Life is such a shit.'

This was the beginning point for more work. It became possible to focus on precisely what it was that, for Joe, made life a shit. Because of experiences in the past, he felt that he was missing out on things. We were able to explore how, when he felt angry, there was often a background thought that he was missing out. He was then able to see how this thought made his life more painful, thus increasing rather than reducing his tendency to miss out on things and feel depressed. He worked out how he could challenge these ideas with more helpful ones. He came up with:

- I can learn to live from day to day rather than constantly looking back in anger.
- My anger is understandable but not helpful. Anyway, what is gone is gone.
- I can be sad about that but don't have to walk around feeling hard done by all the time as this makes it more difficult to live the kind of life I want now.
- In reality, there are some good things in my life, such as my marriage, which I am not making the best of.

He realized that he had been so eaten up with anger about the past that he could not move forward to enjoy life. He also had the idea that he had to hang on to his anger and should remain a living testament of how bad things had been.

Speaking with Different Parts of Ourselves

In the book so far, we have talked about having depressing thoughts, anxious thoughts, angry thoughts, rational thoughts, compassionate thoughts and so on. Sometimes, it is helpful to think of these thoughts as if they represent different parts of ourselves, and use an approach that allows us to name these various 'parts' or types of thoughts. Self-critical thoughts can be called the 'internal bully', self-supportive thoughts can be named the 'inner helper' and so forth. If we give space to these inner selves (types of thoughts), it allows us to observe and listen to the different types of conversations going on inside us. The point is that we are not one-dimensional beings, and in many situations, we can have a mixture of thoughts and feelings.

Sometimes it is useful to imagine that you are an outside observer or, if you prefer, a mediator – someone who is going to invite various parts of yourself to have their say. Here is one way you might do this. Get three chairs. Sit in one of them with the other two facing you. When you are in the chair that you are sitting in, you are the observer or mediator. In one of the chairs facing you, imagine the internal bully. Then, ask yourself, 'What does my bully [self-critical thoughts] say about this or about me?' Then write down all the things that come to mind. When you have done this, go over it, perhaps reading it aloud. Say, 'Okay, I want to check that I have understood the bully's point of view. You, bully, are saying that [your name] is a no-good person because he/she did not work hard enough on _____ , or failed at _____ ' – whatever self-critical thoughts you are having about yourself.

Now focus on the other chair, from which you can imagine your rational and compassionate self (your inner helper) will have a say. The inner helper might say:

Well, it's easy for the bully. Anyone can knock things down and criticize. The bully might think it's tough and strong, but real strength comes from supporting people when times are hard – not in lashing out at them. Bullying is not helpful. [Your name] needs support and encouragement. The evidence is that the bully is going in for a lot of all-or-nothing thinking (overgeneralizing, discounting the positives, self-labelling and so forth).

Let the rational/compassionate mind (represented by the inner helper) focus on the evidence, and *give examples* of how the bully is indulging in all-or-nothing thinking, etc.

The idea here is to help you externalize and clarify your various inner thoughts, to bring them out into the open. By carrying out this exercise, you will be allowing yourself some space to get to know your self-criticisms and the degree to which they might be affecting you without you realizing it. This will help you gain some clarity on what is going through your mind. It also allows you to try listening to your inner helper.

We can't hold many thoughts in our heads at once. So this process – of allowing the various parts of yourself (the various thoughts that are in your mind) to have their say in a controlled way – can help to make clear which thoughts and evaluations are most important to you. You can try it with different types of thought: anxious thoughts, angry thoughts, sad thoughts, etc.

As you ask the questions and listen to what is said (thought), you as the mediator want to bring some harmony to your inner world. You want to bring some inner peace. So you will always be on the side of the inner helper. You might also gain more insight into your inner self-critical part so that it won't get away with the things that it has done (e.g. all-or-nothing thinking). Again, the idea is simply to help you become more aware of your negative thoughts and to try challenging them.

Something else you might find helpful is a 'playful' style, e.g. playing each part as if you were trying to win an Oscar. Now this is not at all easy when we are depressed, but this does not mean we cannot try to be playful and take our inner thoughts less seriously. Another thing you might ask yourself is, 'Does the bully remind me of anyone? If so, who?' Then consider what you would really like to say to that person or persons – I mean, *really* like to say. Look around you – you are alone with just three chairs. You can say whatever you like – absolutely anything.

If you find that you are having a hard time getting your compassionate mind to deal with the inner bully, remember some of the things I've written in this book and try saying them. Put some feeling into this. Remember that the compassionate/rational mind can help to control bullies.

If it is still difficult to bring your self-critical bully under control and you find the exercise makes you feel worse in an unhelpful way, then this method may not be for you. Instead stick with writing things down.

Writing About Yourself

Sometimes it is useful to try shifting perspectives on how we see ourselves. One way of doing this is to write a short letter about yourself, from the point of view of someone close to you who cares about you. Such a letter might include:

- I have known [your name] for about twenty years. To me, he/she has been _____ .
- I find him/her _____ .
- I think he/she struggles with _____ .
- I like him/her because _____ .
- His/her strengths are _____ .
- It would help him/her if he/she could _____ .
- I think he/she needs to _____ .

Write whatever comes into your mind, although on the whole, I would avoid focusing on negative things – something that, when you arc dcprcsscd, comcs all too casily. This exercise is designed to help you develop the habit of getting other perspectives on yourself. If you like, show what you have written to someone you are close to and trust and see what he or she thinks.

Changing Negative Images

When we are depressed, we often feel as if we are in a deep hole or pit and our internal images are very dark and harsh. Because this internal world can blacken our lives, it is sometimes helpful to work with these images directly. If you feel in a deep hole, imagine a ladder coming down to you and that you are climbing out, rung by rung. It would be nice to jump out in one go, but that's only possible for a superman or superwoman and I have yet to meet one of those. Each time you succeed at something, that's one more rung up.

If your inner image is dark, try imagining getting some light in by installing some windows, or build a door and get out. Try not to accept the image passively but start to change it so that it becomes more healing.

Carol had thought about getting out of a difficult relationship and coping on her own, but her internal image was always of living in some dark, cold place that nobody ever visited and which she never left. Carol thought that some of her dark images might have had their origins in being left in a cot in a dark room as a child. By focusing on one of these images and using active imagination (i.e. moving into the image), it became clear just how dark this image of being out of the relationship actually was. Then it became possible to explore and change the image. She imagined what she could do in this place to change it, how she would like her own place to look, how she might decorate it, what pictures she might put on the walls, what flowers she might buy, what friends she might invite around, and so on.

The key thing about images is that, once you have a sense of them, you can work on how you would like them to change. Avoid simply bringing the image to mind and then feeling worse because you are not working to change it. It is changing the image that is important.

Sometimes people enjoy painting. Now when we are depressed we tend to paint dark pictures, but it can be helpful to try to paint healing ones. Think about the kinds of images that are healing. These may be of a country scene or of water – a seascape, for instance. Again the key idea is to acknowledge the dark images but also to introduce light and healing.

To Do or Not to Do?

The main reason for doing things is that they should help you.

The primary idea is to avoid only doing things because you feel you have to do them – this often leads to exhaustion. Sometimes, in depression, we really do need to do less, not more.

Betty told herself that she had to do things because her therapist had said that this would make her feel better. So she was really doing them because she had been told to, not because she saw the value in doing them. Before embarking on an activity when you are depressed, keep in mind the following questions:

- If I do this, will I feel better for doing it?
- Am I doing enough positive things for myself?
- Am I only doing this because I have to, or have been told to?
- Do I give myself enough praise when I succeed?

Changing Values

We learn some of our values and attitudes because important people in our lives have told us that some values are good and/or punished us if we did not conform to them. Our attitudes towards sex, religion or expressing anger are often learned in this way. Sometimes we adopt values by copying others, even those in society in general. For example, there is concern today that thinness is so highly valued as a female trait that many young women are getting caught in over-restrictive diets that can spiral into anorexia. We take certain of these values into ourselves (i.e. internalize them) and they become our values and the ways that we judge ourselves.

Getting out of depression sometimes means that we have to re-examine our values and our attitudes. We may find this enormously difficult and painful because we may lose our sense of who we are and have to accept new risk. And to make matters worse, we may feel a great sense of disloyalty in changing our values from the ones our parents have given us. Sometimes we cling to values that are quite harmful to us because, in the back of our minds, we still hope to succeed with them and make our parents (or others) proud of us.

Sam had a high need to achieve and do well because his father had told him that only achievement counts in the world. Sam knew that his achievement style and intense self-criticisms were doing him no good, and he also worked out that the voice of his inner critic sounded very much like his father. And yet, despite this insight, he could not let go of the idea: 'If I don't achieve anything, I am worthless.' For him to give up these values required him to give up the idea that he would, one day, get it right and prove himself. That had always been his hope, and to abandon that seemed like letting his father down and leaving himself with nothing in life to aim for. It took a long time for him to see that, while achieving things was nice and gave him a buzz, it was not helpful to base his whole self-worth on it; that putting all his eggs in one basket was a severe restriction on his sense of worth; and that his father had been wrong to imply that Sam was nothing without achievement.

To help you explore this, write down two columns. In the first, write down the values that you think that you have learned from others. In the second, list the values you would like to impart to someone you love – e.g. a son or daughter. Here is an example.

Possible attitudes/values I have learned from others in my life	*Attitudes I would like to impart to someone else (e.g. a child or friend) to help them be happy*
Women should not enjoy sex.	Sex can be fun and enjoyed. Everyone has the right to a satisfying sexual life.
You should not express anger.	It is important to be able to express your true feelings and not hide them. Anger can be turned into assertiveness.
Other people's needs are more important than your own.	Everybody's needs are important. If you only attend to other's, you will become out of touch with your own needs and become just a servant. Eventually you will get depressed and be less able to care for anyone.
Being depressed is a sign of weakness.	Depression is a painful state of mind that needs to be understood. Throughout history, many millions have been depressed.

Far from being weak or no good, depressed people are often following their values to the letter, bending in every conceivable way to try to make them work. If such people fail at this, they don't re-examine their values but attack themselves vigorously. In fact, it is the strength of their efforts to maintain their values that can, at times, drive them into depression. The main problem here is that, although they may try to 'fight' the depression, do all the things they believe they should do and stick rigidly to their (learned) values and judgments, they end up enduring their depression but not actually challenging it. They think that, with just a little more effort, they will win through. But challenging depression may mean exploring values and attitudes that are no longer useful. Working hard to get well may mean working hard to change some of our attitudes – not just following them more vigorously.

Life Scripts

Another way to think about attitudes and values is to tackle them in the form of 'life scripts' or as typical roles we easily slip into. These offer an identity. For example, think for a moment about what kind of person you are. Try completing this sentence: 'I am the kind of person who _____ .' You may have many endings, not just one.

What did you come up with? Did you have things like 'I am the kind of person who cares for others/is a hard worker/should never show anger'? Or 'I am the kind of person who always loses out/gives in/gets left behind/fails at the last hurdle'? Or 'I am the kind of person who waits to be chosen rather than actively chooses/does not show off'? The point about life scripts is that they are like parts in a play. At times, it can seem as if we are performing a part written by someone else. We might even blame fate. But over the next few days ponder on how you might answer this question and see if any new ideas come to your mind. See if one of your life scripts – i.e. a role – seems to repeat. If so, write these repetitions down and think about where this script might have come from. Gently consider what you would have to do to change it, how might you act in different ways if you had different values. To begin with, just play with a few ideas.

Another life script you might try is: 'I am the kind of person who is not or does not _____.' Here you might note: 'I am the kind of person who is not selfish/deliberately hurtful to others for fun/cheats on others.' Or 'I am the kind of person who does not enjoy sex/put my needs first' and so on. To form an identity often means discovering both things we think we are and things we think we are not.

If you identify a life script – a style of living that makes you 'you' – think about how you might wish to change it. What would you need to do? Can you go some way towards being more as you would like to be? Recall change can be slow, step by step.

Key Points and Exercises

- You can make flash cards with negative thoughts and alternatives to act as reminders.
- Allow your emotions to speak. Give them a voice and then explore their inner meaning.
- Use chairs to enable yourself to express out loud the various types of thoughts that might be going through your mind.
- Consider some of the images that you have in your mind when depressed and try to introduce more soothing and healing images.
- Consider some of your basic life values and attitudes and decide if they are useful to you. For those that aren't, try changing them by thinking about the values you might want to impart to someone else. Those values are more likely to be your own, genuine values and attitudes.
- All of us live out various roles or 'life scripts'. These can be changed if we give ourselves the space to consider what they might be and how we might tackle them step by step.

PART III

Special Problems Associated with Depression

In this section, we will apply the ideas discussed in Part II to specific problems in depression, some of which may apply to you and some may not. I have written this section so that the chapters make more sense if you work through them in the order given. If you don't understand certain sections, skip them and come back to them later. Some chapters cover the same ground and same issues but from different points of view.

12

Approval, Subordination and Bullying

Approval

We begin Part III with the issue of approval because a desire to be approved of, recognized, wanted, appreciated, valued and respected is often at the heart of many of our personal conflicts and worries when depressed. When we explore other problem areas, such as shame, anger, disappointment and perfectionism, we will find that the issue of 'approval from others' is often in the background, if not in the foreground.

Some people may become vulnerable to depression because they have an excessive need for approval, sometimes called 'approval addiction'. A person may believe that approval is always good and necessary and disapproval a disaster. Some individuals have a need to impress others and be seen as special. Others feel completely downcast if they are criticized. Yet others feel unlovable or abandoned if they don't get constant approval. Sometimes, the loss of approval affects us badly because we take what others say about us to be the whole truth. If others say that we are unlovable, useless or silly, we feel that this is true (even if their judgments are rather extreme and ignore the positive aspects of ourselves). Or we may overgeneralize, concluding that if one person thinks badly about us, then others will too.

Approval, Shame and Acceptance

For some people, an excessive need for approval comes from a need to make up for feelings of intense inadequacy and shame – i.e. there is a belief that 'If others approve of me, I can't be so bad/

inferior.' However, before exploring ways in which we can become less sensitive to the need for, and loss of, approval, it is important to recognize that the need for approval is very much part of human nature. Think, for a moment, what our world would be like if no one cared what others thought of them, if no one worried about gaining approval.

Much of our competitive conduct is related to gaining approval – whether it be passing an exam, winning a sports competition or beauty contest, or even having friends say nice things about our cooking. We often do these things to court other people's approval, to feel valued. We would like them to see us as able and competent, in order to raise our status. We also have a need to belong to groups and to form relationships and so avoid being seen as inferior or rejected altogether. Indeed, people will do all kinds of crazy things to win the approval of others, be this of friends, parents or even God. And the fashion business would have a hard time if we were not concerned with gaining the approval of peers by following the latest fashion. So by obtaining approval, we raise our own status and feel accepted in our groups and relationships.

Keith, an ex-soldier, said that getting drunk and being seen as tough was a way of gaining approval from other men. To be regarded as weak would result in not being accepted and shamed. He had suffered terrible hangovers rather than risk being seen as 'not one of the guys.'

Debby grew up in a very wealthy family where associating with certain kinds of people or having left-wing political views was very disapproved of and seen as shaming. In therapy, she struggled to find her own values and develop a way of living that suited her rather than follow the lifestyle of her parents and social group. Debby was often in conflict with what she felt she 'ought to do' and what she 'wanted to do'. The approval of her parents mattered a great deal to her, and her hardest task was breaking free of the fear of possible family condemnation and finding her own values.

There have been many accounts of the agony that people have felt when they have wanted to marry out of their class or religion – and thus risk the disapproval of others close to them. So, following family traditions, or adopting totally the values of the group we are in, can play an important role in our approval-seeking behavior.

Nearly all humans have a basic fear of disapproval, especially when it comes from those we value or look up to, or on whom we feel, in some way, dependent. If we do not value the person, his or her approval matters rather less, unless he or she has some power over us – for instance, as a boss might.

Don't criticize yourself if you recognize that you are an approval seeker – frankly, most humans are. The problems come if you are too dependent on it, feel overwhelmed by the loss of approval, and become self-critical without it. You need to try to keep the desire for approval in balance – not all-or-nothing (e.g. I must be totally approved of, or I don't give a damn).

Approval and Self-Judgments

Unfortunately, our need for approval can become a trap when we pursue it to an excessive degree. When this happens, it is not just fear of rejection or not fitting in that causes us problems but our whole sense of ourselves can be affected. We take the approval or disapproval of others to be judgments on our whole selves. We may become very self-critical if we do things that do not meet with approval or are criticized. Coping with disapproval is easier if you come from a loving background because then you are more likely to have developed a basic sense of being 'okay as a person'. But even if your background was not such a good one, there are many ways of learning how to cope with disapproval and reduce an excessive need for approval.

In general, it is helpful to recognize that it is not a good idea to put too much faith in other people's judgments of you. This does not mean that specific criticisms are never valid, but global labels (e.g. 'weak', 'stupid') and put-downs say more about them than you. Even our nearest and dearest can be disapproving some of the time or fail to notice things about us that we would like them to give special attention to. This can lead to disappointments but not serious problems unless we start to attack ourselves or those we love.

For example, Liz had a new hairstyle and hurried home to show Carl. He had liked her old hair style and was unsure about the new one, so he was cagey about whether he liked it or not. Liz felt deflated and started to think, 'I thought he'd really like it but he doesn't. Maybe I made a mistake. Perhaps others won't like it.

Why can't I do anything right?' Liz started to feel inadequate and angry with Carl. Note how Liz's disappointment turned into:

- *All-or-nothing thinking*: 'he doesn't like it,' rather than 'he's unsure' or 'he likes it a little' or 'he may come to like it when he's used to it.'
- *Overgeneralization*: 'others won't like it,' instead of 'I like it and the people in the shop said it looked good. Just because Carl is unsure doesn't mean that everyone won't like it.'
- *Self-criticism and self-attack*: 'why can't I do anything right?' instead of 'a hair style is a hair style and not evidence that I do things right or wrong.'

Liz had developed various fantasies that the new hairstyle would really impress Carl, and it was a disappointment when this did not happen. If this sort of thing tends to happen to you, consider some of the pointers for coping outlined in Chapters 13 and 17, on shame and frustration.

Some people have feelings of inner emptiness if they do not constantly gain the approval of others. Wants, wishes and what were once thought to be good ideas seem to evaporate the moment another person does not go along with them or seems to disapprove. If this is the case for you, think about the possibility that you can start to find your own self by exploring your own preferences. Search inwards rather than outwards. Review the section on the empty self in Chapter 10. Ask yourself: What things can I value that do not depend on other people's approval? Even if someone disagrees, this is not 'all-or-nothing' – e.g. they are right and I am wrong.

Mind Reading

When we become depressed, we can need so much reassurance that we become extremely sensitive to the possibility that others do not like or approve of us – they might be deceiving us – and we can engage in what is called 'mind reading'. In this situation, rather small cues of disapproval are seen as major put-downs or rejections. A friend hurries past in the street and does not seem to want to talk to you. If you are depressed, you might think: 'My friend does not really like me and wants to avoid me,' rather than: 'He/she seems rushed and hassled today.' So if you are unhappy with someone's attitude towards you (perhaps because they were critical or ignored you), it is important for you to reflect on the evidence. Ask yourself:

• Did the critical remark or look really represent a major putdown?
• How would I have felt about it if I was not depressed?
• Am I mind reading and thinking that the person thinks more negatively about me than they actually do?
• Am I assuming that a small disruption in the relationship is a sign of a major breakdown in it?
• Am I thinking in all-or-nothing terms or overgeneralizing? For example, am I saying, 'If someone cares about me, they must never ignore or criticize me.'
• What will I think about this event in a week's or month's time – am I likely even to remember it?
• Am I expecting others never to have a bad day and be grumpy and irritable?

The Subordinate Self

The Subordinate Approval Trap

The subordinate approval trap often begins when you feel low in self-worth but you work out that you can feel better about yourself if others approve of you. So you set out on a life's task of winning approval – which, on the face of it, may sound like a good idea. But the way you seek to gain approval might involve various unhelpful things. For example, you might try to be what the other person wants you to be. You might avoid owning up to your own needs. You might hide your anger. You might be overly accommodating, hoping that the other person will appreciate this. Sadly, what can happen is that other people may get used to you simply fitting in, and the odd nod of disapproval can have you hurrying back to please them. So you end up feeling like a doormat and worthless. However, you know how to deal with feeling worthless – you try to win other people's approval – and so around and around we go, as Figure 7 shows.

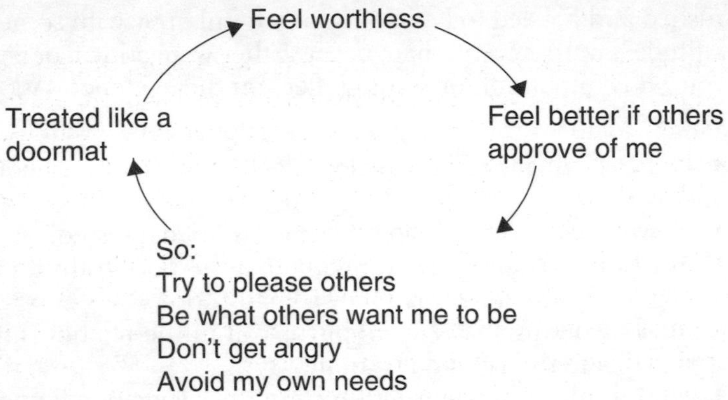

Feel worthless

Treated like a
doormat

Feel better if others
approve of me

So:
Try to please others
Be what others want me to be
Don't get angry
Avoid my own needs

Figure 7

Getting out of this circle requires that you are aware that you are in it, and that it is, to a degree, you who are setting yourself up for it. Next you need to challenge the idea that you are worthless. Remember that this is a self-label and is more likely to be kept in place by your inner bully up to its old mischief. Perhaps you might go back a few chapters and recall how to challenge your inner bully. Remind yourself that 'worthless' is a label and unhelpful. Try not to discount the positive aspects of your life. Focus on what you can do rather than what you can't. What would your friends say about you? Remind yourself of some of the disadvantages of constantly seeking approval and some of the advantages of learning how to accept disapproval without attacking yourself.

Approval feels good but you can't base your self-esteem on it. Try to praise yourself more and avoid disbelieving it when you do. Treat yourself as you would treat a friend. Remind yourself that you do not have to be anyone's servant. Try being assertive about your own needs (see Chapter 16).

One of the major problems with an excessive need for approval is that it can lead to a subordinate sense of self. It is as if we can't do much on our own initiative but must always get permission. We feel that we have to ensure that whatever we want to do is approved by others. This kind of subordination increases our vulnerability to depression.

The Puppet

A puppet, as we all know, is a toy that moves when the strings are pulled by a puppeteer. Pull the strings up and down and the puppet dances; let the strings go slack and the puppet flops. At times, if we become too dependent on approval, we are in effect making ourselves into puppet people: if other people approve of us, we feel good, but if they disapprove, we flop.

Of course, approval may matter a lot when it helps us get a job or get on in a relationship. However, a serious difficulty arises when we make negative judgments about ourselves if we don't get the approval we want. If you are wondering if you have puppet tendencies, think of a recent event that upset you which involved either disapproval or criticism. Now write down your thoughts and check if the disapproval sparked off any negative thoughts in you. If it did, consider what the rational/compassionate mind would say.

Here's an example: You put what you thought was a good idea to others at work but they are not impressed and said that it was poorly thought out. Your negative thoughts might include:

- Oh no! They must think I'm not very bright.
- This is terrible. I've damaged my reputation.
- I should have thought it through more.
- I am stupid to have opened myself up to such criticism.
- Why do I always put my big foot in it?

You might challenge these negative thoughts with the following alternatives:

- Well, it's disappointing that my idea did not catch on, but reputations are not damaged in single incidents like this. Maybe I'm upset because my pride's been hurt a little. I can live with that.
- Other people get criticized, too – not just me.
- Nothing risked, nothing gained.
- If I can learn to cope with this type of criticism rather than telling myself how bad it is or how stupid I am, I'm going to be better able to cope in the future and will increase my confidence.
- My self-esteem doesn't need to depend on what others think about my suggestions unless I tell myself it does.

- Even if I fail, this does not make me a stupid person. And in any case, failure is rarely all-or-nothing. There are parts of my idea that are still good – I just need to work on them more.
- I am letting my disappointment mask all the positive aspects of my self.

Pleasing Others

It may also help if you consider whether you work too hard to please others in order to win their approval. If so, you may end up as a subordinate with a loss of a sense of your own identity (see below). One of the big disadvantages of being overly dependent on others' approval is that you may do things that you don't really want to do – and then later feel resentful. So one advantage of learning how to avoid being too upset by a lack of approval is that it helps you become more independent. This does not mean that we become selfish and do not care for others, or selfishly follow our own course regardless of other people's feelings, or turn others into servants to fulfil our own needs. Rather, it means that we can be pleased with approval but not devastated without it.

Research suggests that, in mild depression, there is an increased tendency to try to please others, but as depression worsens, people actually give up trying. No one is entirely sure why this is. It may be because of a build-up of resentment; it may be because these people no longer believe in their ability to be pleased; it may be because they are simply too exhausted.

A Loss of Identity

Similar to the need for approval is the need to feel appreciated and not taken for granted or exploited. The latter need can involve trying to get other people to see us as valued individuals and not just subordinate to them – we want to be valued as people in our own right, with some status and control over our own destiny. The development of such a personal identity is helped by living in a way that others seem to value or give some credit to. The problem comes when, in situations and relationships, we feel that we have become highly subordinate because of having to 'please the other'. We don't feel valued for ourselves, but only as servants to others.

The most extreme example of this is in various forms of abuse (especially sexual). The abused person may feel that they have no real identity of their own but only that given by the abuser.

When we feel ourselves to be subordinate to others, that we are being used by them in a way we do not like, all kinds of changes happen in us. Beth and Martin had a good sex life. Martin was always keen, and at first Beth took this to mean that he really fancied her and she was a 'turn-on' to him. That made her feel good. However, gradually she came to think that, in other areas of their life together, he did not seem so caring. Eventually she had the thought, 'I am just a body to him.' This thought, of being used by Martin and being highly subordinate to his sexual needs, had a dramatic effect on her. She lost all interest in sex, became resentful of Martin and wanted to escape. Moreover, she felt that he had gradually taken over her identity and that she had lost any of her own. Men can have similar feelings but these usually focus on money-making – e.g. men are more likely to think: 'My wife only stays with me because I'm a soft touch, a good pay packet.' Whatever the source of feeling exploited and only a servant to the other, the result is often resentment and a belief in a loss of identity.

However, Beth's thoughts got out of perspective as she became more depressed. Slowly she was able to change her thinking:

- It remains true that Martin fancies me and I don't need to discount that aspect of our relationship.
- I can talk to Martin and tell him that I'm unhappy with other areas of my life.
- I can take more control in my marriage. If I feel exploited, maybe it's because I'm not asserting my own needs enough.
- Martin is not really an unkind man, but he is rather thoughtless at times. I need to help him be more attentive.
- Maybe it's my resentment and unexpressed anger that are also causing problems here.

It had been Beth's feeling used and unappreciated that had sparked off her negative feelings, but she had not had an opportunity to focus on them, challenge their extreme nature and take more control in her marriage. When she did this, she saw that there were problems in the marriage, but she felt more able to try to sort them out. And perhaps she had rather allowed Martin to be inattentive for too long. What Beth also realized was that she and Martin needed to engage in more mutually enjoyable activities, not just sex.

A loss of identity can occur when we are in conflict about whether to live for ourselves or for others. Such conflicts can become all-or-nothing issues rather than faced as difficulties in balancing the various needs of each person in a relationship. Nell gave up her job to have children and support her husband, but she gradually found this less and less fulfilling. Over the years, it had become accepted that her husband Eric should do all he could to advance his career, and in the early days, this had seemed like a good idea. But when he was offered a good promotion that involved relocation, Nell became depressed. What had happened?

Nell felt that she had lost her identity, she didn't know who she was any longer and she wanted to run away. She did not want to move to another city but, on the other hand, felt she was being selfish and holding Eric back. Although she had for many years voluntarily subordinated herself to his career, and at first had valued this, she gradually had come to think of herself as merely his satellite, spinning around him, and simply fitting in with his plans. Slowly her subordination had become less and less voluntary. However, she felt it was wrong to assert her own needs, and she was very frightened of doing or saying things that might be strongly disapproved of. Even her own parents said that she should do what she could to support Eric and she worried about what they thought of her. As she became less satisfied with her position in the family, she found it difficult to change it because she thought she was being selfish and 'ought' to be a dutiful housewife. She thought that doing things that might interfere with her husband's progress would make her unlovable. But relocating and leaving her friends was a step too far. As for Eric, he was stunned by Nell's depression, for he had simply come to expect her to follow and support him. He had not learned anything different. In fact, Nell's depression was a kind of rebellion.

The first thing Nell had to do to help herself was to recognize the complex feelings and deep conflicts she was experiencing. I then recommended that she watch the film Shirley Valentine – in which a housewife goes on holiday to Greece with a woman friend, leaving her husband behind, and then decides to stay on – and to consider her depression as a kind of rebellion: not as a weakness or personal failure (as she did at first), but as something that was forcing her to stop and take stock of where she was and where she was going. An important idea was to see the depression as making her face certain things, and this, although painful, could be an impetus for change. When she gave up blaming herself for being depressed and telling herself that she was selfish for not wanting to move house, her depression lessened. We then did some of the exercises for the empty self (see pp. 159–61).

Sometimes people feel that they have to accept a subordinate position because they have lost confidence in other areas of their lives. This was certainly true for Nell, so the next thing was to explore with her her loss of confidence. She wanted to go back to work but felt that she was not up to it. Underneath this loss of confidence was a lot of self-attacking – for example, thoughts of 'I'm out of touch with work,' 'I'm not good enough,' 'I won't be able to cope,' 'I might do things wrong and make a fool of myself,' 'Everyone is more competent than me.' Nell had also become envious of her husband's success and his independent lifestyle, but again, instead of seeing this as understandable, she told herself that she was bad and selfish for feeling envious.

Confidence is really related to practice. Think of driving a car. The more you do it, the more confident you will be, but if you rarely drive, you won't have the chance to become confident. It is the same for social situations. Women who have given up work to look after children can sometimes feel very afraid at the thought of returning to work later in life, and this can simply be a matter of being out of practice. If this happens to you, think of whether you lack confidence due to a lack of practice. Avoid the tendency to criticize yourself. Work towards building your confidence step by step. Get the evidence rather than assume that you wouldn't be able to cope. If you give up too quickly, it may be because you are self-attacking.

Nell was also beset with various problems that are not unusual in depression, including intense conflicts of whether to live for herself or for others (partner, children etc.). She was also receiving many signals from her social environment that indicated that she was considered selfish to want to 'do her own thing'. Now, if you have these kinds of conflict, avoid developing all-or-nothing thinking – for example, 'I either do exactly what the other wants of me or I do my own thing.' It is a difficult balance to maintain but it is useful if both the needs of self and others are to be catered for. As Nell became more confident she was able to work out some of the issues about moving with Martin. She felt that her voice was being heard.

These conflicts are not untypical of people who feel highly subordinate in relationships. Sometimes the need to please others, gain approval and feel appreciated and valued has led them further and further down a road of being subordinate and self-sacrificing to others. Slowly, the thought comes that they are nothing other than what the other person wants them to be. Feelings of being unappreciated and used can be powerful in depression.

Conflicts Over How to Live

It will take time, but you may slowly be able to take more control of your life. If you can come to terms with a possible loss of approval, this is going to place you in a better position than before your depression: others will not be able to frighten you with their possible disapproval.

At times, people feel inhibited about saying what they really feel because they are worried about what others will think of them. They may worry about being seen as selfish and thus unlovable or inadequate. Kim was married to a wealthy businessman, and before she came to see me, she had been given drugs and told that her depression was biological. She herself could not understand her depression – after all, she had as much money as anyone could want and her husband was not unkind and did not beat her. She thought she should be happy, but instead felt weak for being depressed.

Within a few sessions, Kim began to talk about how she had come to feel like a painted doll. She had to appear with her husband at important functions and often felt 'on show'. Her husband was often away on business trips, and when he returned home tired, she felt that he used her to relax. She began to express her own needs – she wanted to go to university and wear dirty jeans –

but she also thought that her needs were selfish and stupid for a woman in her position and would court serious disapproval. She believed that, because her husband could provide her with any material thing, she was being ungrateful and selfish for wanting to live differently. She said: 'Many people would be delighted to have what I have.' She also had many self-critical and self-doubting thoughts about going to university: for instance, 'I'm too old now,' 'I wouldn't fit in,' 'Others will think I'm odd,' 'I'm not bright enough,' 'I'll fail.' Of course, she did not try to discover the evidence for any of these beliefs – and the depression was taken as proof that she would not be able to cope.

When Kim began to help herself to get out of her depression, she started to:

- Learn to take her own needs seriously.
- Change the self-labels of 'ingratitude' and 'guilt' to 'need to develop'.
- Avoid discounting the positives in her current life (e.g. 'Nobody is interested in me for myself,' 'I'm only a doll for my husband').
- See her depression as a signal that her life needed to change, rather than as a sign of weakness.
- Understand how her thoughts were driving her further into, rather than out of, depression.
- Talk more frankly with her husband.
- Find out whether she could cope with university.
- Avoid attacking herself (especially in social situations).

Some people who feel highly subordinate to others can also feel so inferior that they think they don't have the power to change. Once they can give up seeing themselves as inferior and inadequate, they open the door to change.

Subordinate to a Way of Life

In a way, Kim felt as much subordinate to a way of life as to any particular person. Sometimes, it is making money that causes problems, or maintaining a certain lifestyle. A family may have become so dependent on the money that a couple make that their lives revolve around money-making and intimacy falls away. Both partners feel trapped by the demands to 'keep going'. But the evidence is very clear on this: after a certain point, money does not add to happiness. If relationships are totally subordinated to the need to make money, there is often a reduction in intimacy and happiness.

There is increasing concern about these problems in our society today. The fear of losing a job can lead to working long hours. However, even in these situations it is important to try to do what you can to work yourself out of feeling trapped. It can help to share your dilemma with others and try to devise ways to get free of the trap, at least to some degree. Are there some positive activities that could be done that would help? Has the relationship become too split into 'the one who cares for the children' and 'the one who works'? And, most important, is the trap partly due to one person having lost confidence in him/herself? Does he or she see his/her own needs as selfish or impossible?

Sadly, at times people find themselves in situations where there seems little opportunity to develop personally. They feel power-less. They may live in poverty and feel overwhelmed by the needs of looking after children or just coping day to day. Sometimes there are very few positive activities in the person's life and this can be one place to start to change (see Chapter 5). However, the important thing is to see the depression as something that has been activated in you and not as a personal weakness.

Approval and Relationships

We have various kinds of relationships, some intimate, others friendly/social and still others that occur in the workplace. When we feel highly subordinate, we think that we need approval and appreciation from others whom we see as more able or powerful than us. However, we may not think that we should also give approval and show appreciation to these people. So, for example, a boss might learn how to praise his/her workers, but the workers are rarely taught how to praise the boss (they are more likely to be taught how to complain). It is surprising how many of us think that approval has to travel down through a hierarchy, not up.

This is because we think that those above us don't need approval – they are so much more powerful than we are that our approval does not matter to them. We can be so busy trying to gain their approval and do things to please them that we forget how to show appreciation of what they do give us. For example, Lynne had a great need to be approved of. When I asked her how she showed that she valued her husband Rob, she said, 'By doing things for him, keeping the house clean.' My response was: 'Well, his approval of you makes you feel good, but what do you say to him about how you value him?' Lynne went blank, then said, 'But Rob doesn't need my approval. He's all right. Life's easy for him. I'm the one who is depressed.'

When they were together, Lynne and Rob tended to blame each other for what they were not doing for each other:

LYNNE. You never spend enough time with me.
ROB. But you're always so tired.
LYNNE. That's right – blame me. You always do.
ROB. But it's true. You're never happy.

Around and around we went. Neither Rob nor Lynne could focus on how to offer approval to the other. Instead, they continually focused on the negative and thus there was little to build on. They rarely said things like 'You look nice today' or 'It was really helpful when you did that' or 'I thought you handled that well' or 'You were really kind to think of that.' Lynne tried to earn approval but was not able to give it. It was painful for her to come to see that, in placing herself in a subordinate position, she felt that others should attend and approve of her (and she'd work hard to get this approval) but she did not need to show approval of others. She saw them as more able than her and believed that her approval of them did not matter.

Depression can make us very self-focused in this regard. Sometimes depressed people are resentful of their partners, and giving approval and showing appreciation is the last thing they want to do. It can be useful, therefore, to consider how we can praise those around us – not just do things for them, but show an interest in them and recognize that all humans feel good if they feel appreciated and not taken for granted.

Parent–child relationships can also be like this. Even as adults we might seek the approval of parents but not take an interest in them as people in their own right. Lynne wanted recognition from her mother but rarely praised her.

Relationships are like flowers: they cannot grow unless they are nurtured and fed. And feeding a relationship means that approval has to go both ways. At times, trying to look after children, holding down a job and so forth can make it all too easy for relationships to be taken for granted – the only time a couple may spend together is at the end of the day when each is exhausted. So try to plan activities which are mutually rewarding and enjoyable. Spend time together on positive things and show each other appreciation for sharing those things. Build on the positives rather than be separated by the negatives.

Nonverbal Communication

As I have suggested, humans have a basic need to feel approved of by others. This begins almost from the first days of life. For example, babies are very sensitive to the faces of their parents. If babies are happy and smile at their mothers and they smile back, the positive feelings between them grow. But if mothers present a blank or angry face, the babies become distressed. When mothers and babies are on the same wavelength and approving of each other, we say that they are 'in tune' or are 'mirroring' each other. Throughout childhood, approval signals from parents help us to feel loved and wanted, and later in life they help to make relationships gel and friendships to build. Approval nearly always feels good (unless we are discounting it in some way). It gives us the feeling that we are accepted and wanted and that our efforts are valued (see Chapter 4).

The nonverbal communication of some depressed people is very unfriendly. They look grumpy and fed up most of the time and rarely think about how this will affect others. Yet when others become distant, they feel worse. Unless one is very depressed, it is often helpful to try to send friendly nonverbal messages – to smile and be considerate of others. You may protest, 'But aren't you just suggesting that I cover up my feelings, put on an act?' The answer is yes and no. Yes, to the extent that you need to be aware that a constantly grumpy appearance is not a good basis for developing positive relationships – a depressed attitude can push others away. Moreover, if you try to smile and be friendly, this can affect your mood positively. However, the answer is also no, to the extent that, if there are problems that you need to sort out, then they need sorting out – don't hide what you feel. But being grumpy and making no effort to be friendly actually sorts out very little – it can lead to brooding resentment in both you and others.

Being Bullied

It is one thing to be criticized and to learn how to cope with that, but it is another to be on the receiving end of bullying. There is now much evidence that being on the receiving end of a lot of criticisms and put-downs (called high expressed emotion) is associated with mental ill-health. These criticisms and put-downs can be verbal, nonverbal or even physical attacks. Indeed, in adult life, approval is not only signalled by the words people use but by the types of attention they give, the smiles, facial expressions and nods. Sometimes, we find ourselves living in a world where approval signals are hard to come by but put-downs are rather common.

As we have seen, the need for approval begins early in life and is conveyed in the facial expressions of child and parent. But even as adults, the sense of being approved of or criticized can be conveyed by nonverbal communication. A smile or a frown can say a lot, and a hug can do much to reassure us. A depressed person may say: 'My husband/wife doesn't need to say anything. I can just tell by the way he/she looks at me that he/she disapproves of me.' Again, there is nothing abnormal about this. In both humans and animals, nonverbal communication can be powerful. If you were going to train as an actor, your talent would be judged not just by your ability to remember lines but by how you say them and your nonverbal expressions and other body language.

Many depressed people become very sensitive to nonverbal communication. Seeking reassurance and sensitive to not getting it, they can become easily upset by how people respond to them nonverbally. Depression makes us very aware of the judgments of others, and nonverbal signals are taken as cues to how others are judging us. We can feel put down and bullied because we exaggerate the degree of threat in a particular interaction with someone.

Although it is quite common in depression to overestimate the degree and implications of criticism, it can also be the case that put-downs are not exaggerated. The problem then becomes whether anything can be done to change the situation or whether it is best to try to get out of the relationship.

Bullying and Intimate Relationships

When someone is able to make us feel bad 'by a look', in effect they are exerting a certain power over us, so it important to recognize this sensitivity to nonverbal communication and learn how to handle it. If you are living with someone who is depressed, it might help you to realize that your nonverbal attitude can be important. Remember that we often convey warmth (or a lack of it) not just by what we say but by how we say it. I would like to explore a rather extreme example.

Mark rarely said positive things to Jill and acted as if he were disappointed in her. In therapy, he would rarely look at her but instead scanned the room as though uninterested in what was going on. Even when he did say some positive things to Jill, it was said in such a hostile and dismissive way that you could understand why she never believed him. The problem here was not just Jill's depression but Mark's difficulty in conveying warmth. Many of his communications bristled with hostility and coldness; he saw depression as a weakness and was angry at Jill's loss of sexual interest. She came to dread Mark's moodiness and how he would look at her.

Sadly, both Jill and Mark had become locked into a rather hostile and disapproving style. She experienced him as a disapproving dominant male, and her life was spent trying to elicit his approval and get some warmth from him. When she failed, she blamed herself and became more depressed, with a strong desire to escape the relationship –which also made her feel guilty and frightened. She held the view that she should make her relationship work regardless of the cost or how difficult it was. She prided herself on not being a quitter. But sadly, only if she subordinated herself to Mark's every need could she elicit approval from him. Moreover, she came to believe that all men were like this.

These kinds of problems often require marital therapy. However, if you blame yourself for such problems or are ashamed of them, this might stop you from seeking help. If you feel frightened and are not sure where the next put-down is coming from (be this in a close relationship or at work), it is possible that you are caught up in a bullying relationship. The degree of your fear can be a clue here – although consider whether you would be fearful if you weren't depressed, because sometimes we become fearful of others because of depression. I have certainly come across many couples who fight a lot, feel resentful and so forth, but are not necessarily frightened of each other. So fear may be a key.

The first thing is to be honest with yourself and consider if a frank exploration of your relationship and its difficulties would be of benefit. Sometimes it is the bullying partner who feels ashamed about examining feelings of closeness and how to convey affection. Mark, for example, came from a rather cold and affectionless family and felt uncomfortable with closeness. He acted towards Jill in the same way that his father had acted towards him and his mother. As Jill came to recognize this, she gave up blaming herself for his cold attitude, and although this did not, of itself, cure her depression, it was a step on the way. She learned that trying to earn approval from a person who found it virtually impossible to give was, sadly, a wasted effort. Eventually the relationship ended.

So the lesson of all this is: Don't blame yourself for another person's cold attitude towards you. If you do you are giving too much power away to the other person. Research has shown that a woman still living with an abusive partner will often blame herself for the abuse inflicted on her, but will come to see it as not her fault if she moves away. So try using the 'responsibility circle' (Figure 5, p. 141) and see how many things you can think of that might be causing the problem. What are the alternatives for the other person's cold attitude?

Another thing you can try is to openly discuss these issues with your partner. It may be that the relationship has drifted to such an extent that you have forgotten how to value each other and are taking each other for granted. Try to put aside a special time when you can be close and talk about things. Review your relationship together. See if you can pinpoint where it went wrong and what was happening at that time. Try to be honest with each other. If you are, you may say some unpleasant things to each other, but try to share these in the spirit of reconciliation. Remind yourself that the reason for having this discussion is to improve closeness – not just to get your own back. And you may need to examine closely whether you are guilty of all-or-nothing thinking: 'I must stay in a relationship, come what may.'

Finally, sometimes it is necessary to recognize that a relationship is abusive and that it will be extremely hard to get out of your depression unless you also get out of the relationship.

Bullying at Work

A key theme so far has been that, although we can be very sensitive to the opinion of others, we must be careful not to swallow their views of us hook, line and sinker. There is increasing concern today at the amount of bullying that goes on in families and schools and at work. To be on the receiving end of a bully's attacks can be pretty depressing. As a society, we need to learn how to be more accepting of others and less unkind. As individuals, we also have to learn how to protect ourselves as best as we are able from the effects of bullying.

You can sometimes spot a bully because you will not be the only one who experiences his or her attacks. So it can be useful to get the views of others – get the evidence that it is not just you. For example, in the case of Jill and Mark, many of their mutual friends saw Mark as a 'difficult' person. When Jill thought about this evidence, it helped her to give up blaming herself.

Colin became depressed when a bullying boss came to work at his company. The boss would attack and criticize his work, and gradually Colin lost confidence in his own abilities. He began to help himself when he changed his thinking:

- Just because the bully says I'm no good does not make it true.
- I've done good work in the past, and my colleagues think my work is good.
- The boss is using all-or-nothing thinking and disregarding the positive aspects of my work.
- Other people have the same problems with him that I do.
- Maybe I want his approval too much and feel enraged when I don't get it.

Another set of Colin's beliefs had increased his depression: 'I should be able to cope with this. I'm letting him get to me. If I were a real man, I'd put him in his place. I shouldn't let him get away with it. I'm weak.' Thus, his (in)ability to stand up to the bully was taken as evidence of his lack of manliness and weakness.

Disapproval and criticism by others can be used to judge ourselves. Once Colin gave up seeing his problems with the boss as a test of his manliness, he was able to work out other ways to deal with it. In this case, he accepted his limitations and sought a transfer to another department. I agreed with him that, in an ideal world, the bully would be brought to account – but Colin was taking too much personal responsibility for sorting out his boss and he simply did not have the power or support to do it. Colin understandably remained angry about this, but his depression subsided when he gave up seeing himself as weak. Sometimes the best response to a bully is to get away, if this is possible, and/or get others to support you. Don't turn it into some kind of individual test.

In sexual harassment, however, specific individuals may be picked on. Others may not experience the bully in the same way. If this happens to you, again try to obtain support from others and to be as assertive as possible. Raise the issue as openly and frankly as you can at work. Don't be stopped from raising the issue with thoughts of 'it's only me'.

Key Points

- If we become too focused on gaining approval, we can become like puppets and subordinate to the needs of others.
- We can get caught up in a subordinate approval trap, in which the only way we see to gain approval is to become more subordinate and pleasing to others – to sacrifice our own needs and wishes.
- We can become subordinate to the lifestyles of others, or even to a lifestyle we may, at one time, have chosen. This can lead us to feeling that we have lost our own identities.

continued on next page

- When we lose a sense of our own identities we are actually saying that we have lost control of where our life is going. This is often associated with confusion and a loss of confidence. The best approach is to take your own needs and preferences seriously and avoid attacking yourself, which undermines confidence.
- Just as you need approval and signs of acceptance, so may others around you. It is important that you don't discount this aspect.
- Sometimes we accept the judgments of a bully as true reflections of ourselves, and/or we think we ought to be able to put the bully in their place – and we are weak if we can't. However, sometimes the best response is to seek help from others and/or get away.

Exercises

Use the 'thought form' (p. 384) to work through these exercises. Write down your negative/depressing thoughts, try to identify the kinds of thinking styles you might be using (e.g. all-or-nothing thinking, discounting the positives, self-blaming, etc.; see Appendix 2) and then look for the evidence against these ways of thinking. Use the rational/compassionate mind to consider and suggest alternatives.

- First, consider how you deal with approval. Do you discount it in some way? If so, the next time someone says something nice to you, try accepting it without 'reading between the lines'. Monitor your thoughts if you discount praise, and challenge those thoughts.
- Consider what goes through your mind when something that you did that you thought was good is hardly noticed by others. Are you making more of this than you need to? Check yourself for self-attacking thoughts (e.g. 'If I were

continued on next page

more powerful, good or did this even better, they'd notice'). Try the alternative thoughts of: 'Well, I would like them to notice, but if they don't, this does not mean it's no good. I can still value something even if others don't. In fact, it may be my ability to hang on to what I value, even if others may not see much in it, that makes me a unique person.'

- If you feel that you must please others, write down your thoughts about what would happen if you don't. Are you afraid of their reactions? Are you putting yourself down and labelling yourself as, say, selfish? If so, work out some alternatives. For example, 'If I don't want to be a satellite to someone else, I need to try to put forward my own views. What thoughts stop me?' How could you think in a different way that takes both yours and the other person's views into account?

- If you are on the receiving end of bullying, check to see if you are blaming yourself. If so, how could you give this up? Are you taking the bullying as a judgment on yourself in some way? If so, how would a compassionate friend speak to you?

13

Confronting Shame

Of all the emotions that are likely to reduce our ability to be helped, to reach out to others and to treat ourselves with compassion, shame is the most important and destructive. Indeed, people can feel ashamed about being depressed, and try to hide it from others as a result. If you can recognize your inner shame and work to reduce it, you will do much to heal yourself.

The word 'shame' comes from the Indo-European word *skam*, meaning to hide. In the biblical account, Adam and Eve ate of the apple of the tree of knowledge, became self-aware and realized their nakedness. At that moment, they developed a capacity for shame and the need for fig leaves – or so the story goes. Part of their shame was fear that, having transgressed against God's instructions, they would be punished. In general, shame – like embarrassment, pride, prestige and status – is related to how we think others see and judge us, and how we view ourselves.

Shame evolved from the need to behave submissively to threats from more powerful others. If an animal low in the status hierarchy is threatened by a more powerful individual, it can reduce the threat by backing down, showing it is anxious and trying to run away. This defensive response is triggered quickly. Because shame is linked to our submissive defences, this is why when we feel ashamed we can behave submissively, averting our eyes and wanting to run away or hide.

However, human shame can also be triggered by our own powerful self-critical thoughts. Just as our mental sexual images can make us feel sexy, and stress-related thoughts can trigger our stress systems (see Chapter 2), so telling ourselves we are inferior or bad

210

in some way can trigger our submissive systems. The potential for shame is universal; but sometimes it can get completely out of hand. Shame is now regarded as one of the most powerful and potentially tricky issues in helping people with depression, because it often involves concealment or an inability to process 'shameful' information.

The Feelings of Shame

Shame is a complex phenomenon, with various aspects and components. Among the most important ones are the following:

- *Internal negative self-evaluative thoughts.* These include beliefs and feelings that one is inferior, inadequate or flawed. Many of our self-attacking thoughts (e.g. I am useless, no good, a bad person, a failure) are in essence shaming thoughts and self-evaluations.
- *Social or externally focused thoughts.* These are beliefs that others see us as inferior, bad, inadequate and flawed; that is, others are looking down on us with a condemning or contemptuous view. This is linked to stigma.
- *An emotional component.* The emotions and feelings of shame are various, but include anxiety, anger, self-disgust and self-contempt.
- *A behavioral component.* There is a strong urge to hide, avoid exposure and run away; or (when anger is the emotion) to retaliate against the one who is 'exposing' the self as inferior, weak or bad.
- *A bodily or physiological component.* Feelings of shame are stressful and activate our stress systems. Shame also affects our mood chemicals and is not helpful in trying to foster positive moods.

The most powerful experiences of shame often arise from feeling that there is something both different and inferior, flawed or bad about ourselves. We may believe that, if others discover these flaws in us, they will ridicule, scorn, be angry and/or reject us. In this respect, shame is fear of a loss of approval in extreme form.

We can feel paralyzed by shame and at the same time acutely aware of being scrutinized and judged by others. Shame not only leads us to feel inferior, weak or bad in some way, but also threatens us with the loss of valued relationships – if our shame is revealed, people won't want to help us, be our friends, love or respect us. A typical shame-based view is: 'If you really got to know me, you would not like me.' A major feeling in shame can be aloneness. We can feel isolated, disconnected and inwardly cut off from the love or friendship of others. Shame can give us the feeling that we are separated (different) from others, an outsider.

Feeling Ashamed and Being Shamed

We have noted that people can have negative thoughts about themselves, such as seeing themselves as inferior, inadequate or bad in some way. These are part of *feeling ashamed*. However, we can also experience others as critical and putting us down in some way; that is, we experience *being shamed* by others. Now, sometimes we can be shamed by others but not feel internally bad. For example, imagine a man who visits prostitutes. If he is caught he may be very upset about being found out and shamed. He worries about what others think about him, and his reputation among his family and friends. However, he himself may see nothing wrong in visiting prostitutes. He does not see *himself* as bad or inferior for obtaining sex this way. So it is not always the case that if people are shamed they will feel badly about themselves. In depression, however, it is more common for people to have both types of shame. They feel others see them as inferior, bad or inadequate; and they see themselves also as inferior, bad or inadequate.

When you are working with your own sense of shame, then, it is useful to be clear about:

- What you are thinking about yourself. How are you rating yourself?
- What you think others are thinking of you.

When you do this, you will see how often shame feelings are related to fears of loss of approval. In this chapter we will focus mainly on *internal* shame; that is, the kind of things you say to yourself that trigger feelings of shame in you, make you behave submissively and undermine your confidence.

The Focus for Shame

According to the psychologist Gershen Kaufman, there are at least three areas in which shame can cause us much pain. We can feel shame about our bodies, shame about our competence and abilities, and shame in our relationships. There is an additional one that is especially common in depression: shame of what we feel. Let's briefly look at each of these.

Shame of the Body

Some people don't go to see their doctors because of shame. There are all kinds of conditions that people regard as shaming: piles (hemorrhoids), impotence, bowel diseases, urinary problems, bulimia (where people vomit after eating binges). Shame, perhaps more than any other emotion, stops us from being honest with ourselves and seeking help, and there is general agreement that doctors could be more sensitive to this. Sadly, too, people who have any kind of disfigurement can also feel shame, especially if others laugh at them, reject them or appear repelled by the way they look.

People who have been sexually abused often have an acute sense of body shame. They can feel that their bodies have become dirty, contaminated and damaged. In extreme cases, these individuals may come to 'hate' their own bodies. Talking about the experiences and feelings of abuse can in itself produce strong feelings of shame, and for this reason people may hold back from discussing them. However, healing this shame requires coming to terms with one's body and reclaiming it as one's own.

Concern with the way we look is, of course, a driving force behind fashion. However, some people feel so awkward and ashamed of their bodies that they will do almost anything to themselves to try to avoid these feelings. Men might spend hours at a gym body-building, and women might put great effort into dieting to make themselves thinner. Make-up and plastic surgery may also be used to avoid feelings of body shame.

It is one thing to be mildly dissatisfied with one's body, but body shame often involves strong self-condemnation and anxiety at being seen by others. Valerie, for example, could not bear to look in a mirror. When she did, she would think, 'You look awful. Why are you so ugly?' This feeling of body shame was linked to an underlying belief that she was not lovable because of the way she looked. She also discounted any positive comments her husband made ('He's just saying that to make me feel better').

Shame About Our Competence and Abilities

This kind of shame relates to performing physically or mentally. For example, although Melanie would have liked to have played tennis, she had poor eye–hand coordination. She would dread trying to play at school, because every time she hit the ball out of court (which she often did), she suffered an acute feeling of shame.

Pete would become very angry with himself when he was unable to make things work. When household appliances broke down, he took it as a personal criticism of his abilities and manhood. When his car wouldn't start, he would think that, if he were a proper man, he would be able to understand mechanical things and would be able to fix it. He hated taking it to the garage and showing his incompetence to the garage staff, and so always asked his wife to take it.

In my own case, my poor English has often been a source of mild shame. Dyslexic children often experience much shame and feelings of being defective and inferior.

The main point here is that attempting to do things and failing can be a source of shame. It is made worse when we rate ourselves as bad, and attack ourselves for failing. As a rule, it is easier to cope with mild shame if we don't attack ourselves. The next time you feel embarrassed at a failure, check to see if you are self-attacking and try to bring your rational/compassionate mind into play.

Shame in Relationships

You can sometimes tell that someone has a relationship shame problem because he or she usually responds badly to criticism and conflicts. Shame-prone people are liable to become angry, sulk or give in quickly. Some like to be in control in relationships and beyond criticism. Such people have difficulty owning up to their own vulnerabilities for fear that, if others became aware of them, they would be marked down as weak and inadequate.

There is also increasing concern in our society that some people (especially, but not only, men) are very prone to shame when it comes to expressing feelings of affection in relationships. Some feel awkward when confronted with gentleness, touching and hugging. It is as if there is an invisible wall around them. In situations of close intimacy, their bodies stiffen or they back away. Men may hide their shame by clinging to the idea that 'grown men don't do that sort of thing' or that to be tender is to be 'soft' and 'unmanly.' This can cause problems in how they act, as intimate friends, lovers and fathers. For example, children often seek out physical affection, and it can be very hurtful to them if their fathers push them away when they try to get close.

Shame of What We Feel

We sometimes try to conceal our true feelings for fear of the consequences. We can be ashamed of feeling anxious, tearful or depressed; and also of feeling angry – as if the very fact that we have these feelings means that there is something wrong, flawed and/or unlovable in us.

For many years, Alec suffered from panic attacks. He dreaded going to meetings in case the signs of his anxiety showed. He was so ashamed of his anxiety that he did not even tell his wife. Eventually he broke down, became depressed and could not go to work. Then the story of his long suffering came out. From a young age, his father had told him that real men don't get anxious; they are tough and fearless. When Alec had been anxious about going to school, his father had been dismissive and forced him to go – shaming him in the process. By the time he was a teenager, Alec had learned never to speak of or show his inner anxieties.

Susan, who was married, met another man to whom she felt strongly sexually attracted. She flirted with him and would have liked the relationship to become sexual, but she felt deeply ashamed about her desires and believed that they made her a very bad person. As she came to understand that such (sexual) feelings are natural, and to explore what it was about the relationship that so attracted her, she discovered a desire for closeness that she could not get from her husband. This, of course, raised the question of what she could do about that; but it helped stop her being ashamed of her feelings and allowed her to accept that she, like other human beings, wanted closeness – and good sex.

Jenny's mother had told her that sex is dirty – just something that men enjoy because they are more primitive and superficial than women. Later, when Jenny had sex, she could sometimes push these thoughts aside, but afterwards she was left with the feeling of being dirty and of having betrayed her mother's values. When she monitored her thoughts during the day, she noticed that, whenever she had sexual thoughts and feelings, she would also think: 'These are bad thoughts; a good woman doesn't have these feelings. Therefore I'm dirty, and if my mother knew what was going through my mind, she would be disgusted and disappointed with me.' Jenny then distracted herself from her sexual feelings and turned them off. However, once she had come to recognize that she was having these kinds of thoughts (and she had to really focus to 'catch' them going through her mind), she was able to say to herself:

> *This is my sexual life and it does not belong to my mother for her to control. If I feel sexual, this is because I feel sexual, and it has nothing to do with being dirty. My sexual feelings also give me energy and are life-enhancing. I don't need to act out my mother's sexual hang-ups in my own life.*

Andrew was ashamed of his homosexual desires. Brought up within a strict religious framework, he thought that they were a sin against God and that he was a bad, worthless human being for having them. Although it was a struggle, he began to explore the possibility that there were alternative ways to think about and explore his sexuality – without being ashamed of it.

Gary was ashamed of his anger and rage. When he became angry, he felt terrible and unlovable. He said that he just wanted to act like a decent human being, and, more than anything, he felt that his anger made him a horrible person. Indeed, the bully in him often told him that he was horrible, ungrateful, selfish and self-centred. As a result, he could not explore all the things that hurt him and the reasons behind all his anger. Instead, he simply tried to keep a lid on his anger rather than acknowledge its source and heal it.

At times, Patricia felt very tearful, but she would not allow herself to cry – she was too ashamed. Leo hid the extent of his drinking out of shame. Zoë was too ashamed to talk about the fact that her husband was abusing her. Amanda could not go far from her house just in case, needing to use the bathroom, there was none available and she would wet herself . . . There are many examples.

It is only too clear from these examples that shame can operate in many areas of our lives. It can be a huge block to healing and coming to accept ourselves. We feel ashamed at revealing our pain and difficulties – so we hide them.

Deeply shaming experiences are not easy to forget. They can weave themselves right into the fabric of our being. Shame can lie within us, ready to pounce. And when we feel shame, we often ruminate on it, going over and over it in our minds.

The Origins of Shame

If shame is so powerful, where does it come from? Well, one answer is that we all have the capacity within us to feel shame – that is, it is part of our evolved minds. In effect, shame alerts us to all those situations that could be detrimental to us – such as being rendered inferior and subordinate, rejected and ostracized. These have always been serious threats to animals and humans, and over millions of years we have evolved, within our brains, the capacity to be alert to them and take defensive action. Shame operates on the 'better safe than sorry' rule (see Chapter 2). In other words, the brain makes the decision: 'It is better to conceal this [aspect of ourselves] or change it rather than risk rejection.'

There are a number of other theories about the origins of shame. According to one view, evolution has equipped children to enter the world as social beings who need positive things from others. We come into the world with an enormous need for relationships, care, joyfully shared interactions and recognition. The treatment we receive at the hands of those who look after us will have a major effect on whether we move forward with confidence (the result of the many positive experiences encountered while growing up) or with a sense of shame, of being flawed, not good enough, lacking value or worth. Research has shown that the way the caregiver and infant interact has important impacts on the infant's nervous system, emotions and sense of self.

Shame can arise from at least three different types of reactions to the treatment we received from our parents or others who have cared for us in our early lives: thwarted efforts to be recognized as good and able; pressure to conform; and direct attacks and puts-downs.

Failure to be Recognized as Good and Able

Consider the following scenario. Three-year-old Tracy sits quietly, drawing. Suddenly she jumps up, rushes to her mother and proudly holds up her drawing. The mother responds by kneeling down and saying, 'Wow – that's wonderful! Did you do that?' Tracy nods proudly. 'What a clever girl!' In this encounter, Tracy gets positive attention, and not only experiences her mother as proud of her, she also has emotions in herself about herself – she feels good about herself. However, suppose that, when Tracy went to her mother with her drawing, her mother responded with, 'Oh God, not another of those drawings. Look, I'm busy right now. Can't you go off and play?' Clearly, this time the way that Tracy experienced her mother, the interaction between them, and the feelings in herself about herself were quite different. Tracy would be unlikely to have had good feelings in herself and may have had a sense of disappointment and probably shame. Her head would have gone down and she would have slipped away. Thus a lack of recognition and a dismissal of ourselves, when we try to display something attractive to others, can be shaming. Experiences like this happen in even the most loving of homes and the child learns to cope with them; but if they are common and arise against a background of insecurity and low parental warmth, they can, over time, be quite damaging.

One of my patients who read this section said that it brought back memories of herself as a child, when she would be sent to her room to play and 'just keep out of the way'. Throughout her life, she had never felt deeply wanted and had developed a sense of being in the way and a nuisance.

When people fail to win approval or praise, they can often feel shame. Remember Anne, who felt her dinner party had been ruined because she had overcooked the meal? Her experience was one of shame – an intense anger with herself and wanting to hide.

Donna's parents were very ambitious. They wanted the best for her, and wanted her to do her best. If she came second or third in class, they would immediately ask who came first and indicate that coming second or third was okay but not really good enough; with a bit more effort, she could come top. Donna came to believe that nothing other than coming top was good enough to win the approval from her parents that she so desired. Anything less always felt like a disappointment for them and herself. Well, you can guess what this all led to – an underlying belief that, unless she did everything perfectly, she was flawed and had let herself and others down. Lack of perfection was failure, and failures were always deeply shaming: so Donna was rarely able to focus on what she had achieved, but thought only about how far short she had fallen.

Pressure to Conform

We all have a very strong desire to conform and be accepted. We want to feel that we belong somewhere. We follow fashion and express the same values as others so that we can signal that we are one of the group. We are highly motivated to try to be valued by others rather than devalued. Men, for example, may try to conform to cultural stereotypes of being tough, competitive, strong and independent, and not showing their feelings (which could be taken as a sign of weakness). Women may feel ashamed if they can't reach the standards set by others of their set. They are not supposed to be hypersexual or aggressively competitive. They are supposed to be sexually coy, caring, attractive, non-aggressive, sensitive and loving. All around us are values and standards to which we are supposed to conform if we don't want to be shamed and stigmatized

We may even try to avoid shame by going along with others, showing that we are made of the 'right stuff', even if, in the centre of our beings, we know that our action is immoral. Keith, an ex-soldier, told me that getting into fights was often more to do with avoiding the shame of not fighting than with any real enjoyment in, or desire for, a punch-up; yet no one wanted to 'break ranks' and point this out. Conforming to cultural values to avoid shame is a powerful social constraint. To risk exposure to shame is to risk not being accepted and not belonging.

Direct Attacks

We also know, of course, that children and adults can be shamed directly by being told that they are stupid or bad, that they don't fit in or are unwanted, and by being physically attacked. Indeed, some people will deliberately use the threat of, and the human built-in aversion to, shame to control others. So shame does not only arise because approval and admiration are withheld; direct verbal and physical attacks can shame, too.

The Shaming Loop

As we enter depression, we can get caught up in various 'circles' of negative thinking and behavior, and shame can lead to several forms of self-perpetuating difficulties. At times, these can give rise to what I call a 'shaming loop' (see Figure 8). This is particularly true of teenagers, adolescence being a time when the approval of peers and the potential for shame can have particularly significant effects. Many children are prone to being teased; some, sadly, more so than others. Coming to terms with teasing can be important for adolescents, and there are positive ways to do so, such as finding other friends or learning to ignore the teasing. Some individuals, however, turn to all kinds of things to ensure that they are not rejected in this way. Simon, for example, told me that he stole from local shops to give things to 'friends' so that he would be accepted and win some status/prestige from them. Sadly, through much of his adult life he had felt that he had to give 'tokens' to others before they would accept him.

It is not always the case that feeling inferior leads to social withdrawal – but it can do, especially when people label and attack themselves. When feelings of inferiority do lead to social withdrawal, then such individuals are also more likely to be rejected because they signal their feelings of inferiority to others.

Unfortunately, adolescents particularly, but also adults, do not find withdrawn behavior attractive. So the very thing that these people were hoping to avoid – being seen as inferior and being rejected – can happen because of the way they behave. However, if you stop being self-critical and labelling yourself as inferior, and learn to expect criticism from time to time as a matter of course rather than a personal rejection, you are less likely to become withdrawn and thus less likely to be ignored or rejected. One cannot avoid criticism, but one can learn not to be knocked out by it.

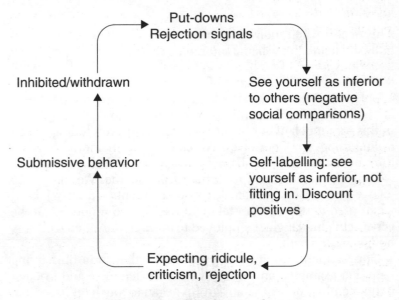

Figure 8   The 'shaming loop'.

Avoiding Shame

If shame is so powerful, how do people cope with it? One way is to avoid it, by avoiding being seen as inferior, weak and/or vulnerable. While the methods below may work for a while, problems can arise if they are adopted over the long term.

Compensation

This involves efforts to prove to yourself that you are good and able, and to avoid at all costs being placed in an inferior position. Sometimes we engage in vigorous competition with others to prove our own worth to them and to ourselves. It is as if we are constantly in a struggle to make up for something or prove something. Of course, we are trying to prove that we are not inferior, bad or inadequate and thus can be accepted rather than rejected.

Concealment

This occurs when individuals hide or avoid that which is potentially shameful. Body shame (including shame of disease) may lead to various forms of body concealment. In the case of shameful feelings, we may hide what we feel. Other people are always seen as potential shamers who should not be allowed to peer too closely at our bodies or into our minds. When we try to deal with shame in this way, much of our lives can be taken up with hiding – even hiding things from ourselves. We can repress memories because they are too painful and shameful to know and feel.

Laughter may be used to distract from shame. We may make jokes when we feel shame, to divert others' attention from it. Joking, when used to stop us from taking ourselves too seriously, can be very useful; but laughter employed to avoid shame often feels very hollow underneath.

Concealment can at times produce another form of shaming loop. For example, Janine would become defensive and irritated if the members of her therapy group began to touch on issues that caused her shame. This made the other group members irritated in turn. They felt she was not being honest or facing up to her problems. This actually caused Janine to feel even more shame, and so she closed down even further. Thus her way of trying to hide her shame actually produced more shaming responses from others.

Violence/Attack

'If you shame me, I'll hit/hurt you.' This is retaliatory shaming. Violence, especially between men, often arises as a shame avoidance strategy – a form of face-saving.

Ray had been caught stealing at school. When his father found out, he gave him a 'good thrashing'. What happened here is that Ray's father felt shamed by his son's conduct, believing that his son had disgraced him and the family. Not able to recognize or deal with his own shame, the father had simply acted out his rage on his son. This, of course, compounded Ray's shame and anger. Had Ray's father not felt so ashamed of his son, but instead been concerned to help him, he might have been able to sit down and explore what this stealing was about.

Natalie and Jon had a disagreement in public, and Natalie contradicted Jon. When they got home, he threatened her, saying in a very menacing way, 'Never show me up in public again, or else!'

Now, usually shame and counter-shaming interactions do not reach the stage of violence. None the less, they can involve a good deal of blame and counter-blame. Each person attempts to avoid being placed in the bad or wrong position. Let's recall the interaction between Lynne and her husband Rob from the last chapter.

LYNNE. You never spend enough time with me.
ROB. But you're always so tired.
LYNNE. That's right – blame me. You always do.
ROB. But it's true. You're never happy.

This blaming and counter-blaming is a form of 'shame-passing'. It is as if someone has to agree that he or she was wrong. The moment we shift to a more positive way of resolving the conflict, the shame cycle might be broken. For example, Lynne could have said, 'I really enjoy the time we spend together – how could we organize our time to do it more often?' Rob could have said, 'Well, I can understand how you would be upset by our not having much time together.' They would avoid 'all or nothing' blaming and could try to work on the positive aspects of their relationship and try to resolve their problems.

Projection

Projection is used in two ways. In the first type (mind reading), you may simply project on to others your own opinions of yourself. So if you think that your performance is not very good and label yourself as a failure, you believe that others will think the same. You assume that you are not very lovable, so you take it as read that others will think so, too. You feel that crying is a sign of weakness, so you think everyone else does, too.

A more defensive kind of projection involves things about yourself that you are fearful of or have come to dislike. You hide these from yourself, but see them in others. So it is the other person who is seen as the weak, shameful one – not you. Condemning homosexual desire, for example, may be a way of avoiding acknowledging such feelings in oneself (which are feared), seeing them only in others who may then be attacked. Sometimes bullies hate the feelings of vulnerability in themselves and so they attack others in whom they see them. Some bullies label others in the same way that they would label themselves if they could ever reveal their own vulnerability or hurt. Such people project those aspects that they see as inferior in themselves. Racist and sexist jokes can be a result of this.

If people criticize or attack you, it is possible that they see something in you that they don't like in themselves. For example, Sandra often cried about feeling alone. Her husband Jeff would become quite angry at this, which Sandra took as a criticism of her crying. But it turned out that, as a child, Jeff had himself been criticized for crying. Not only did he view Sandra's crying as a criticism of himself (he thought it meant she was not happy living with him), but he also hated the feelings of vulnerability that might lead to *him* crying. Thus, Sandra's crying reminded him of things he was ashamed of in himself.

So, if people put you down or try to shame you about something (e.g. for crying or failing or needing affection), ask yourself: How do *they* cope with these things? How do they cope with crying or failing? If you reflect on this and recognize that they don't allow themselves to cry, or that they become quite angry when they fail, or that they have problems with affection, then it is wise to consider that perhaps they are criticizing you because they can't cope with these things themselves. Whatever you do, don't get caught up in the idea that they are right and you are wrong.

Shame, Humiliation and Revenge

Humiliation is both similar to and different from shame. Both involve painful feelings, of being put down, harmed or rejected. We believe that the other person (e.g. parent, partner, boss) is sending signals that we are unacceptable, inadequate or bad in some way. In shame, we take this as evidence that there is, in truth, something bad about us; but in humiliation, we may not feel this. To use an extreme example, people who are tortured may be humiliated but not feel shamed, because they do not see themselves as bad.

So much depends on whether we blame ourselves or others for the insults or hurts we undergo. Of course, this may not be a clear-cut issue, for we can blame both ourselves and others. And we can feel that, as a result of others' bad actions towards us, we have been turned into bad people ourselves. For example, those who have been abused might feel humiliated (and terrified) by the abuse and blame their abusers; but they may also feel that, as a consequence of the abuse, they have been damaged and rendered inferior.

Feelings of humiliation, where we feel unfairly criticized or injured, can ignite powerful desires for revenge. Indeed, you can tell the extent to which you feel humiliated by the intensity of your thoughts about the injustice done to you and the strength of your desire for revenge. For some people, their fantasies of revenge are frightening and so they are hidden away. In such cases, acknowledgment of anger is a first step. For others, the anger and desire for revenge are constantly present, and they need to discover ways to work through the humiliation and let it go.

It is quite important to consider whether your humiliation is the result of a serious and genuine injury, or whether you have a sensitivity that makes you fly into rages if you are criticized. Quite often psychological help is necessary to work this out. As I have said before, self-help books are not a universal substitute for professional help, although they may give you the insight and courage to seek it. As with many things in life, there is wisdom in recognizing what we can do for ourselves and where we need help from others.

You may be vulnerable to feelings of humiliation now because of things that happened to you in the past. However, sitting on a lot of desires for revenge is not helpful to you. This is not to say that there might not have been very harmful things done to you;

rather, it is to say that, if these feelings are not worked through, they can lead to a lot of mistrust of others and a tendency to want constantly to get your own back. This is actually a terribly lonely position. You can take the first steps to change by acknowledging your pain and hurt and deciding to seek help. You may also need to grieve for past hurts and losses.

Now, it is one thing to have a desire for revenge on someone we do not care about; but what happens if it is someone you *do* want to have a close relationship with? Ted's father knocked him about as a child, and yet Ted also loved his father and wanted to be close to him. In therapy, Ted found it extremely difficult to recognize the feelings of humiliation that his father had inflicted on him and his own desire for revenge. But until he did recognize this, he was not able to move on to forgiving both himself, for his vengeful thoughts, and his father.

Blocked Revenge

Sometimes a strong desire for revenge that is blocked can be associated with depression. For example, someone has been physically attacked in the street or seriously injured in a car crash, but the guilty person gets off with a light sentence – or evades arrest altogether. When we feel a grave sense of injustice that we cannot put right, we can feel terribly frustrated and defeated. People who experience blocked revenge can be caught up in awful ruminations and feelings, often leading to difficulties in sleeping. This continual brooding keeps the stress system highly active, as they go round and round in circles; and even if they know this, they may be reluctant – understandably – to give up their preoccupation. Professional advice and support may help.

Shame and Guilt

We will be looking at guilt more fully in the next chapter, but it is worth making a few comments here about shame and guilt. Shame, as we have said, involves being seen as inferior, worthless or bad in some way. It often invades the very sense of ourselves. Guilt, however, is focused on other people. We see that we have harmed or hurt them, and our feelings are about wanting to repair that hurt. In shame, we hide and conceal things; in guilt, we reach out to repair.

Now, shame and guilt often run together. For example, Betty had hit her children, for which she felt guilty. However, she was unable to reach out to them and repair their relationship because she felt too ashamed about what she had done. Instead of just focusing on her particular behavior and understanding the reasons why she had acted in that way at that time, she felt that her action made her a bad mother and even a bad person. It was this shame, which she had locked away, that stopped her from looking at the issues and trying to make her behavior more as she would like it to be.

In most situations, if we behave badly – and we all do from time to time – it is useful to focus on that action and ask ourselves questions about it. Think about the circumstances of the action and use the compassionate/rational mind to consider if it could have been avoided. If we start to attack ourselves and feel internally completely bad, this will paralyze our ability to work through these problems, to adapt, change, grow, and try to put things right.

Shame and Responsibility

If you feel ashamed because you believe that you are responsible for something bad that has happened, use the 'responsibility circle' (see Figure 5, p. 141) to try to discover all those other factors that were impinging on you at the time. Even very distressing occurrences such as being abused when you were young turn out not to be your fault. For example, the abuser was older than you, might have had poor impulse control, might have threatened you; there may have been no one to turn to who would help or listen; you may have been confused or only trying to do your best to win love.

If you have hurt others, acknowledge this honestly without putting yourself down. The chances are that you did not harm others for the fun of it. You were probably hurt or stressed, and you may have been trying to cope with a difficult situation alone. Maybe you were confused and simply didn't know what to do, or did not realize that your behavior was hurtful. Perhaps you wanted revenge because of past hurts.

Sometimes we simply have to accept and digest our responsibility, learn to forgive ourselves and others, and not expect that we can go through life without (at times) hurting others. In an ideal world, we would all be loving to each other all the time; but sadly we do not live in an ideal world. The more you are able to acknowledge honestly your power to hurt and the reasons for it, the easier it will be to come to terms with it and change.

Healing Shame

Self-Consciousness

One of the main difficulties with shame, and something that can really paralyze us, is self-consciousness. We become acutely aware of ourselves and how we exist in the world 'for others'. Our attention is focused in on ourselves. Indeed, in shame it can be as if we are outside ourselves looking in. We become aware that our faces have turned red, or that our voices are shaking, or that we are not saying anything interesting. In shame, there is a monitoring of our actions and appearances and a highly negative evaluation. We might think: 'Oh no, I'm not doing this well. Others will think I'm stupid. I'm making a fool of myself. I'm foolish.'

Ruth hated driving, not because she felt she did it badly, but because she was always acutely aware of other drivers. She was worried about what they would think if she made a mistake, did not drive fast enough or did not seem confident. She constantly monitored her own driving and looked at the other cars in her mirrors.

People with body shame have a constant sense of their body as they think it must appear to others. Intense self-consciousness can make it difficult to show off, initiate things or get close to others. As a result, some people dislike taking the initiative, or feel that they need permission before they can do things. Then, if they do initiate something, like going out or having sex, they may constantly monitor the responses of others to make sure that they are enjoying it and don't think they made a bad decision. It's possible to become so focused on these concerns as to lose the enjoyment of the activity itself.

This self-monitoring of your own behavior and appearance, and the negative judgments that go with it, can be highly disruptive. To overcome this, it is first necessary to notice how you monitor yourself. Try to catch yourself when you are doing it and see how often you give yourself put-down messages. Then learn to recognize and challenge your internal bully.

Challenging Your Internal Bully

Personal shame that depresses people nearly always involves the internal bully, which gives you thoughts and feelings of being inadequate, useless, bad, weak and so forth. The internal bully lives in the state of depression; it feeds off it. Just as in some science fiction movies, where an alien or evil entity feeds off fear and the heroes/heroines realize that once they are not afraid the evil entity can't survive, so it is with the internal bully. Once you stop listening to its messages and bring your rational and compassionate mind to bear on it, it tends to shrivel.

Let's look at some bullying and shaming messages and ways to challenge them.

Inner bully says	*Rational/compassionate mind says*
You failed at this task, therefore you are a failure, useless.	Failing is a disappointment, of course, but this is all-or-nothing thinking. One failure does not make me, a human being, a failure.
	That's the trouble with you, bully. You're always so simple in your accusations and, dare I say, boringly repetitive.
	If you are so keen on success, how come you put me down so much that you take away all my energy to try?
	The best way to help people if they are struggling is to encourage them and give them a boost. As I see it, you are just into shaming and blaming – that's not helpful.

I'm going to face my limitations and what I feel ashamed about. If I listen to you, I'll just want to run away and then I won't learn anything, grow or mature.

So I failed. Big deal. Who hasn't failed in life? I'm disappointed and upset about this, but learning to fail and then recover is the real mark of health, not simply beating myself up over it.

Crying is a sign of weakness.	Crying is a sign of pain and hurt – not weakness.

Maybe it is our ability to cry that makes us human.

When we lose the ability to cry, we may lose the ability to feel and to heal.

Even if others see crying as a weakness, this does not make it true. Maybe they also have a shame problem about it.

After all, if we were not meant to cry, why do we have the physical capacity for it?

Crying is often about feeling sad or lonely, and this is an important message to listen to. The more I can acknowledge my tears, the more in touch with my feelings I may become.

Direct Engagement

Coming to terms with shame involves accepting it, facing it and working through it. In many cases, people are more likely to recover from shame if they explore it. Confronting and healing shame, rather than avoiding or compensating for it, may be a source of personal growth.

To accept our shame, we have to give up seeing ourselves in terms of 'all-or-nothing' negative labels, such as 'inferior' or 'inadequate'. Rather, we need to be specific about what it is we are not happy with, and then try to change that or come to terms with it. If we stick with negative labels, we stay in hiding and withdraw. Then our chances of recovery are reduced.

Relating with Others

In overcoming shame, it can be helpful to learn to relate to other people in a different way. We have to come out of hiding. It may be that you'll want to seek out professional help with this. The main issues here are how you feel with your helper and whether he or she can understand and work with shame. However, it is also possible that there are people close to you who would be helpful if you allowed them to be. At times we can block ourselves from connecting with others because we cannot face revealing what we feel ashamed about. However, just because you think something is bad does not mean others will.

Since shame is usually about hurt, sometimes it is possible to tell others what has hurt us and explain our feelings. It is important that we don't discount their efforts to help with ideas of 'They can't/won't understand.' Try to think: 'Maybe they won't understand, but do I have the evidence for that?' Of course, if you do have evidence that the other person is rejecting and critical, then he/she may not be a good person to confide in; but try not to assume it before you know better.

If people try to be helpful, respect their efforts rather than discounting them. Again, avoid thinking in all-or-nothing terms – i.e. they must understand completely or it's pointless. Maybe a little understanding is helpful. Maybe it's part of a step-by-step approach. Try to avoid attacking others if they do not understand in the way you would wish, as this will just put them on the defensive.

Coming out of shame is often a slow opening-up process. We gradually learn to reach out to others, and become more compassionate with them and with ourselves. Once you make the decision to come out of hiding, numerous possibilities become open to you.

Key Points

- We all have the potential for shame.
- Shame can be focused on many things – our bodies, our actions, our feelings. The origin of these feelings may be recent or in the past.
- Shame grows in us when we label ourselves as bad, inferior, inadequate, etc.
- Commonly it is when we want to feel good about ourselves, loved, wanted and valued, but seem unable to elicit this from others that we feel shame.
- Feelings of shame often come from our internal bully, and it is not a good idea for anyone to be controlled by a bully.
- Shame can be a paralyzing experience, and we may spend a good deal of our lives trying to conceal it or make up for what we think is shameful.
- Recovery comes from gradually acknowledging what we feel ashamed of, learning to treat it with compassion, and recognizing that many depressive styles operate in shame (e.g. discounting the positives, all-or-nothing thinking, overgeneralizing, self-labelling and even self-hatred).

Exercises

- Complete the following sentences:
  I feel ashamed about myself because _____ .
  I feel ashamed of myself when I do/fail to do _____ .
  I feel ashamed of myself when I feel, think or fantasize about _____ .
  I feel ashamed of myself because in the past I _____ .

Now that you have outlined some of the things you feel ashamed about, you can start to use your rational/compassionate mind to face these honestly and heal them. To do this, review pp. 101–3 and also 118–19.

continued on next page

- Write down some alternatives to the thoughts of shame you might have. For example: I am *not* a bad/inferior/worthless person because _____ .
- Try using healing imagery. Imagine yourself when you feel ashamed: what is (or was) happening to you? Now imagine that someone who cares about you has come to help you. What do you need from them? Ask for it. Imagine what they say to you – maybe they put an arm around you. Let their compassion flow to you. Decide how you will change to overcome your shame. Next imagine how you would act if you were less shame-prone and think about the steps to take to make this come true.
- Try to change the way you behave. For example, if you feel you must always wear make-up before going out, try going out without it. Check on your thoughts and challenge them. Remind yourself that this exercise is designed to lower your fear of what others might think about you.
- Leave your house untidy if people come to visit. Try to develop a more informal approach with others you know. In other words, focus more on the friendliness rather than on appearances.
- Take the first steps to initiate positive activities with other people. Decide if you are a person who waits to be chosen or are a chooser. Try to exert more control over positive choices, not just vetoes.

14

Coping with Guilt and Caring Too Much

Guilt, like shame, can play an important role in increasing vulnerability to depression and maintaining it. There have been many theories about the differences between *guilt* and *shame*, and debates on these still bubble away. We touched on these in the last chapter and can now explore them more fully.

Differences between Shame and Guilt

First, guilt has a different focus from shame. In guilt we usually focus on the *harm* or *hurt* we have caused other people by our actions, thoughts or feelings. So guilt is often about feeling *responsible* for others – to make them happy or protect them from harm. Shame, you will recall, is more about harm to oneself (being a bad person in some way). Second, guilt tends to focus on specific events – 'I feel guilty because I did that or thought this' – whereas shame is focused on feelings about the self, such as being inadequate, flawed or unattractive. Third, whereas in shame we want to hide and cover up, in guilt we want to repair things and put things right. Fourth, guilt (often) arises where there are conflicts over things that we want, or want to do, that may harm others. Guilt is commonly associated with conflicts where one person's gain is another person's loss.

To clarify these distinctions, consider the reactions of two men, John and Tom, both of whom have affairs. When their respective wives discover their infidelity, John thinks, 'Oh dear, my wife will give me a hard time now. Maybe she won't love me so much. Suppose she tells our friends? How will I face them? I think I had better hide for a while.' John's focus is not at all on the pain he has given his wife, but only on himself. His main concern is the damage the discovery may do to him. His response is shame-based. Tom, however, feels terribly sad for the hurt he has caused his wife and the damage he has done to the relationship. He recognizes how bad he would feel if the situation were reversed and feels remorse. Tom may also worry about his wife loving him less and what his friends might think of him if they found out, but principally he is focused on the harm he has done and the hurt he has caused. His response is guilt-based.

Guilt feelings are often related to *fear* and *sadness*. When we have done something that has caused hurt or done harm there can be feelings of *sorrow*, and these in turn are linked to feelings of remorse and regret. It is these feelings that make us want to put things right. So, for example, John may not feel that much sorrow for what he had done, because he is focused purely on the damage to him that may follow from the discovery. Tom, however, feels deep sorrow to see his wife so hurt.

You will note from this example that although Tom feels guilt and is far more in touch with the pain he has caused than John, he is unlikely to be free of shame. Suddenly, confronted with a deeply hurt wife, he may (perhaps for the first time) really appreciate how hurtful his actions have been, and this could trigger negative (shame-related) thoughts. So, although this chapter is going to focus on guilt, we should be clear that guilt can trigger shame (and self-attacking thoughts, e.g. 'I am a cheat and a bad/ unlovable person'); indeed, in depression it commonly does. Both guilt and shame are *self-conscious* emotions – meaning that they focus attention in on the self. The heightened self-consciousness of guilt can easily tip into shame and negativity when we are depressed. Guilt, as a trigger for shame, is important to spot.

Caring and Guilt

The American psychologist Martin Hoffman sees guilt as related to sympathy and empathy. But this is not the whole story. For a torturer, hurting others might be a pleasure – especially if 'they talk' – and an empathic torturer is worse than a non-empathic one. The non-empathic torturer puts the gun to your head, the empathic one puts it to your child's head. So there is more to guilt than just empathy. Adult guilt also involves a capacity for compassion and a desire to care for others. If we don't care about others, why would we be bothered with guilt? One does not need to care for others to feel ashamed, but one does to feel guilt. Indeed, one of the reasons we can behave so badly and hurtfully towards others is because we neither have sympathy for, nor care for, the person. Similarly, if we stop caring or feeling sympathy for ourselves, we can also treat ourselves very cruelly and unkindly.

Caring, Reputation and Approval-Seeking

Guilt requires some emotional capacity for caring. It is not related to a status hierarchy or to feeling inferior in the way shame is. Guilt evolved along with our capacity to care for others. However, before we look at this more closely we need to clarify something important about our motives for engaging in caring behavior towards others. Not all *acts* of caring involve *genuine feelings* of care or compassion. In fact, many don't. Sometimes we are kind and nice to others because we want them to think well of us. We want to have the *reputation* of being nice, caring people. We are caring because we want to be liked, loved or admired. This is approval-focused caring. If we fail at this, what we feel may be not guilt (because our motives weren't focused on the other) but shame: 'Oh no, I forgot Bridget's birthday party. She will think *I am* really thoughtless and be angry *with me*. Why *am I* so forgetful? *I am* stupid to make these mistakes.' You see how much is focused on the self?

Let's think about Tom and John again. Suppose John decides that he must be extra nice to his wife because in that way he might *win back* her love, or make life easier *for himself*, or because he might feel better *about himself* – this is approval- and shame-based caring. Tom, however, wants to help *his wife* to feel better. This is guilt-based caring.

So we can see that both caring for others (being nice to people) and putting things right when they go wrong can be motivated by a desire to make ourselves feel better (shame-based) or to make others feel better (guilt-based). However, as in so many things, the picture is rarely black and white; in most cases it is a matter of balance, and our caring behavior is not purely of one or the other kind. Let's look at this more closely.

Rescuing Heroes and Self-Sacrifice

For many people, doing a good turn for others and helping out when needed feels good, especially if others show gratitude and appreciation of our efforts. Letting our friends or family down, on the other hand, can feel bad. Now, trying to earn others' gratitude and thus feel good about ourselves is a typical human thing to do; we like to feel needed. For some, though, this desire can become exaggerated.

For example, David had fantasies of developing a loving relationship with a woman by rescuing her from a difficult life situation. The fantasy was vague. It could have been that she was lonely, or in a bad relationship with another man. He wanted to be someone's shining knight and rescue her. The key point was that he felt that if he found a woman who needed him, then her *gratitude* to him would be the basis for love. He needed to be needed. As you might imagine, he was far more uncertain that he could be loved simply for himself – he had to be useful to a woman before she would love him. And you can imagine the kind of person he felt he had a chance with. He never thought he'd get anywhere with strong and able women, and also he felt they would overpower him easily. Gratitude and appreciation are of course important aspects of affectionate relationships; but sometimes people set out to put themselves in relationships where they can earn them, because getting others' gratitude and appreciation is the *only way* they feel loved. This approach to relationships is a form of approval-seeking or gratitude-seeking (see Chapter 12).

Looking at the same desire negatively, we need others to be in difficulty so that we can rescue them. Some theorists see this style as developing in childhood, where children try to heal the wounds and difficulties of their parents and so to make their parents love them out of gratitude. This is not uncommon in children whose parents have been depressed or suffered in some way, or had difficult lives. The child's role as rescuer is established early on, and they can feel much guilt and shame if they fail in this role. Fear of this kind of failure, and the anticipation of how good they will feel about themselves if they are successful (make the parent feel good or better) set up a style of relating to others, where to feel good about oneself one has to be helpful to others.

This style can be called the *rescuing hero*. Now, many of us have this element to our personalities and I am not at all suggesting one should try to get rid of it. If I care for someone and we both feel good about it, then we both gain. If you are wondering if you have this style of relating to others, then think for a moment what it is that you would like to do (or be) to earn the love and respect of others. How much of your fantasy involves obtaining others' appreciation, gratitude or admiration for being able to make things better for people? How much of it is really approval-seeking? Saving the world from a disease or alien invasion is the stuff of many of our fantasies as children and (judging by Hollywood movies) adults too. We want to be heroic saviours – and why not!

But, as with all our other emotions and dispositions, we need to keep this aspect in balance with others. If it comes to dominate excessively, it can result in vulnerability to depression. Extreme rescuing heroes and self-sacrificers often try to be nice – sometimes super-nice. And they are commonly attracted to the helping professions like psychotherapy. This can also give them a sense of power and control over others. Some patients intuit that their therapist is 'doing' therapy for his or her own reasons – because being nice to people and helping others makes the therapist feel good. They may be right. But even therapists can't be nice all the time; and what do you think happens when they have to say 'no' to others, assert their own needs over those of others? Or when compassion fatigue sets in, or when they become depressed and lose interest in others, or simply lose the energy to be caring? You've guessed it – shame and guilt. Indeed, in the 1970s there were many books written on how guilt arises from an overdeveloped need to be nice, and can get in the way of healthy lifestyles. And, of course, if others don't play the game and express their appreciation for our niceness and helpfulness then we can feel put out and let down.

Rescuing heroes are prone to burnout, exhaustion and hiding their negative feelings towards others. They may have problems with being assertive in pursuing their own wants and desires, through always trying to be 'so understanding'. Sometimes they don't fully recognize that some of their behaviors are aimed at eliciting love and appreciation – at being seen as a 'thoroughly good person'. Various writers have claimed that some people can care or love too much, and are vulnerable to depression because they behave too submissively. In my view the problem is more commonly one of needing to be seen as, and to feel oneself to be, a caring person. Whether or not this always involves genuine feelings of care I am not so sure.

Guilt, Caring and Depression

So far we have linked guilt to caring because guilt arises from believing that one has harmed or might harm others, or has not done enough for them. We have also noted that some of our caring behavior comes from a wish to make ourselves feel good and worthy. How does all this relate to depression? Well, it does in a number of ways. First, when people become depressed they often lose the capacity to feel care for others and can feel deeply guilty and ashamed about this. Second, sometimes when people become depressed they more honestly face up to the fact that some of their caring and putting others first has been motivated by the wish to be liked, loved and approved of, and not necessarily from care or compassion for the other. Third, guilt and the concern not to hurt others can create many complicated dilemmas in life that can also be traps. Let's look at these links.

Losing the Capacity to 'Feel' for Others

Depression knocks out many of our abilities for positive feelings. We can lose interest in ourselves, and in others too. Becoming aware that we have neither the energy to care nor feelings of caring can be a blow to our self-esteem.

Sam had been a caring man for his family and friends but when he became depressed he felt unable to show interest in his family. His anxiety stopped him from doing things with them, like going on holiday, that previously he would have planned, organized and enjoyed. When one of his children informed him he was going to be a new grandfather he felt inwardly dead about it. Our conversations went something like this:

> SAM. I just don't feel anything for anyone any more. I don't know what has happened to me. When Julia told me she was expecting I didn't feel anything. I know my reaction must have hurt her and I felt terrible about it. I would so much like to be there for her, but it just seems such an ordeal. My first thoughts were, 'Oh God, I am going to have to take the responsibility of being a caring granddad. I don't want the hassle of that.'
>
> PAUL. Well, sadly depression can do this. And even when we are not depressed we can have such thoughts. But when we are depressed our inner resources are low and the body simply does not have energy to put into caring feelings. If there is no fuel in your car it does not matter how much you push the accelerator, it won't go anywhere. This does not mean *the car* is bad or deficient, only that the fuel tank is empty. So we need to have a way of thinking about your loss of ability to care for others, 'to be there for them', so that your guilt does not become another source of self-attacking.

Working with this aspect of Sam's depression was focused on his guilt feelings for not feeling for others close to him. It turned out that he was often prone to guilt feelings and was normally very sensitive to others and loving. Sam was experiencing guilt for his lost abilities to 'be there for others' and aware of how much his depression was hurting others. Yet he could not do anything about it. And he could not address some of his anger and difficulties in relationships because to do so felt like a betrayal and (of course) made him feel more guilty. Also, his guilt feelings turned to shame; for example, he told himself he was selfish and an unlovable person. Therapy had to focus on how he needed to overcome his depression before his feelings for others could return.

Mothers can be especially prone to guilt when they lose loving feelings for their children. They tell themselves, 'I should not feel like this, I should always feel loving towards them.' Concern that their feelings and behaviors are harming their children can be a source of painful guilt. If this triggers negative ideas of the self such as 'I am a bad mother', then there is both guilt and shame.

Being a Burden

There are some depressions where people feel that they are being a burden to others. They may even have the view that others would be better off without them. This is a dangerous way of thinking, because it fuels suicidal thoughts. Sam sometimes felt like this. If you think like this, let me state clearly: this is the depression talking, and *it is never true*. Sadly, I have seen the damage a suicide can do to families for years to come. And when people recover from depression they are very relieved they did not harm themselves. If you think others would be better off without you, then you need to be clear in your mind that everyone, including you, would be better off if you could recover from your depression – that's just common sense – but, no matter how dark your feelings are, *no one* gains from a suicide.

So let's be honest about this. Sure, depression is burdensome – but so are many other types of illness. We do not need to pretend otherwise. When we are children we could not survive without being dependent on others. When we get sick we often need looking after – life is like this. There are times when we have to take as well as give. Sometimes we have to learn how to cope with being cared for, for a while; to learn that sometimes we have just run out of fuel and then we can't give out as much as we would like. If you are haunted by feelings of being a burden, then seek professional help as soon as you can. Tell yourself, 'This is my depression talking. There is nothing bad *about me* for feeling this way. However, I can focus on what I need to do to get well rather than how bad (guilty and/or ashamed) I am for being depressed. There are over 300 million depressed people in the world, so it can't be my fault if my depression makes me feel this way. Let's go step by step and focus on what I can do rather than what I can't.'

This is what we worked on with Sam.

PAUL. At the moment you're preoccupied with the fact that you don't feel pleasure in your daughter's pregnancy, right? And you feel sad at this loss and the possibility that it hurts her?

SAM. Yes.

PAUL. Okay, suppose you were to put that to one side; to admit, as you have, that your feelings are not functioning that well right now; that's sad for you, but what might you do that she would like?

SAM. *(thinks)* Well, I guess I would normally send her a card or something.

PAUL. Okay. How would you feel if you did that?

SAM. Better, probably, but it wouldn't seem genuine. I should do this because I really want to, because I feel something. *(Note the underlying belief that all caring should come from a deep feeling of caring. We could have explored this belief, and later on we did, but here we took a different track.)*

PAUL. Sure, if you weren't depressed you might well feel something. But look, we know that at the moment you won't, so there is not a lot of point in telling yourself you should feel something. Your feelings may come back as you recover. The first step is helping you do things that you want to do, regardless of what you feel. Feelings will be the bonus of getting well. So even though there may not be much feeling in it right now, sending a card would be something you could do.

Because Sam was preoccupied with his guilt feelings about not feeling overjoyed at his daughter's pregnancy, but felt indifferent, he had been paralyzed and unable to act in ways he'd normally do. This made him feel even worse. By breaking into this paralysis we were able to help him begin to make changes and not expect that his behaviors should be matched with passionate feelings of caring. So he did go to the shops and sent a card and some flowers. His daughter was touched by this, and this was a small step forward.

We also learnt from this exercise that Sam had been telling himself that if he just went through the motions of caring then this was not genuine caring, and if it was not genuine caring it was a fake, and if it was a fake it was worthless. Remember how some people can be tormented by the ideas that their behaviors are fake (see Chapter 9)? Sam gives another example of this.

Sometimes people lose affectionate feelings for others (and feel guilty) because there are unresolved conflicts of anger or envy about. I will discuss these in the following chapters; here I want simply to make the point that whatever might be causing the loss of caring feelings, there are things that one can do and ways of thinking about the problem that need not lead you into self-attacking. Ask yourself, 'Am I expecting too much of myself? Am I expecting my feelings to work as they would if I were not depressed? How would I feel if I were not depressed or stressed out? Even though I may not have much feeling for it, are there things I could do that would help me feel better.'

Guilt, Dilemmas and Traps

Few of us take pleasure in purposely hurting others, especially those we care about, but sometimes this is just inevitable and we need to face that. Carol had stayed in a relationship for some years because she could not face hurting John. She was fond of him, but the love had gone out of the relationship some years earlier. Her mother had had a similar relationship with her father, and she had felt sorry for both of them. They had stayed together, they had told her, 'for the sake of the kids'. Many children in such situations, far from feeling gratitude to their parents, can feel a sense of guilt. Carol was one of those people who felt it her role to make people happy. She was one of life's rescuing heroes. So, to be a cause of unhappiness (e.g. to John by leaving him) was almost unbearable. And, as we noted above, guilt is most likely in times of conflict, where one person's gain is another person's loss.

Now, no therapy can help people avoid dilemmas in life and sometimes these are acutely painful. There are no right or wrong answers; no cost-free solutions. All one can do is to help people think about their dilemmas in ways that allow them to move forward with them rather than get stuck in guilt and shame. In essence, Carol's psychology had set up a trap – sometimes called the compassion or guilt trap. She was not free to do what she wanted (to leave the relationship) because she felt too guilty about the pain she would cause John. Underneath this there was a bubbling resentment (for which she felt guilty) and depression. She could see no way forward.

Carol's therapy focused a lot on issues related to her guilt and her inability to tolerate it. She had to acknowledge the painful fact that her guilt often led her to being dishonest in relationships. She would do things for others to avoid upsetting them. By the end of her therapy she had worked out that ending the relationship might be for the better. She would be sad about it and John would be hurt, but if she stayed she would only get more resentful and depressed. Once she had faced the possibility that she could go, that she could face her guilt, sorrow and sadness, she felt less trapped. The therapy had loosened the bonds that were immobilizing her. I don't actually know if she did leave John, as their relationship had improved slightly through her being more honest with him; but she told me that she had more insight into what locked her into unhelpful relationships, and this released her a little. Maybe facing the fact that she *could* leave made the need to leave less urgent. I don't know.

Guilt and Escaping

Just as we can feel a burden to others, so we can feel burdened and overloaded by the responsibilities of life. If you are carrying a heavy load that's hurting your back, the most natural thing is to put it down. Similarly, when we feel over-burdened by responsibilities (e.g. for others) the most natural thing is to want to put them aside. This, however, can be a source of guilt for some people because they fear letting others down. Or it can go further. Not only may people lose interest in caring for others; as they get depressed they can have strong desires to get away from them, to escape. For example, a young mother who is not sleeping and has become exhausted may want to run away from everyone making demands on her. In our own studies we have found that desires to escape are strongly associated with depression (see Chapter 3). Sam, for example, felt he 'just wanted to get away' from his family, in part because he saw himself as a burden to them, but also because he felt the responsibilities he believed he ought to take on were themselves too burdensome. And, of course, some people want to escape because there are too many conflicts around them, or there is not much to sustain them where they are, or they feel smothered and constrained. What ever causes us to want to run away and escape, we can feel very guilty about wanting to do that.

If you have strong escape desires, then remind yourself that these are common in depression. Try to work out what *specifically* you want to escape from. Do you need to create more space for yourself and look after your own needs more? Worksheet 4 (p. 354) in Appendix 1 addresses this issue. Here we should note that guilt about wanting to escape can stop people exploring *why* they wish to leave, or what they need to do to change their current situation, or even whether they would indeed be better off leaving or taking time out. Guilt can lock us into circles of thought and feeling. Taking on too much responsibility, we feeling burdened, then want to escape, then feel guilty; to cope with the guilt we try harder, but then feel more burdened – and so on. In this situation it is important to allow yourself to take an honest look at your life and see what needs to change to make you feel less burdened. Are you expecting too much of yourself? Have you become exhausted? Do you feel like this when you are not depressed? Imagine you were talking to a friend. How would you see it for them? How would you help them? How could you help yourself explore the problem without self-attacking or getting caught up by 'shoulds' and 'oughts'? What might a rational/compassionate approach be?

Guilt and a Sense of Deserving

Evolution has designed guilt to warn us about hurting others. Now, one way we can hurt others is by exploiting them, by taking more than our fair share. People who are prone to excessive guilt often talk in terms of 'entitlement' and 'deserving'. Some depressed people, however, can worry that they don't deserve certain things – that they haven't done enough to earn them. When wealthy westerners see third world poverty we can feel a quiver of guilt as to why we are so wealthy and they are so poor. We would like to think the world is fair, or at least that we can bring about fairness. Even quite young children can show concern for fairness. Sadly, the world is not a fair place.

Fairness and a sense of deserving are part of our psychology, but we must learn to keep it in balance. Some depressed people feel they don't deserve to be happy – that somehow if they are happy they will be punished for it. In their book, everything has to be earned. However, such a sense of 'deserving from earning' can be unhelpful. Imagine a man who wins a lot of money on a lottery but then thinks, 'I don't deserve this.' He can't enjoy his winnings because he is preoccupied with a sense of guilt over (not deserving) his good fortune. Now, the question for you is: if good things happen to you, can you enjoy them? Can you really appreciate them and take joy from them? Or are you a person who constantly thinks, 'I don't deserve this'? If you do think like that, then write down the advantages and disadvantages of allowing yourself to enjoy good fortune. What do you gain from not allowing yourself to accept the good things that happen to you? What do others gain by your undermining yourself in this way? Are you wanting to be seen as one of life's victims, an identity which is threatened by accepting good fortune?

People can be tormented by guilt and shame because they can't enjoy their good fortune. Such a person may say, 'I've got so much going for me. I'm not poor, and I have a fairly good relationship with my partner, but I am not happy. I feel so guilty that I can't appreciate things. Maybe I don't deserve them.' This is a bit like Sam from a few pages ago. Instead, of working hard to find out exactly what they are not happy about, they keep telling themselves they *should be happy* and feel worse for not being so. If this is the case for you, then write down what you are satisfied with in your life. Try to *be specific* about the things you are not happy with. Recognize that there are things that you are happy with and things that you may not be happy with. Next, note that if you are unhappy in one area of your life this can affect the feelings about other areas – that's natural. If you break a leg, it doesn't matter how well the rest of your body is functioning, the broken leg still hurts like hell. Telling yourself you shouldn't be in pain because at least you don't have cancer does not help much. Of course, learning to appreciate the good things in one's life can be important in depression because it helps us avoid all-or-nothing thinking and over-focusing on the negative. But there is not much to be gained by feeling guilty at not being happy. You can see then that the question of 'deserving' does not enter into it.

Guilt and Greed

For some people, wanting more of something can feel like being greedy, and this ignites guilt. We might feel we are too demanding or are not entitled to what we want. Remember how in Chapter 10 we noted the feelings of being a nuisance? Well, this is another aspect of the same kind of feeling. People can feel guilty even for coming to therapy and taking up the therapist's time. They tell themselves things like, 'I am taking up time here that should be given to more needy others.' Guilt about fulfilling our needs when this may take away from others can be one of the reasons why we never learn enough about our needs to know how to satisfy them. By feeling guilty that one wants more of something, whether this be love, affection, care or understanding, we never get to the bottom of why we want those things and how to increase the chances of getting them. You can challenge such thoughts about wanting too much with alternatives, for example:

> *Who knows what is too much? Surely the key thing is to understand more about why I am feeling depressed and taking the steps I need to so that I can overcome it. By taking my needs and feelings seriously I may discover things about myself I didn't know before. I may learn new ways of coping and treating myself better. By engaging with my needs I will be able to throw myself into my therapy or self-help process wholeheartedly rather than only doing it half-heartedly because I tell myself I don't deserve it.*

If you think like this you will be more able to appreciate what you have, but also to work on those areas of your life, or your self-beliefs and feelings, that do need changing.

Let's now look at some other ways a sense of deserving and guilt can get in the way of overcoming depression and becoming content.

Survivor Guilt

Lynn O'Connor and her colleagues in San Francisco have studied guilt over a number of years and noted there are different types of guilt. One form of guilt they have drawn attention to is called *survivor guilt*. This type of guilt first came to the attention of researchers when it was found that people who had survived traumatic experiences like incarceration in prison camps were depressed. They felt bad (in part) because they had survived while others had died or had been seriously injured. They asked themselves, 'Why did I survive and others die?' Sometimes there was a feeling that they didn't deserve to live, or didn't have a right to be happy when others had died. Feeling happy made them feel guilty. A recent study has found that people who have survived a life-threatening illness and knew others who shared the condition but who did not survive, can feel not only sadness but also a depressive sense of not deserving or 'why me'?

Guilt at Being Better Off than Others

Lynn and her colleagues also reasoned that this kind of guilt can operate in many types of relationship where we find ourselves better off than others, for example, from an awareness that we have superior qualities, or better opportunities. Imagine that you and a good friend take an important examination to (say) go to university or get a job, or you both enter a competition like a beauty pageant. You are both keen and share your hopes of passing or winning. You pass but your friend does not – s/he fails. How do you feel?

There are times when we know that we can't do anything to help others; and knowing that others are suffering while you feel helpless to do anything about it can be depressing – especially if you are doing well yourself. Sonia had landed a good job in advertising. She was over the moon about it. Her husband Dave, however, was not doing so well. His firm was going downhill and eventually he was put on short time. Sonia started to feel guilty about her success. When she came home she didn't share good experiences she had at work or her sense of how exciting it was, because she felt it would upset Dave and make him feel worse. She was also worried that Dave would resent and envy her for her good job. She loved Dave, but she also began to resent his low mood and anger at how things had turned out for him. And then she also felt guilty at feeling resentful. After all, things were going well for her. The guilt of upsetting Dave with her own good fortune stopped her from sharing things with him. As time passed, she found that she would stay longer at work to be with enthusiastic people rather than in the more subdued mood that prevailed at home – but this also made her feel guilty. Key beliefs were: 'I shouldn't want to spend more time at work when I know that Dave needs me at home. I should be there for him. I shouldn't enjoy my life when Dave is not enjoying his. I am selfish.'

Sonia needed to clarify the issues and recognize that, for her, wanting to be with enthusiastic people rather than a husband afflicted by low mood is natural. For Sonia, the important point was to help her see that labelling herself as selfish and feeling guilty about feeling resentment were unhelpful.

In some families, induced guilt is rife. Sonia had grown up in a family with a mildly depressed mother. As she entered adolescence and started to go out at night, her mother would often tell her how lucky Sonia was and how much more difficult it had been for herself when she was young. 'I never had the opportunities you have,' she'd say. Her mother would tell her how much she loved Sonia, not by noting how good-natured or talented Sonia was, but by pointing to all the sacrifices she (as mother) had made for her! Sonia was unwittingly being trained to operate on guilt and gratitude. She came to believe that she should always put the needs of others first and that if others were suffering or needed her, she should be there for them. After all, she was so lucky, wasn't she? It is in fact common in therapy to find that people who are sensitive to guilt, who feel uneasy with success and just enjoying life, often have had depressed parents. They need to care for others, to help others; and quite often they gravitate into the helping professions.

As we have seen, then, when something good happens to some depressed people they often wonder if they 'deserve' it or have a right to enjoy it. These thoughts are often not fully conscious, but are in the background of their minds. If you ever worry about showing off your talents because you fear that others will feel badly in comparison to you, and so you play them down, the chances are you are operating on some kind of guilt issue. You may also have a belief that others will *envy* you. 'If they see my good fortune or talents they will envy me or dislike me or try to pull me down.'

Just as some people feel they don't deserve their good fortune, and so sabotage their ability to enjoy life, so others are all too ready to use the idea of deserving to support and justify their good fortune. Some months ago the newspapers published the fact that a wealthy financier had been given a £3 million 'golden handshake'. When asked whether he was a 'fat cat', he responded with, 'No. I worked hard for my firm and deserve it.' No obvious guilt here. How much more refreshing to have heard, 'Well, I have had the good fortune to be reasonably bright, with an ability for hard work; I've been given a good education and had the connections to get a good job.' As you see, the notion of 'deserving' is in the eye of the beholder.

Responsibility Guilt

Lynn O'Connor and her colleagues have also pointed to a form of guilt that comes from taking too much responsibility for other people, especially their feelings. Taking an interest in others and helping them as best we can is of course no bad thing, but sometimes we take this too far – as we have already seen in a different context when discussing 'rescuing heroes' above.

Rescuers often take too much responsibility for others. Some women blame themselves for their husbands' drinking or violence. One woman felt that her husband drank because he felt unloved, and that if she could love him more he would stop. Thus in her mind she felt guilty for not loving him enough to heal his inner pain. This kind of thinking, however, takes responsibility away from the other person and stops them having to confront their own problems. To put it negatively, we can literally rob people of their responsibilities. It is as if we were saying to the other, 'You are not responsible for your own happiness or bad behavior. It is all down to me. I am responsible for what you feel or do.' Put like that, it doesn't sound so good, does it? People can only grow and mature by taking responsibility for themselves. Although you may think that blaming yourself and feeling guilty is helpful or protects them, this is unlikely to do them much good in the long run.

In this situation it can be useful to draw out a responsibility circle (see p. 141). There may well be aspects of any situation that are indeed your responsibility and under your control; but always try to keep a balance here. Avoid all-or-nothing thinking: 'It's either me or them.' Sometimes when people confront their own pain, especially if it's people you care about, you may feel sad for them. But this does not mean you have to feel guilty, as if you were not doing enough to help them. Support them, yes; but don't take on the responsibility for their change or healing their minds – only they can do that.

In some cases of serious depression, called 'psychotic depression', a person can come to believe that they have caused serious major events. For example, one of my patients believed that a phone call she had made to a friend, in which she had voiced her anger with her son for borrowing her car, had been tapped by the police, and now her whole family would be arrested and their lives ruined. Her guilt at 'telling tales' on her son had become part of a serious psychotic guilt experience. At first I was not able to help much in her acute depression, and in fact came to be seen by her as in league with the police. However, once she was in hospital and her antidepressant medication began to work, her delusions lessened and we were able to work together – and she made a full recovery. Thankfully, in most depressions things don't go this far; but it is not uncommon for seriously depressed people to believe that they have caused harm to others for which they might be punished. We don't really know why, in some psychotic states, guilt takes on such proportions. It may be guilt for unconscious aggressive feelings. Be that as it may, for such depressions medication and medical help are often essential.

In less severe cases, as people become depressed they can also feel more guilty. They may start to focus and dwell on things they have done or not done that they think have harmed others. If this is the case for you, then think about how you would see this if you weren't depressed. May be there are things that you need to come to terms with or forgive yourself for, but dwelling on guilt won't help you here. At times it may be necessary to talk these things over with others or get professional help, because depression can so easily make us lose perspective. Ask yourself, are you self-attacking? What would a rational/compassionate view on this be?

Abandoning Guilt

I discovered my own 'rescuing hero' side with a wise and compassionate supervisor who drew my attention to the fact that I was not discharging people from therapy as I should. He helped me discover my own thoughts along the lines of: 'Maybe I haven't done enough to help them. Maybe they will need me in the future.' I had mild guilt and shame feelings of discharging people because I might be abandoning them (letting them down), and so they would not like me.

Remember Carol's story, related above? She stayed with John out of guilt for the hurt she might cause him if she left. Carol had another thought typical of people in this situation. If John found someone else it would be a relief! She could separate with no guilt. However, this had turned her relationship into a trap. And consider Tim. Tim found it difficult to leave his job for a better one because he felt guilty at abandoning his staff. He hated his job, but the feelings associated with leaving his colleagues behind were intense for him. However, if he didn't take the opportunity he would be trapped in a position he deeply disliked without any prospects. So he had to learn to tolerate the sadness of going and moving to something better for himself, while leaving others behind. He nearly didn't go.

When it comes to ending a relationship or separating from others, we often have many mixed feelings, and one of them can be the guilt of leaving and saying goodbye. This can be more acute if the person we are leaving seems to need us. In the lives of some depressed people there is often a history of guilt at leaving the parents. When Ruth wanted to go away to study, one of the things that stopped her from going to her favored university was the prospect of leaving her mother, who from Ruth's childhood had turned her daughter into her 'closest friend'. Although Ruth was close to her mother too, the relationship was fairly one-sided in terms of who was benefiting from it. Ruth remembered many occasions when she had not gone out with friends so that her mother wouldn't be lonely. Ruth had major guilt problems in separating from her mother, and thinking of her as 'being left alone'. But from the outside it was clear that unless Ruth had faced this, she would not have been able to claim her own life. Parents are responsible for their own lives and can cause children real problems by turning them into their carers or depending on them for friendship. For most animals, including humans, the role of the parent is to train their offspring to be able to enter the world, even at times to push them out into it. It is not to keep them away from it in relationships of dependence.

Grief and Guilt

The biggest separation is, of course, death. When someone we love dies it is not at all uncommon to feel (at least a bit) guilty. We remember all the times we said unkind things; the times we could have done more for the person and didn't; the visits we could have made and didn't. This is all normal and not uncommon. We are only human, after all. However, sometimes there have been unresolved conflicts with the dead person and we feel painfully guilty that we were not able to sort them out before they died. Many Hollywood movies have been made in which relationships work out at the last moment before death and a reconciliation occurs. There are few dry eyes in the house. But that is Hollywood; real life is not often like this.

Guilt can be one of the many complicating factors in grief and can stop you working through your grief. The problem with guilt and death is that because the other person has 'now gone', we may see no way we can repair things or put them right. So we feel blocked. If this is true for you, then getting counselling or therapy might help you move forward. As always, be aware of the negative self-attacking thoughts you might have.

Through talking to others, you may gain new insights and see possibilities for change. I remember a person early in my career who taught me a lot about how things can 'just happen' in therapy. We had been working on his relationship with his father and how they had not got on that well. When his father died, Ben felt intense sadness and guilt for a separation that had lasted for years and which neither had been able to heal. Then one day Ben had a dream about his father. I don't recall the details, but Ben came to therapy in a changed state of mind. He said something like, 'You know, I can see now that both my father and I are proud men. Neither of us could share our feelings that easily. I see how much he suffered because of this. It seems so silly and pointless to me now. His death has brought home to me how important it is to say what we feel and not hide behind these barriers. By dying when he did, he has given me the chance to be different from him. In a way I guess that is a gift he has given me.' Ben was very tearful at this point. He had looked at his guilt in a different way, and had been able to learn from it rather than being paralyzed by it.

There can be times when a death is a relief. Maybe one has had to look after a dying person, whose death sets both free. Even this can, however, induce guilt, as if we should not feel relief at the release from the burden of caring alongside the sadness of the loss. But a hundred years hence, much that we see now will be dead. This is the cycle of life. Death makes room for new life. The evolutionists have their views about it and the religious have theirs. The only point I am making here is that to feel relief at the lifting of a burden is natural to life. You may wish to focus on your sadness, but you don't need to be stricken by guilt.

Existential Guilt

Can we feel guilty for things that harm only ourselves? The existential writer Yalom, in his book *Existential Psychotherapy* – a fascinating work on these issues, including those associated with death – answers 'yes'. In his view, to believe that we have not lived to our full potential, that at times we have taken the coward's way out and have not been 'true to ourselves', can induce what he calls existential guilt – that is, guilt for how we live our lives. We put up with things which in our heart we know we shouldn't tolerate. One of my own self-guilt areas is in having been a smoker. In my heart I knew it was bad for me but I just couldn't be bothered to put in the effort to stop. I knew I was harming my body, and my family asked me to stop – and I was always going to, 'next week'. This type of guilt is helpful to own and face up to, because it helps us take steps to change. When we deny it or pretend we don't feel guilty for things we know can harm us, then we may be less likely to change. Having said this, it is usually better to find positive reasons to stop doing harmful things – guilt simply alerts us to the need for change.

Inducing Guilt

Roy Baumeister and his colleagues have written much about guilt, including how it can work positively in relationships. Imagine what relationships would be like if we never felt it! Certainly, there are times when children and adults alike have to recognize the hurt they have caused others and learn to experience and cope with guilt; and there are times when adults have to point this out to their children. However, some people actually try to induce guilt in others in order to make them do what they want them to do.

For example, we might say to a lover, 'If you leave me I couldn't cope without you,' or even 'I will kill myself'! We try to shift responsibility to others. This tactic may work to a degree, but you always run a risk here. If you are a guilt inducer and go around telling people how bad they make you feel, or try to control them by inducing guilt and making them feel sorry for you (or bad about themselves), you will run into problems. You may end up with resentful others around you.

Again, one has to be honest here. Think of the last time you had a conflict. Did you say things you (secretly) hoped would make the other person feel guilty? Even if you were successful, how would this help them feel closer to you or more keen to be with you? Think of people you know who make you feel guilty. Do you like being around them? Do you like being around people who make you feel sorry for them? Sadly, no. In the next two chapters we will look at dealing with conflicts and how to be assertive. So try to recognize your guilt-inducing tactics (which we all use from time to time). Once you are aware of them, then you can choose to be different and find new ways of sorting out your differences and conflicts with others.

Working with Guilt

Tolerating Guilt

Carol's story, described above, warns us about the unintentional dishonesty that can creep into our lives if we are too guilt-prone. As noted in Chapter 3, our feelings, such as anxiety, anger, jealousy, shame or guilt, are there because evolution has designed them that way. But we need to understand them, not just act them out. If every time we felt anxious we ran away, we'd soon end up with serious problems of managing our lives. If every time we felt angry we lashed out at people, we would not have any friends. With guilt as with so many other areas of life, it is often a matter of learning to cope with and tolerate our feelings. We need a balance – not too much and not too little. Indeed, if we can't tolerate at least a little guilt or shame, we will run into problems. If, in every conflict that produces guilt, we back down, we will soon feel overwhelmed and paralyzed. So sometimes therapy is about learning to tolerate our negative feelings.

There are some depressed people who are, in effect, intolerant of shame and guilt. They may feel these things acutely, but instead of working with the feelings, understanding them and learning how to accept them as part of life, they will do everything they can to turn them off and avoid feeling them. There are many reasons for this. Sometimes it is because these feelings have been overwhelming in childhood and they have not had the opportunities to work with them and accept them. And often it is because these negative feelings trigger terrible attacks on the self.

Anger and Guilt

Usually, guilt does not involve anger at others. (This is another aspect that distinguishes it from shame and humiliation.) But sometimes people feel angry if they can't own up to their feelings of guilt and recognize that they may have hurt someone. Consider an example. Tom forgets Jane's birthday and when he gets home she's clearly upset about it. Here is a guilt scene.

JANE. Tom, it's my birthday and you forgot. I feel really upset about it.

TOM. Oh, Jane, I am so sorry. You are right. I was so busy. It was really thoughtless of me. Let me put it right by taking you out tonight.

Let's assume that Jane accepts the apology and the offer. Here Tom has acknowledged his guilt (at having hurt Jane), apologized and made an offer to 'put things right'. Jane, for her part, is not intent on punishing Tom but accepts and forgives.

But suppose it went like this.

JANE. Tom, it's my birthday and you forgot. I feel really upset about it.

TOM. Oh, come on, Jane, you know I have been so busy . . . I can't remember everything, I'm stressed out right now. (angrily) Look, I am sorry, okay!

In this scenario Tom can't cope with his guilt and feeling bad, so

256

he turns it around and blames Jane, asking her (angrily) to accept the fact that his work took precedence over her. His 'sorry' is not a 'sorry' at all. The evening will now be affected by bad feelings, because Tom does not deal with his guilt but tries to cover it up. Many therapists would see this as turning guilt into shame, but it is also a form of guilt intolerance.

Another possibility is:

JANE. Tom, it's my birthday and you forgot. I feel really upset about it.

TOM. Oh, Jane, I am so sorry. You are right. I was so busy. It was really thoughtless of me. Let me put it right by taking you out tonight.

JANE. Well, it's too late for that. I think you are a mean, thought-less sod.

In this scenario Jane does not accept the apology. Perhaps she thinks, 'If he loved me he would not forget,' and acts on that assumption, maybe also withdrawing and sulking. She is intent on wounding Tom – inducing shame and guilt. This will get neither of them anywhere.

The point here is that because guilt often arises from conflict there is always the possibility either that the guilty person won't face up to it or that the one who feels hurt will escalate the situation into yet more hurtful conflicts. As a rule of thumb, when you hurt people with your thoughtlessness – and you will, we are not perfect – own up to it. Allow yourself to feel the guilt and pain you have caused. This does not make you a bad person; far from it. It keeps you in touch with your caring feelings and compassion.

If you do feel sorry for your poor behavior, then it is useful to express this as sadness rather than as anger. If you express your apology in an angry, dismissive or cold way, people won't believe it is genuine. Many apologies fall flat because of the way they are given. Also, as a general rule, if someone who has hurt you appears to be genuinely sorry, then it is helpful to accept it. Attacking them further is usually not productive.

Becoming More Aware of Your Guilt Areas

Guilt is an unpleasant feeling; but rather than turning away from it, it can help to recognize it and think about it. The first thing is to write down the typical triggers for your guilt. Get to know the typical situations that are likely to arouse guilt in you. You can do this when you feel guilty, but also when you feel calm and are reflecting on yourself. Once you have clarified your guilt areas, then write down your typical thoughts, paying close attention to the things you are thinking about yourself. Always remember that self-attacks are usually most unhelpful. They will only increase the signals going into your stress systems (see Chapter 2). If there are things you need to apologize for or make good then do so, but be clear that this is not just being submissive. Acknowledge openly that as a fallible human being you can unintentionally do things that hurt others. Don't go overboard on this with negative self-attacks, but be honest and do what you feel will help.

Work out how much your guilt feelings lead you to take on a rescuing hero stance in life. Is this helpful to you? What do you risk by doing this? Will you get burnt out? If there are times when you have to say 'no' to people, be aware that you might feel guilt to some degree; but you don't need to always back down.

Guilt and Forgiveness

Among the ideas that can help you with guilt over things you have done in the past are those of forgiveness and acceptance. Forgiveness is discussed more fully in Chapter 16; but we can note here that inner forgiveness can be an important aspect of change.

Kieran had walked out on his family fifteen years earlier. As he grew older and matured, he was haunted by terrible guilt at what he'd done. But he could not face it; so he drank. It took him some time to recognize that when he married he was not emotionally mature enough to cope with a young family. But he had to face up to and grieve for the pain he had caused. Until he could confront this grief, sorrow and guilt, he could not come to terms with his life. His guilt had turned to shame, which paralyzed all good feelings about himself. He saw himself as a worthless inadequate who always let people down and who could never be trusted. Thus (he believed) he'd never be able to have a loving relationship. This kind of self-battery did him no good at all; nor did it help him to relate to others or to try to develop a more supportive relationship with his ex-wife and son, which he wanted to do. The steps to forgiveness often require us to fully acknowledge what we have done, face our guilt and pain, learn from it, make amends if we can, and give up attacking ourselves.

Distancing Oneself from Guilt-Inducers

Annie found that every time she got off the phone having talked to her mother she felt depressed. As we unpacked this mood change we found two other feelings: guilt and anger. Her mother had a knack of making Annie feel guilty (e.g. for not visiting enough), and always wanted to pour out her woes, with the expectation that Annie should do more for her. Annie felt angry at not being able to stand up to her mother. Despite this, she kept phoning, because she thought she ought to and felt guilty if she didn't; and so she kept stirring up low moods.

My first intervention was to suggest a ban on phone calls (I had to take the responsibility for this). Second, we looked at what was a reasonable level of responsibility and what was not. Annie acknowledged that her mother had always been like this and had alienated other members of the family too. Third, we discovered that Annie had a secret hope that one day her mother would change and give her the love and approval she wanted as a daughter. Accepting that this was unlikely was painful. Fourth, and later on, we helped Annie monitor her thoughts very carefully as she spoke to her mother on the phone, and to challenge them as they happened. During the conversation, she held a flash card on which she had written thoughts like:

> *I know Mother will try to make me feel guilty, but then she always has and she does it to others too. It's not me, it's her style. She is not going to give me the approval I want, so there is no point in secretly hoping and then getting angry. I don't have to feel responsible for her happiness, and in truth there is not a lot that I could do.*

The key idea was helping Annie to keep a balance and break up her guilt–anger cycle. Sometimes we have to learn to cope with those who seem able to make us feel guilty by noting and challenging our own thoughts and feelings of excessive responsibility and anger. Sometimes it is important to keep our distance, and acknowledge that while we may feel guilty about this, we can tolerate it if we don't engage in excessive self-attacking or tell ourselves things like: 'I am bad or unlovable for keeping my distance.' And, of course, it can help to talk to sympathetic others or therapists if there are complex conflicts with guilt-inducers that we would like to resolve.

Key Points

- Guilt is a natural part of life. We can't go though life, with all its conflicts and difficulties, without feeling it. On the positive side, guilt helps us to recognize our hurtful behavior. On the negative side, it can be very inhibiting to us in recognizing our own needs.
- Guilt often arises when we think we haven't done enough for people, have had to refuse people what they want of us, or have to separate from them.
- We can learn to identify our guilt areas and clarify our typical thoughts and feelings.
- Especially important is when feelings of guilt trigger self-attacking (shame-related) thoughts and feelings.
- Sometimes we need to learn how to tolerate guilt feelings, and the sorrow associated with them, as part of life (like anxiety or anger), rather than trying to never feel them.
- If you feel guilty about being depressed, letting others down or being a burden, then try to remember that you would prefer not to be depressed – you are not a joyful depressive! If you feel suicidal for being a burden, then be clear: this is the depression talking – and seek professional help. You owe it to yourself to do what you can to recover from your depression rather than let it dictate your actions.

Exercises

Identify your key guilt areas:

I feel guilty when I ....

I would feel guilty if I were to ....

Guilt can be helpful or harmful, so let's think about this.

- In what ways does acknowledging your guilt and working with it help you? You might think, for example, 'It allows me to recognize when I am hurtful to others, to face up to this honestly and make reparations if I need to. This is part of growing and accepting myself as a fallible human being.'

- In what ways does acknowledging your guilt and working with it not help you? You might think, for example, 'If I turn my guilt in on myself with shaming self-attacks, then this will not be helpful and does nothing to repair the situation.' Or: 'If I avoid guilt feelings rather than learn to tolerate them, then I might always give into my guilt, not look after or recognize my own needs, and then at some level feel resentful.'

So, when you feel guilty this can be helpful if you face it. But you can ask yourself the following questions:

- Am I trying too hard to be nice? If so, what am I trying to achieve by this?
- Am I taking too much responsibility on myself for other people?
- Is responsibility-taking something I picked up in childhood and now need to reassess in my life? If so, how might I have come to think this way, and how might I change?
- Am I able to be assertive when I need to be, even if others may not be happy with that?
- Am I telling myself guilt is always bad (all-or-nothing thinking)?
- Am I trying to avoid painful dilemmas by not feeling guilty?
- Do I feel guilty if I succeed when others fail, and if so, does this hold me back with no real benefit to anyone?
- Do my difficulties with guilt make me too submissive?

continued on next page

You can challenge some of your negative thoughts about guilt with these questions:

- What is the evidence for feeling guilty in the first place? What is the evidence against?
- What are the alternatives for my current beliefs?
- If I'm honest, are other people really expecting too much of me?
- Am I expecting too much of myself?
- What would I say to a friend in a similar situation?
- What do I need to do to reduce any guilt and control it? How could I do that?

It can sometimes be useful to write out a *life review*. Start by writing: 'I have learnt to feel guilty because . . .' Then write for yourself your own story of how you think this may have happened. Then write out: 'The challenge for me now to overcome this problem is to . . .' This will help you to work out what you can do to challenge your typical guilt thoughts.

15

Coping with Anger

Strong feelings of anger are common in depression. Freud believed that unexpressed anger actually causes depression, as if anger can be turned inwards. However, we now know that, in some depressions, feelings of anger actually increase; people become more angry and short-tempered with others, not less. Nevertheless, Freud was correct to draw attention to the fact that sometimes anger and disappointment are directed at the self, and that people can be very fearful of their anger.

Anger is often related to feeling frustrated, blocked, thwarted, ignored or criticized. Something or someone is not as we want it or him/her to be. In evolutionary terms, anger gives us the energy to overcome the blocks to our goals, or to fight harder (counter-attack) in a conflict situation. Thus, anger can be a natural response. Anger can also be used to threaten others and coerce them to do as one wants. Various forms of retaliation (revenge) fit this function. Of course, we can work to overcome obstacles to our goals without feeling angry, and we can also coerce and threaten people without necessarily feeling anger – but in depression, efforts to coerce others often involve anger.

This emotion can also be experienced as powerless or impotent anger – that is, we feel unable to do anything about what we feel angry about. This may be because we think that nothing we do will work, or that anger is bad and makes us unlovable, or that we have no right to feel angry. All such thoughts can lead to a feeling of powerlessness. When we feel this way, we also feel subordinate to others, that other people have far more power than we do. Although depressed behavior can have a powerful effect on others, depressed people rarely see themselves as powerful.

Anger depends on certain kinds of thinking. If someone harms you accidentally, you are likely to feel less angry than if you think he or she did it on purpose. The problem here is that, even though someone may not have harmed you on purpose, you still have to deal with the feelings of being harmed. For example, when we are bereaved, we obviously know that the person did not intend to die, but the death can still generate much anger: 'How could he/she leave me like this?' Indeed, intense anger in grief is not an uncommon experience. Sometimes this can be directed at others – for example, at doctors who were unable to save the person.

Like frustration, we can be angry with things outside us in the world (e.g. other people) or we can be angry (and bully) with ourselves. To put this another way, we can blame ourselves for our difficulties (or states of mind) or blame other people. The same is true in how we express anger. It can be directed outwards (e.g. at other people) or inwards (e.g. at ourselves). We can even become angry with ourselves for feeling angry.

What Triggers Anger?

A common theme that ignites anger is a perception of some kind of threat, damage or block to things we personally value. Examples of some of these are damage or threats to:

- our sense of self (be this physical or self-esteem)
- our possessions
- our plans and goals
- our way of life

Commonly, we might see others as transgressing against us in some way, doing things we feel they should not do. But not all anger is related to transgressions. The most important source of anger is a threatening situation. These threats are usually associated with a sense of damage, of being harmed/thwarted, and can show up in various ways.

Frustration related   Frustrative anger occurs when things in the world don't go as we want them to – e.g. the car won't start in the morning. The damage in this case is to our goal to get to work on time. Stress and depression can lower our tolerance for frustration and thus our susceptibility to feel anger. When stressed, we may feel generally more vulnerable to things that can damage or block us, and there are also some basic self-beliefs that can affect our tolerance for frustration – for instance, 'This shouldn't happen to me', 'This is going to seriously interfere with or block me in what I want to do.'

Injury related   We can feel anger when others pose a threat to us and/or injure us in some way. Physical or verbal attacks can lead to feelings of anger. Anger is likely to be greater if we think the injury was deliberate, or the result of carelessness, than if we think it was unintentional or unavoidable. The anger that we feel towards an intentional injury can be revenge, and the impulse is to harm (counter-attack) the other verbally or physically.

Exploitation   A very common theme in anger is exploitation. This is when we think someone is taking advantage of us, using us or taking us for granted. As we have seen, most of us have a desire to feel appreciated and for relationships to be equitable. Be it in child–parent relationships, between friends and lovers, or even between countries, perceptions of being exploited or taken advantage of can lead to anger and its consequences.

Lack of attention   Anger can arise when others don't give us the attention we want. They may ignore us or dismiss our point of view. For example, Emma wants Chris to spend more time with her and help around the house, but he says that he's too busy. Or maybe Chris says he will help but does not keep his promise. Emma feels angry with Chris. However, with this kind of anger, we rarely want to harm the other person, but rather behave (e.g. scream and shout) so that he or she does not ignore us. We want to renegotiate our relationship, not necessarily destroy it.

Envy and jealousy   This kind of anger arises when we think that someone is getting more of something than we have. Linda thought that she would win the beauty contest but didn't, and she felt envious anger towards the winner. In envy, we want what someone else has, be this material possessions, a position in society, a popular personality, intelligence and so on. In jealousy, we think that someone we value might prefer to be with a person other than ourselves – for example, a married woman shows an interest in another man and her husband has pangs of jealousy. This type of jealous anger (if expressed) acts as a threat to the woman, suggesting serious consequences if she were to defect or cheat on her husband. Sexual jealousy is more likely when a partner sees the other as a possession.

Lack of social conformity This anger relates to the feeling that others should do as they are told. Parents become angry with children who disobey them. A religious person becomes angry if the members of his church do not obey the rules. We may become angry with our government over how they spend our money. The basic belief here is: 'Others should conform to and obey the rules of conduct that I believe are important.' The anger occurs because, in some way, we see the other person's conduct as potentially damaging to our own interests or way of life.

Compassionate anger This is when we feel anger by seeing harm come to someone else – for instance, when we see people starving and feel angry that this has been allowed to happen. The anger fuels the desire for us or others to do something.

There are two aspects common to all these situations: first, things are not as we want them to be; and second, we place a high value on the things that we are angry about. If they become less important to us, then clearly we are less prone to be angry about them. For example, if it does not matter to Emma if Chris helps with the housework, she is unlikely to feel angry if he does not help out. If you would be relieved if your partner found someone else and thus made it easy to end your relationship, you are unlikely to feel strong jealousy. In helping ourselves with our anger, it is possible that we may discover that we are overvaluing something, drawing conclusions about a situation that may not be warranted or seeing more potential damage in a situation than there is.

The Shades of Anger

Anger itself is not 'all-or-nothing', 'black or white' – it is more shades of pink. For example, imagine a line that starts off white and gradually becomes pinker until the other end is red. At the white end, there is no feeling at all, nothing matters. At the other end, one is enraged. The trick is to be somewhere along this line where you can keep control, but not in the white area or the red area. Anger is like a car that we need to learn how to drive. You don't want to drive everywhere at 100 miles per hour, but neither do you want to leave the car locked in the garage because you are frightened of it.

Sometimes depressed people do not know how to drive their anger. They continually lock it up and enter only as far as the vaguely pink area – at least as far as expressing their anger goes. That's fine if you are confident in doing that and don't need to show your anger. But it is not so good if you do need to reveal it and feel weak and inferior if you back down too quickly. If you feel that your anger tends to get out of control, you can learn other strategies – how to apply the brakes when you need to by, for example, breaking off encounters that are becoming too heated (too much in the red zone). Instead, you could give yourself space to calm down. Learn to control your anger rather than allowing it to control you.

Anger is often defensive in the sense that we are defending ourselves against a block to something or from criticism or being ignored or dismissed. When we behave defensively we often go for 'better safe than sorry' thinking and our emotions are triggered quickly (see Chapter 2). This is why many psychologists think that beneath the veneer of an angry person is a very vulnerable one – not someone who is confident or strong. Confident people rarely need to get angry as they are less easily threatened and more assertive. It is because anger implies that we have felt something as a threat or block that it can be so 'hot' and difficult to control. In working with our anger, we need to discover why we feel threatened and then work with our feelings of vulnerability.

Why Anger Expands

Why can anger feel so powerful? Why does it hit the red zone? It is not uncommon to find that what triggers it can be quite trivial. We might suddenly find that we are seething with anger over rather small events. It appears as if our anger has expanded. In some depressions, there are 'anger attacks', when people find themselves enraged for reasons they can't put their finger on. Some researchers believe that, in some cases, anger attacks are to do with the depression itself (and the biological changes associated with it). It has also been noted that some patients on certain antidepressant drugs can experience increases in anger. If you find that you have become far more irritable and angry since starting an anti-depressant, go back to your family doctor, who may recommend a change in medication.

But there are also psychological reasons for 'blowing up' over a trivial event. Let's think about the example of Emma and Chris given above. Suppose Emma says to herself, 'If Chris really cared about me, he would help with the housework.' Clearly the anger is not just about the housework but about the fact that Chris's lack of help is being taken as a lack of caring. Emma may also feel taken for granted. Thus, what seems like a trivial event actually has a much larger meaning.

When you think about the things that make you angry, it is useful to ask yourself some questions:

- What is it about this situation that I really value and feel could be damaged?
- Let's suppose I cannot change the situation. What does this say about my future?
- What am I saying about me if this (the source of the anger) happens? Am I drawing negative conclusions about myself?
- What am I saying about the other person? What motives am I reading into his or her action?

Another question that can be very useful is to ask is: 'In what way does this situation hurt me?'

In depression, as a rule, it can be helpful to focus on the feelings of hurt rather than on the anger. If we focus on the anger, we could miss the fact that it relates to feeling vulnerable or damaged in some way. Indeed, by being angry we can sometimes block out deep fears of being abandoned, ignored and hurt. Behind anger in depression is commonly a lot of hurt, a need to grieve for past hurts and problems of shame. If the person can work through the grief, both the anger and the depression may subside.

If we focus on our hurts rather than on our anger, we might gain more insight into our anger. In Emma's case, she saw that she believed that Chris's lack of help had the extra meaning of 'not being cared for', which led to the idea that maybe he did not value her or thought she was worth caring for, which led to the idea that maybe he was right. When Emma explored this, she realized that caring was not 'all-or-nothing' and that there were in fact many other instances (evidence) that showed that Chris did care.

So our anger can expand when we overestimate the damage that can be done to us. Here's another example. Derek was working on a project that required help from others. However, they did not finish their own work on time and he became furious. His thoughts were: 'If I don't get this project in on time, that will be a very bad mark against me.' He had a fear of being seen as inadequate by his boss. 'They are making me look incompetent to my boss. This could affect my chances of promotion. Therefore, these people, by not doing their work on time, are shaming me and ruining my whole future.'

When Derek focused on his own fear of shame, he began to see that he often got angry with anyone who might 'show him up'. This led him to consider why the approval of those (mostly men) in authority mattered so much to him. This in turn revealed the poor relationship he had had with his father and his belief that 'I must please those in authority, otherwise they will be angry and ignore/discount me.' These thoughts ignited many of the feelings and fears he had as a child. So his anger was powerful because of the meanings he put on the situations that triggered it. Later, Derek was also able to see that his belief that 'his whole future would be ruined' led to a high degree of anger.

Derek learned to deal with his anger by making a number of flash cards:

- When I feel anger, I need to slow down and monitor my thoughts.
- If I don't slow down and monitor my thoughts, I am likely to see many events as a re-run of my childhood.
- When I get angry, I often overestimate the damage that can be done to me.
- What is the evidence that this situation is damaging? How can I cope with it without getting angry?
- I don't have to feel ashamed by every block or setback.

Having the flash cards gave Derek just that extra bit of space to avoid letting his anger run away with him. It helped him to take his foot off the accelerator.

Robert became enraged when he went to a hotel and found that he had been put in the wrong room and the young assistant did not seem to care. He ended up telling her that he did not think the hotel should employ people like her. When he got to his room, he felt ashamed and depressed about his over-reaction, sat on his bed and burst into tears. What had happened here? Later, in therapy he was able to work out his thoughts as the following:

- Why can't people get things right?
- This assistant obviously sees me as a fool and a soft touch.
- If I were manly, I would sort this out without any difficulties.
- People should respect me and not treat me this way.
- I must be seen as a weak, useless bastard.
- But that's not fair – I'll show her that I'm somebody to be reckoned with.

In just a few seconds the problem had grown out of all proportion and had become a question of respect, manhood and being seen as a soft touch. The assistant's attitude had triggered Robert's underlying fear of being someone not worthy of respect and his sense of inferiority – all of which he defended with rage.

But later, while still sitting on the bed, he recognized that he had behaved aggressively to the assistant. He then thought:

- I'm losing control.
- What's happened to me? I used to be caring of others.
- Maybe I'm just a selfish person who has to have his own way.
- I am unlovable and bad for being like this. I hate myself for being like this.

So we can see how Robert's anger expanded because he had over-estimated the damage to his self-esteem and had believed that this was a test of his manhood. In fact, it is not that uncommon to find that depressed people can have rages and then feel intensely unlovable and hate themselves for it (i.e. anger with themselves for being angry). Consider the man who became enraged with

another driver while driving with his family. His children were
frightened and started to cry so he screamed at them, too. Later,
he felt ashamed and guilty. He thought that he had ruined their
day and was a horrible man to 'go off like that'. At 3 a.m., feeling
alone and unlovable, he started to think that they would be better
off without him and contemplated suicide. His anger was a sign
that he was not coping and was feeling very vulnerable underneath the rage. Anything that blocked his desires was taken as a
personal put-down and fuelled an underlying sense of inferiority
and weakness.

So, understanding the values you place on the things that make
you angry is a first step. Then consider the ways that you feel hurt
and vulnerable. If you sometimes feel that you lose control, try to
avoid globally attacking yourself and instead look for alternatives.
The following are the ones that Robert eventually came up with
for himself:

- Okay, I did go off the deep end and that is disappointing.
- However, I know that I'm not always or even usually like this.
- I need to recognize that I'm under stress right now and that my
  life is not easy, so my frustration tolerance is low.
- I need to learn to back off when my feelings are hitting the red
  zone. However, a low frustration tolerance does not make me a
  bad person – even if some of my actions are undesirable.
- I will help myself if I learn to be more assertive rather than
  aggressive. If I label myself as bad, I will only feel much worse,
  and when I feel bad and ashamed of myself, my frustration
  tolerance level goes down further.
- I can forgive myself for this, apologize to the hotel assistant if I
  need to and move on. Hating myself is failing to treat myself
  with compassion and recognize the stress I'm under. If I treat
  myself better, I'm more likely to treat others better.

You may have noted that the anger in the various examples
outlined above could also be seen as 'shame anger'. The anger
acts as a defensive measure against being put down, feeling small,
discounted or rejected. Indeed, in situations when you feel anger,
it is always worth thinking that shame may be part of your feelings. You can get into shame/anger spirals where you are angry at

being shamed and ashamed of being angry. The first step to get out of this is to avoid attacking yourself.

Shoulds and Oughts

One reason why we can feel anger is when we are using 'shoulds' and 'oughts'. Robert, in the example above, had thought: 'Others should not behave this way.' Unfortunately, we can't write the rules for how others will behave. If we are not careful, we can get stuck and simply go over and over in our minds what another person should or shouldn't do. At times, these 'shoulds' are related to other thoughts, such as 'If X loved/respected me, he/she would/wouldn't . . .' You can change these ideas by telling yourself:

- I would prefer that others did not do this.
- However, I cannot write the rules for their conduct.
- Each person is free to behave in their own way.
- If I don't like the way they are behaving towards me, I can learn to be assertive and put my point of view.
- I do not have to personalize every conflict situation and see it as a personal attack on my worth, selfhood, manhood or whatever.

Who is to Blame?

A boy runs into the busy street. When the danger has passed, the boy's mother screams at him and smacks him. The mother is blaming her son for putting their relationship under threat and for the panic she had felt, as well as ensuring that the boy will remember this event – a lesson not to be forgotten. Later the mother may blame herself for having been so aggressive towards her child.

Blaming others is often a first response in anger. But in depression people frequently feel bad about themselves for getting angry. How can you treat yourself kindly if you have become so angry? Again, we need help from the compassionate/rational mind. It may help us with such thoughts as:

- It is indeed upsetting to become very angry.
- It may mean that underneath I am feeling very vulnerable.
- However, my anger doesn't make me completely unlovable as

a person – that would be overgeneralizing, thinking in all-or-nothing terms and self-labelling.
- It is this particular action at this particular time that was rather harsh.
- Remember the times that I've been caring and not angry and how it's possible to do positive things for myself and others.

Sometimes, if we have been angry (especially with children), we feel so guilty that we think we have to make it up to them and start to allow them to do things that we would normally not allow – because of guilt. However, this can backfire because the children, being children, might start to take advantage of the situation, which can trigger our anger again. So, if necessary, apologize for your action and then try to work on gaining more control over it rather than acting out of guilt.

Hatred

Sometimes, because we believe that we have been very hurt or damaged, anger turns to hate. Then the desire is to harm others and this can be frightening. Bella came to hate her mother because of a very physically and emotionally abusive past. She felt that her mother had 'an evil tongue'. She had fantasies about stuffing a pillow in her mother's mouth and watching her choke to death. However, she was desperate to be loved, and she took her hatred and murderous thoughts as evidence that she herself was evil. Her thoughts were:

- Hatred is bad.
- I should not feel like this.
- It is abnormal; others don't feel like this.
- I must be bad/evil for feeling hate this strongly.
- I can't reveal to others the depth of my feelings because they will think that I am evil, too.
- I hate myself for hating.

Her doctor, who had been treating her with drugs, had no idea of this inner life. This is not surprising, for such hate–anger is often not revealed if there is strong fear or shame associated with it. Bella was able to begin to challenge these thoughts and ideas:

We all have the capacity for hatred – it is not itself abnormal. Indeed, sadly, history shows the consequences of hatred, so there have been many who have felt like me. I am not abnormal. To call my hatred 'evil' is all-or-nothing thinking and self-labelling, and leaves out the hurt I have felt because of what happened to me. I did not wake up one day and think that it would be a good idea to hate my mother. These feelings have come from a lot of painful experiences, and it is understandable for me to hate someone who has hurt me so much. However, I do need to learn how to work with my hatred and come to terms with it. I need to learn how not to hate myself for hating. This is because my hatred hurts me and holds me back in my efforts to get well.

Avoid Brooding

If we think about what anger is designed to do, and recognize that one of its functions is to help us to fight harder, we can see the danger of brooding on angry thoughts. These turn on our fight/flight system, when stress hormones and other chemicals are pumped around our bodies, which become tense and alert. But if no 'fight' or 'flight' happens, these chemicals can get up to mischief.

Allen was asked to take early retirement, and a new manager started to undo all the changes that he had introduced in his section. He had various arguments with his boss, but all to no avail. Allen became depressed and had serious sleep difficulties. I asked him to monitor his thoughts when he woke in the middle of the night. These turned out to be: 'The bastard. After all the years that I have worked there and this is how they treat me. There must be some way I can stop them. I can't just roll over and let this happen.' When these thoughts began to run through his mind, he became quite agitated and would pace about the house, going over and over them. If his wife tried to calm him down, he would snap at her and then feel guilty. Then he would say to himself, 'They're even breaking up my relationship with my wife.'

My discussion with him went something like this: 'When you have these thoughts, they activate your primitive fight/flight system and that's designed to hype you up to fight or to run away. However, you've done what you can and there seems to be no way that fighting can help you now – especially at three in the morning. So you're left in a hyped-up state that has nowhere to go except in pacing about and snapping at your wife. You've recognized that, in reality, there is not much you can do.' Allen reluctantly agreed. 'So we have to find a way for you not to activate your fight/flight system because it drives you into depression.'

As Allen came to understand the processes that he was activating in himself, he was ready to start to explore alternatives. So we wrote out some flash cards for him to read if he woke early:

- I am disappointed with this situation, but I have to face the fact that I have done my best and this is the way of the future.
- I have given the company many good years, and it has not been too bad really. I can be proud of that.
- Perhaps the time has come to let go and think about the next phase of my life.
- All these thoughts of fighting and getting my own back only hypes me up and to no real purpose.

We also examined the advantages and disadvantages of taking early retirement, including the fact that he would have more free time and that it would probably be better for his health. Once Allen gave up fighting an unwinnable battle, he was free to explore other strategies – such as how to get the best deal for his retirement. It was not easy, but a year later, he told me that it had been the best decision he'd ever made.

So the key issue is to try to avoid brooding on anger. Try to work out strategies for coping. If there are things that can be done, do them. If there are others who can help you, seek their help. But brooding on injustice, going over the same ground over and over again, does not help. Giving up an unwinnable fight is one strategy, but at other times you may need to learn how to become more assertive and stand your ground (see Chapter 16).

Anger to Avoid Pain

Caroline was angry with her parents because she thought they did not love her enough. As long as she felt angry, she avoided the great sadness and need to grieve that were underneath her anger. Anger gave her some feelings of power. Sadness and grief made her feel very vulnerable.

Anger can be used to prevent the recognition of being hurt, but it is often hurt and shame that need healing and this often involves sadness. Some people may imply that all you need to do is to get your own back on the person who has harmed you or to stand up to them. However, although this can be helpful it is not always so. Underneath, we still have a wish to be loved and approved of. I remember a patient who had done quite a lot of work with another therapist on learning to stand up to her abusive parent and express her anger. But, despite this, she was still depressed and mistrustful. What she had not done was grieve for her lost childhood or allow herself to feel and accept the feelings of vulnerability in grieving.

In working with anger in depression (and I stress 'anger in depression' because not all anger is like this), it is sometimes important to find someone who will help you move through the grieving process. In grief, we acknowledge our pain and vulnerability. And in the grieving process itself, anger is often the first or a very early response – but we have to work through this stage rather than get stuck in it.

Bypassed Anger: Ten Common Reasons for Avoiding Anger

Sometimes people try to avoid feelings of anger altogether. If you bypass anger, you might go straight to feeling hurt, but also feel a victim (powerless subordinate). You will also bypass becoming assertive (see Chapter 16). You may feel that you have no power to do anything about certain situations. You might think that you feel hurt because you are weak, and you may not be able to focus on the fact that it is at least partly the attitude of the other person that is the cause. It is important to recognize your hurts without, at the same time, becoming a powerless victim.

Here are ten self-beliefs that may stop you from exploring your anger and learning how to use it in an assertive way. Following each one, I offer some alternative ideas.

1 Others are more powerful than me. I will never win in conflict with them.
Alternatives: It's not about winning and losing. Even if you don't

achieve the outcome you want, it is important to try to put your point of view. If you tell yourself that you have to win, otherwise it's pointless, you are defeating yourself before you start. If you attempt to put your point of view, at least you will have tried. Trying to be assertive means that you are less likely to be angry with yourself if you don't get the outcome you want.

2 I learned in childhood that anger is bad.
Alternatives: Because your parents could not cope with your anger does not mean that anger is bad. Anger is part of human nature, and it can be useful. Consider compassionate anger (see p. 266). If we never felt angry about things, would we be motivated to try to change anything? Anger is really important because it reveals where you are hurting and what you value. True, aggression and lashing out are not good, but anger turned to assertiveness has many uses. Although your parents taught you that anger is bad, they may not have taught you how to be assertive. Perhaps they did not give you any positive way to deal with conflicts – so maybe the problem was that they did not know themselves. You'll need to learn this for yourself.

3 When I am angry, I am bad and unlovable.
Alternatives: Of course, you might prefer never to be angry but that's not possible. To say that you are unlovable is all-or-nothing thinking and self-labelling and discounts the positive aspects of your life. When you think of being unlovable, you may be thinking of being unlovable *to someone.* So who is the person you feel unlovable to? If it is your partner, you can think of it this way: Relationships are like boats. If your boat can only sail in a calm bay, it is not much of a boat. We need boats that will not capsize even if a storm blows up. If you see yourself as unlovable when you feel angry, you are also saying that your relationship can't cope with the odd storm – but, in fact, clearing the air and being honest and frank with your partner are likely to strengthen your relationship, not ruin it.

Of course, it is true that, at the moments of conflict, you are not sharing loving feelings. But love is like the climate; it remains no matter what we do. Anger and conflicts are like wind and rain – they come and go. Just as one thunderstorm does not change a climate, so your anger does not make you unlovable. You can learn to survive conflict.

4 When I am angry, I am being disloyal.
Alternatives: Sometimes, when you confide in people you trust about the anger you feel towards others close to you, you can have strong feelings of being 'disloyal'. However, confiding in others might help you to get your anger in perspective. If the person you are angry with has done things that have hurt you, keeping them hidden is really colluding in a secret rather than showing loyalty. You confide in others because you want to sort out your feelings. It is understandably difficult if you feel that you are 'breaking loyalties'. However, remember that people have done all kinds of bad things out of loyalty. If you show compassion, you can try to change things in a different way.

5 I must not hurt others.
Alternatives: Deliberately hurting others is not, by most people's standards, a moral thing to do. But the anger we are talking about here is not like that. Rather, you want to use your anger to draw attention to the fact that something is causing you pain or hurt and change. You have no wish to harm others for the sake of it, but to help them see how they are hurting you and to stop them doing it. In this sense, your anger is defensive. Others are far less likely to be hurt if you explain your position and show respect for them rather than attacking them. But if they are hurt, they need to understand why and sort that out. You can't be held responsible for everyone's feelings – that's giving yourself too much power. In any case, you might, in the long run, be more hurtful to them and your relationship if you are not honest with them about your feelings. Think in terms of respectful rather than hurting anger.

6 I can't stand the feelings of anger.
Alternatives: Angry feelings can be frightening if you are not used to feeling them. You may block your angry feelings if you feel that you might lose control. However, you are far less likely to do this if you learn how to be assertive (see Chapter 16).

7 I might lose control and damage people.
Alternatives: It is your responsibility not to do that. But you need

to consider a number of things. First, are you seeing your anger as more damaging than it is? Are you secretly telling yourself that you are a very powerful person and that everyone around is so fragile that they could not possibly cope with your anger? If so, try to think of the reasons why you might wish to believe that. Then work out the evidence for this belief and the evidence against it. Lashing out at people – going into the red zone – is not a good idea, but this is no reason to avoid being assertive with others.

8 I might lose control and make a fool of myself.
Alternatives: It may be that you are prone to feeling shame if you express your feelings, so you can work on that. It may also be true that if you become very angry, you might say things that you do not mean or become tongue-tied. The main thing is to try to focus on the issue, the message you want to convey, rather than your anger.

If you have become angry, try to find out if you are having internal bullying thoughts and calling yourself names (e.g. 'I'm stupid,' 'I'm a fool'). If you are, recognize this is all-or-nothing thinking and discounting the positive aspects of your life. Remind yourself that your anger is one element that you may wish to change, but it does not make you a fool or stupid.

9 I only feel I have a right to be angry if I am 100 percent sure that I am in the right.
Alternatives: There are few things in life where one can be 100 percent right. This is all-or-nothing thinking. Maybe no one is right or wrong, but everyone has a different point of view. Sharing these differences can be a source of growth.

10 I would be ungrateful or selfish to show anger.
Alternatives: 'Selfish' is, of course, a self-label and you are probably discounting all those times when you have given of yourself. Even if you feel grateful to someone, this does not mean that there cannot be disagreements between you. You can show gratitude when the situation warrants it, but positive things can be achieved in not hiding your discontent. Be cautious not to let your gratitude turn into a trap of obligation, for then you may feel more resentful.

Key Points

- Anger is part of life and can be aroused in situations when we perceive actual or potential damage to something we value.
- In depression, we can become too angry and 'blow up' or we can hide our anger.
- We may resort to rather underhanded ways to avoid open conflict, get our own way or get revenge.
- Anger is very often related to shame – our greatest rages often occur in situations where we feel shamed – whether we recognize it or not.
- At times it is important to consider whether we are over-estimating the amount of damage that can be, or has been, done (e.g. to self-esteem).
- Anger itself is not all-or-nothing, and it is useful to learn how to control it rather than allowing it to control us or locking it away.
- Brooding on anger leads to an aroused (hyped-up) state, which is often very unpleasant and not helpful.
- There are a number of primary self-beliefs that make anger difficult to deal with because they do not allow it to be worked through and it stays hidden.

Exercises

- Write down your thoughts about the last time you became angry. Ask yourself questions like: 'What am I saying about this event?' 'What implications am I drawing?' 'What do I think this event (or the other person's attitude) says about me?' 'What am I saying about myself?' When you have written down some of your thoughts, explore whether you are engaging in any of the following: all-or-nothing thinking, overgeneralizing, discounting the positives, thinking in 'musts' or 'shoulds', and so forth (see Appendix 2).

continued on next page

Let's work through the example of Emma becoming angry with Chris over him not helping with the housework. The following are her main thoughts and the possible coping responses she came up with:

I'm always left with the housework while he goes off with his friends.
Well, actually he does help sometimes. I am overgeneralizing here. And I am ignoring some of the other positive things he does to help. Still I do feel strongly that he should do more. I need to sit down with him to talk about it – when I don't feel so angry and upset.

This is really unfair. If he cared about me, he would help out.
Is doing housework the only sign of caring? Chris is behaving in a way that is traditional for males. His father was the same. I may not like it, but I may be exaggerating if I think this shows that he doesn't care about me. I need consistently to point out that this is a concern to me and that he can learn to change.

He just takes me for granted.
I might feel taken for granted, but is this true? What evidence is there for and against this idea of being taken for granted?

Maybe that's all I'm good for. If I was more lovable, he would be more attentive.
I recognized a problem about who does the housework. However, I'm going to feel much worse if I start to think Chris's lack of interest in housework is a lack of interest in me. It is this blaming myself and feeling unloved that is making me depressed. It could just as easily be a typical male attitude. I need to train him!

- If you tend to become too angry, try to spot the danger signs early. Think back to the last time you were angry.

continued on next page

281

What was going through your mind? What were your early feelings? Was there any build-up to it? Could you spot the danger signs – feelings of getting wound up? If so, learn to say to yourself, 'I am entering my danger zone and need to back off – keep my distance.' If you find yourself getting too angry, move away from the other person. Blowing up at others is not helpful. However, if it is appropriate, try to come back to the issue that was behind your anger when you feel calmer. Don't avoid the issue but avoid the strong anger that might lead you to say things you later regret.

- Use the 'count to ten' approach. If you suddenly feel very angry, stop, then count to ten slowly, then take a deep breath. Learn to avoid acting when you have hit the red zone. You may also try leaving the room. The key idea is to distract yourself, and give yourself time to calm down sufficiently to stay in control.
- If any of the 'ten common reasons for avoiding anger' (see pp. 276–9) apply to you, make your own flash cards and try challenging these thoughts. Think of the advantages and disadvantages for changing them.
- If you are frightened of the feelings of anger, try expressing anger when you are alone. Get a rolled-up newspaper, kneel by the side of your bed and hit your bed with it. As you do, speak (or shout) your thoughts about your anger. Allow yourself to feel your anger. Remind yourself that no one can be hurt by this exercise – the point of it is to help you become less fearful of the feelings of anger. When your anger has subsided, you may wish to cry. Allow yourself to do this.

Then, and most importantly, before leaving the room lie on your bed and carry out a relaxation exercise. Think to yourself, 'This anger episode is over and I will let it go.' Imagine a stormy sea that becomes calmer. The idea is to recognize that you can become angry but will also calm

continued on next page

down. Learning how to do this is important, because it helps you avoid brooding on your anger. At the end of the exercise, note that you were able to become angry and to calm down afterwards – so the feelings of anger themselves need not be frightening, even though, of course, they may not be pleasant. But you were able to control your anger by directing it at the bed. This exercise is not designed simply to release anger but to allow you to experience it without fear. Go step by step, and learn that, even when you are very angry, you can still stay in control of your feelings.

Next, when you feel calmer, write down what you said when you were angry – what went through your mind? Explore to see if some of your thoughts were extreme and should be challenged. The next stage is to recognize where you are hurting and what your anger is about.

16

From Anger to Assertiveness and Forgiveness

We now need to think about what we do when we feel angry – given that, in depression, anger is often related to hurt, vulnerability or feeling blocked. The main issue, however, is not to express anger as such – at least not in a raw, over-the-top or impulsive way – but to learn to pinpoint what it is that is really upsetting us, and learn how to act assertively rather than aggressively.

Assertiveness

What is Assertiveness?

Before we can think about acting assertively, we need to clarify what we mean by assertiveness. Research has suggested that assertiveness is related to many types of behavior. Willem Arrindell and his colleagues in the Netherlands have studied assertive behavior and suggest there are at least four components to it:

1 *Display of negative feelings:* The ability, for example, to ask someone to change a behavior that annoys you, show your annoyance, stand up for your rights and refuse requests. This is what most people are thinking of when they talk about 'being assertive'.

2 *Expressing and coping with personal limitations:* The ability to admit to ignorance of something and to making mistakes, and to accept criticism. In addition, the ability to ask others for help without seeing this as a personal weakness.

3 *Initiating assertiveness:* The ability to express opinions and views that may differ from those of others, and to accept a difference of opinion between oneself and others.

4 *Positive assertion:* The ability to recognize the talents and achievements of others and to praise them, and the ability to accept praise oneself.

This chapter focuses primarily on the 'display of negative feelings.' In Chapter 13, which dealt with shame, we discussed how we can accept personal limitations without attacking ourselves. In Chapter 12, on approval, we explored how important it is both to accept and to give praise. In many ways, therefore, some of the types of behavior discussed earlier can be seen as helping you become more assertive and raise your self-esteem.

Non-Assertive, Aggressive and Assertive Behavior

When people have problems in acting assertively, they are either highly submissive, fearful and prone to back down when faced with conflicts, or they become overly dominant and aggressive. The table of non-assertive, aggressive and assertive behavior shown on p. 286 outlines some differences between these forms of behavior, showing the contrasts in non-verbal behavior, feelings and thoughts. Although there are occasions when coming to terms with and expressing angry feelings is useful, I am not encouraging you to express extreme anger, but to become assertive and more in touch with your hurts and vulnerabilities.

Interestingly, non-assertive (submissive) and aggressive people can share similar beliefs. For example, both can think in terms of winners and losers. In a conflict situation, there are thoughts of 'I'm not going to let them win this one' or 'I can't win this one' or 'I always lose.' Aggressive people are determined not to be losers or be placed in a subordinate position. Depressed people can feel that they have already lost and are in a subordinate position. Sometimes this seems like a replay of how they experienced their childhoods. Parents were seen as powerful and dominant and they (as children) felt small and subordinate. Depressed people can, however, be aggressive to those they see as subordinate to themselves (e.g. children). The important thing is to remind yourself that while

Non-assertive	Aggressive	Assertive
Nonverbal Behavior		
Looks down or backs away	Stares and 'looks' angry, threatening	Meet eye contact but avoids 'the angry face'
Tries to signal 'no-threat'	Wants to signal threat – to be obeyed	Wants to signal 'listen to my point of view'
Allows other to choose for self	Chooses for (and imposes on) self and others	Tries to reach agreement
Feelings		
Is fearful of the other	Is angry or enraged with the other	Tries to control both anger and fear
Hurt, defeated	Feels a victim and sense of injustice	Recognizes that one can't have everything one wants
Thoughts		
My view is not important	My view is the most important	All views have a right to be heard
I don't deserve to have this need, want or desire	My wants and needs are more important than other people's	Each person's needs and wants are important
I will lose	I will (or must) win	It is preferable for no one to win or lose but to work out how to give space to each person
I am inadequate or bad	I am good and in the right	Right and wrong is all-or-nothing thinking and labelling. It is preferable to work out what the issues are rather than labelling or attacking the person or oneself
Just here to please others	Others should do as I want	We should try to please each other in a mutually sharing and caring way
Self-attacking	Other attacking	Avoids attacking

it might have been true that, as a child, you were in the subordinate position, you don't have to be now. You can look after yourself and treat others as your equals. You are an adult now. So you might use the motto: 'That was then. This is now.'

One way to feel more equal to others is to try to eliminate the 'all or nothing' from your thinking (powerful/powerless, strong/weak, winner/loser) by telling yourself that 'It is not me against them. Rather, we each have our own needs and views.' To be assertive, then, is to not see things in terms of a battle, with winners and losers. This may mean that you have to be persistent but not necessarily aggressive. The angry-aggressive person wants to win by force and threat; the assertive person wants to achieve a particular end or outcome and is less interested in coercing others or frightening them into submission – and will often accept a fair compromise.

The second aspect of assertiveness is that it focuses on the issue, not the person. To use a sporting metaphor, it involves learning to 'play the ball, not the player'. In this case we speak of our wants or hurts without alarming others or employing negative styles of thinking. For example, these are typical responses of someone who is angry and aggressive towards someone else:

- You are a stupid person (all-or-nothing thinking and labelling).
- You are always so thoughtless (overgeneralizing and discounting the positives).
- I can never trust you (all-or-nothing thinking and discounting the positives).
- You are a selfish bastard (just about all the styles!).

All these statements attack the other person. When people feel attacked, they tend to go on to the defensive. They lose interest in your point of view and are more concerned with defending themselves or attacking back. The assertive response focuses less on threatening/attacking the other person but more on ourselves and the quality of our relationships with others. Thus, in acting assertively we would explain in what way a particular action or attitude is hurtful. For example:

- When you behave in that way, I feel hurt because I think that you don't care about me.

- If you say things like that, I feel you are discounting my point of view.
- I feel much happier when you behave like this towards me.
- I accept that you feel like that, and have a right to, but that is not my point of view.

Can you see the steps here?

1 Acknowledge your anger.
2 Recognize in what way you feel hurt (and, of course, try to discover if you might be exaggerating the harm/damage done).
3 Focus on what this hurt is about and your wish to have the other person understand your feelings and your point of view.
4 Don't insist that the other person absolutely must agree with you.

In assertiveness, we try to remain respectful of the other person. Winning, getting your own back or putting the other person down can have a negative outcome. In fact, even if you are successful (i.e. you win), the other person may still feel resentful and wait for a chance to get their own back on you! Winning can create resentful losers.

Avoiding Spreading Guilt

One word of warning. When you acknowledge your hurts assertively, this doesn't include making the other person feel guilty or ashamed. Sometimes people don't want to share with others what they want to change, but just want to make the others feel bad. When they discuss the things they want to change, they do it in a rather whining, 'poor me' way. Or they may say, 'It's all your fault that I'm depressed.' They may think: 'Look what they've done to me – I'll make them feel guilty for that. Then they'll be sorry.' This is understandable but not helpful. Getting your own back by trying to make people feel guilty is not being assertive. You may at times wring concessions from others, but usually people feel resentful if they have to give in because they have been made to feel guilty.

Sometimes we might even do things to ourselves to try to make the other person feel guilty. After an argument with her mother,

Hilary went home and took an overdose. Later she was able to recognize that she had been thinking: 'She'll be sorry when she sees what she made me do.' Now, nobody can make us do anything – short of physical coercion. It was Hilary's anger that was the problem. Her mother had been critical of her, but at the time Hilary had not said anything, although she had felt anger seething inside her. Her overdose was a way of trying to get her own back. With some effort, Hilary was able to be assertive with her mother and could say things like: 'Look, Mother, I don't like the way you criticize me. I think I'm doing an okay job with my children. It would help if you focused on what I do well, not on what you think I do badly.' This took her mother aback, but after that, Hilary felt on a more equal basis with her mother.

Sometimes depression itself can be used to attack others. Hilary also came to realize that, at times, she did feel happy but refused to let others know it. She wanted to be seen as an unhappy, suffering person, and that this was other people's fault and they should feel sorry for her and guilty. It was also an attempt to evoke sympathy from others – although it rarely worked. She had the idea that, if she showed that she was happy, she would be letting others off the hook for the hard times she had had in the past.

Sometimes there is a message in our depression. It may be to force others to look after us or it may be to make them feel sorry for us. We find ourselves turning away from possible happiness and clinging to misery. It can be helpful to think carefully about how you want others to respond to your depression. It can be a hard thing to do, and you might see that sometimes you use your depression to get your own way or get out of doing things. Try not to attack yourself about this, for you are not alone in doing it. Your decision is whether to go on doing it or whether you can find other ways to make your voice heard.

Avoiding Sulking

Another non-assertiveness problem is sulking, or 'passive aggression'. In sulking, we don't speak of our upsets but close down and give people the 'silent treatment'. We may walk around with an angry 'stay away from me' posture, or act as if we are really hurt, to induce guilt. Indeed, our anger is often written all over our faces even as we deny that we feel angry. We have to work out if our sulking is a way of getting revenge on others and trying to make them feel guilty. Are we sulking in order to punish others?

You may feel powerless to bring about changes. This may be because you believe that direct conflict would get out of hand, or to show anger is to be unlovable or because you think you would not win. However, sulking does have powerful effects on others. Think how you feel when someone does it to you. The problem with sulking is that it causes a bad atmosphere and makes it difficult to sort out problems. When you sulk, you give the impression that you don't care for others. Sulking is likely to make things worse. Another problem is that sulking often leads to brooding on your anger. The more you do this, the more you will want to punish others.

You will find that, if you can learn to be assertive and explain what it is that you are upset about, you will feel less like sulking. Because sulking can have powerful negative effects on others and relationships, I would strongly suggest this is a power that you could give up. You can recognize your tendencies to sulk, work out why you do it and try becoming more assertive. This is likely to take time, but once you decide that you have had enough of being a sulker, you are at least set on a path out. Here are some possible alternatives:

- I sulk because I feel hurt or want to punish others.
- This is not helping my relationships – even if it works at times.
- Maybe I'm saying that the other person should be as I want him or her to be. I can challenge this.
- I can learn to recognize that the other person's attitude is not what I want and try to act assertively.

Anger at Failed Assertiveness

If we hold some of the beliefs about ourselves outlined above, we will have problems in becoming assertive. One extremely common occurrence in some depressions, and even in life in general, is that we can become angry with ourselves for not being assertive. We have probably all had the experience of getting into a conflict with someone and not saying what we wanted to say. Then later we felt very cross for not standing up for ourselves. We felt that we had let the other person win or get away with something. Afterwards we thought of all kinds of things that we could have said but didn't think of at the time. Then we started to brood on this failure to be assertive and our internal bully really got going.

Roger was criticized in a meeting which he felt was mildly shaming. He actually dealt with the situation quite diplomatically but, in his view, did not defend himself against an unfair accusation. Later that night and for a number of days afterwards, he brooded on his failure to say what he had really wanted to say. These were his thoughts about himself:

- There you go again – letting people walk all over you.
- You never stand up for yourself.
- You've shown once again that you're made of mush.
- You've failed again.
- You're a really weak character.

Roger had a strong ideal of himself as a 'person to be reckoned with,' but of course, he rarely lived up to this. As in the case of Allen (discussed in Chapter 15, pp. 274–5), who had to take early retirement, when Roger was out of the situation he started to activate his own internal fight/flight system and brooded on what he wished he had said. At one point, he had fantasies of revenge, of physically hitting the person who had criticized him. As with Allen, Roger's thoughts led to some agitation.

The following are alternative coping thoughts that Roger could have considered:

- I am bullying myself again and getting angry with myself.
- I am exaggerating the degree of harm I sustained.
- I am discounting what I did say and looking at it in all-or-nothing terms.
- I was criticized – in my view, unfairly – but this is not the same as being 'walked all over'.
- Criticisms are not always fair.
- True, if I had thought about it, I might have been able to respond better, but that only shows that there is room for improvement.
- I am sensitive to criticism because I often see it as a major attack

on me as a person. This means that I need to learn how to keep criticism in perspective.

- Other people later agreed that the criticism was unfair, so they don't see me as weak.
- In reality, I don't want to be seen as an aggressive person, and anyway I would rather sort out conflicts amicably and reasonably. I can at least give myself credit for that.

You will be aware by now that the most damaging aspects of Roger's internal attack were the thoughts of having failed and labelling himself as weak. These thoughts placed him in a highly subordinate position and were quite at odds with his ideal self. They activated a desire for revenge. Because of the way our brains work, it is quite easy to get into this way of thinking if we feel that someone has forced us into a subordinate position. So we have to work hard to stop this more primitive brain response from running away with us. Here are some alternative coping thoughts that interrupt this more automatic subordinate thinking style:

- By globally labelling myself as weak, I feel bad. This is all-or-nothing thinking and ignores the positive aspects of my life. It makes me feel much worse.
- It may be true that I need to learn how to be more assertive, but this is going to be hard to do if I take each failure to assert myself as evidence of weakness. There are many areas of my life where I have shown some courage, but in any case, conflicts are often complex and cannot be reduced to simple ideas of weak/strong.
- If I'm not careful, I will have to cope with two problems – the criticisms that come from outside and the criticisms and attacks I launch on myself.
- If a friend had been in a similar situation, I would not have attacked him or her in the same way that I attack myself – for I know that this would have made him or her feel much worse.
- If I feel under threat from the outside, it is preferable that I learn how to give myself some support rather than just running myself down and listening to my own internal bully.

These alternative thoughts are intended to halt the slide into the depressive spiral. We are obviously going to feel some disappointment if we think that we could have stood up to others better than we did, but we don't have to attack ourselves or allow our minds to rush into fantasies of revenge. Moreover, if we approach the problem rationally, we might identify a need to use assertiveness. So we could then plan what we wanted to say (but didn't) and calmly try it out. The problem for Roger was that he never tried assertiveness but only felt disappointed with himself and then became angry. He never gave himself the chance to improve his assertiveness.

We want to be heard and listened to without being seen as aggressive, overpowering or pushy. This may not be an easy thing to achieve. If we are sensitive to these difficulties, recognize that assertiveness is a skill that takes time to learn, and which some-times we will get wrong, we can avoid getting trapped into label-ling ourselves as weak by our internal bullies.

Anger and Assertiveness in Intimate Relationships

Anger associated with depression, in intimate relationships, can result not from single events or short-term problems but from longer-term difficulties. You may have felt that, for years, you have not been taken seriously. In some relationships, one person may feel constantly subordinated to the other, or may be storing up a lot of anger and brooding on events from 'way back'. These can be difficult things to sort out in a relationship. If this is the case for you, it is worth considering marital or relationship therapy. How-ever, it can be very helpful to begin by learning how to be assertive and more open with your partner/family.

Intimate relationships are often riddled with conflicts of inter-est and, sometimes, power plays. These are all quite normal and are what make intimate relationships so challenging. Maybe it's preferable to accept conflicts as challenges and allow yourself to grow and evolve through conflicts rather than trying to avoid them. As with any learning in life, we often get better as we cope with more and more difficult things. It does not matter if you are learn-ing a new language or how to drive a car or training to become a doctor, the more difficult the things are you learn to do, the better you become at doing them. It's a step-by-step process. It's the same with intimate relationships: we grow and develop by passing through difficult as well as good times. By facing your conflicts, you are improving your capacity for intimate relating, not reducing it.

Forgiveness

Reconciliation

Disagreements, arguments and conflicts are normal in nearly all relationships. It is just not possible to see eye to eye all the time, or never to be in a bad mood. Indeed, some marriages can have high levels of conflict, but still survive. How is this possible? Well, it is usually because the conflicts themselves are not feared. However, some depression-prone people do fear conflicts, especially if they think arguments might become heated. We have already explored some of the reasons for this in Chapter 15 (e.g. 'I am unlovable to get angry', 'I will be rejected if I get angry'). But there are other reasons for a fear of arguments. One is a belief that 'something will be damaged beyond repair'.

Some depressed people also have difficulty in reconciling after conflicts have taken place. Couples and families with high levels of conflict but with good reconciling behaviors, and who basically value each other, tend to suffer less depression. When we reconcile and make peace, our anger and arousal subsides. Chimpanzees, our nearest primate relatives, actually seem better at reconciling their differences than humans. Research shows that, after a conflict, they will often come together for a hug and embrace and they rarely stay distant for long.

So why is it difficult for some people to reconcile? In some cases, it is because as children they were never taught how to do it, and now as adults, they feel awkward about it. Perhaps neither they nor their partners know how to make the first move to make peace. Another reason is that one or both parties in the conflict will not reconcile until they are given the dominant position: they must win, get their own way and assert their authority. The one who reaches out to make peace is perceived as the one who has submitted.

For example, Angela said that, when she was a child, it was always her and not her mother who had to say she was sorry. If she didn't, there would be a very bad atmosphere between her and her mother, which she found intolerable. Her mother would sulk, sometimes refusing to speak to Angela until she had apologized. And when she did, her mother would remind her of the conflict and how naughty Angela had been. At a time when Angela was reaching out for acceptance, her mother would make her feel bad, ashamed and guilty again. So Angela developed an expectation that, if she apologized, the other person would use this to make her feel bad about herself and would not accept her peace-making efforts without 'rubbing her nose in it'. She was therefore very frightened of conflicts because there was no way she could reconcile afterwards without always feeling in the wrong.

Jake thought that to say 'Sorry' always meant that he was admitting he was in the wrong. If he had been angry with his children, he would have strong desires to apologize and, yet to apologize was, in his mind, to be seen as weak.

So there are a number of things that can stop us from peace-making:

If I apologize and want to reconcile, it means:

- I was in the wrong.
- I am giving in.
- I have lost.
- I am weak. Strong people do not apologize.
- Others will think I have taken full responsibility for the conflict.
- I am in a subordinate position.

There are various alternatives to these ideas. For example:

- I can apologize for my actions if I think I have hurt someone, but this does not mean that the conflict itself was all my fault. Indeed, it is preferable to think in terms of 'differences of opinions or desires' rather than in terms of blame.
- Assertiveness is not about winners and losers but about being clear about the reason(s) for a conflict and attempting to resolve it.
- The ability to apologize and repair a relationship is a 'positive' on my part, not a weakness.
- I don't have to grovel when I apologize but rather to get together with the other person again because I care about the relationship.
- I can focus on the issue of coming together rather than on just relieving myself of guilt.

Reconciliation, like much else in assertiveness, is a skill that can be learned. It may be difficult at first, but if you set your mind to it, you are more likely to improve. Learning how to 'make up' after a conflict makes them less frightening. You learn that you can survive them and may often benefit from them. Making up is only a submissive position if you tell yourself it is.

Try to avoid sulking, which may be used to punish others. Reconciliation in intimate relationships may involve hugs and other physical contact, but of course, you can't force this on others. If others are not ready to reconcile, all you can do is to state your position – that you'd like to make up. Try to be honest and offer an apology if you need to, and wait for the other person to come round in their own time. If they don't, try to avoid getting angry with them because they don't wish to go at the same pace as you.

One other thing that men especially need to be cautious of is encouraging their partners to prove that they are now reconciled with them by agreeing to have sex. If you do this, it is possible that your efforts at reconciliation will not be seen as genuine, but only as a tactic to get your own way. If your partner does not want to have sex, you may read this as 'Well, he/she does not really care for me, otherwise he/she would.' This can lead to anger and resentment again. If you feel that there is not enough sex in your relationship, this is best sorted out at some other time, calmly, and with no threat of 'If you loved me, you would.'

Some typical thoughts that can make forgiveness difficult include:

- I must make them pay (feel guilty) for upsetting me.
- If I forgive them (or me) I am letting them (or me) off the hook.
- If I forgive them then I can't express my dissatisfactions.
- I will have to be nice.
- Forgiveness is a position of weakness.
- It has more benefits for them than me.

Resentment and Revenge

Forgiveness does not mean that what happened in the past does not matter. Rather, it is the effort made to give up the desire for revenge or punishment. Forgiveness can be a lengthy process that requires an acknowledgment of much hurt. Some people may try to forgive without acknowledging their own pain and anger, but when they do this, resentment usually remains. So forgiveness can be a painful process. However, learning how to forgive is about learning how to let go of hurts. A need for revenge can be damaging to ourselves and our relationships. We may hold on to anger rather than work through it. We may tell ourselves how justified we are to be angry regardless of how useful this is.

Judy felt much anger against her parents for their rather cold attitude, and blamed them for her unhappy life. In doing this, she was in effect saying to herself: 'I cannot be better than I am because my parents have made me what I am. Therefore, I am forever subordinate to them – for they held the power to make me happy. Therefore, I can't exert any power over my own happiness.'

Gradually Judy came to see that it was her anger (and desire for revenge) which locked her into a bad relationship with her parents. Forgiveness required a number of changes. First, she needed to recognize the hurt she felt, which to a degree was blocked by her anger. Second, she needed to see that she was telling herself that, because her parents were cold towards her, she was 'damaged' and destined to be unhappy – that is, she was giving up her own power to change. She realized that she felt a 'victim' to her childhood. Rather than coming to terms with this, she felt subordinated and controlled by it. While it is always preferable to have had early loving relationships, it is still possible to move forward and create the kind of life one wants. As Judy came to forgive her parents (but not condone them), she let go of her anger and felt released from the cage in which she had felt trapped.

If we strongly resent someone or something, we can also feel that we are 'the other's victim'. This is a subordinate position that may seriously interfere with our ability to feel in control of our own lives. We may also develop deep distrust of others, which makes it difficult to have meaningful relationships. Forgiveness – letting go of the desire for revenge – is one way out of this. When we forgive, we are saying, 'I let the past go and am no longer its victim.' One patient of mine said that, by giving himself the power to forgive, he was giving himself the power to live. Forgiveness is not a position of weakness. Some people find that 'letting go' feels like a great release.

To forgive ourselves means that we treat ourselves with compassion. We do not demand that we be perfect and not make big mistakes from time to time. There are many spiritual traditions that recognize the great importance of forgiveness. Buddhists have a meditation that they call 'loving kindness', designed to help individuals treat themselves with more compassion and learn the art of forgiveness.

Key Points

- It is the message or meanings in anger that need to be considered rather than the anger itself.
- In learning how to be assertive, we focus on the hurt and the issue(s) behind conflict rather than attacking either ourselves or the other person.
- Non-assertive behaviors include aggression, inducing guilt, sulking and fearfully backing down.
- Anger at our own lack of assertiveness is a common experience. This self-directed anger can be more damaging to us than the lack of assertiveness.
- Because anger and assertiveness nearly always arise in situations of conflict, it is important that, after the conflict has passed, there is reconciliation and forgiveness. These may not take place if there are specific beliefs that stop them – for example, 'to apologize is to admit I was in the wrong or that I am letting people off the hook.'
- Forgiveness is actually an assertive action because we give ourselves the power to forgive and thus release ourselves from feelings of having been a victim for which we must seek revenge.

Exercises

Focus on examples of assertive behaviour. These include:

- Avoid attacking the other person for that will just put him/her on the defensive.

continued on next page

- Work out what you want to say, focusing on a specific issue.
- Be prepared to 'trade' and compromise. Avoid seeing either as signs of weakness.

Here's an example involving Emma and Chris, who we met in Chapter 15 (pp. 268–9). Emma was angry about Chris's lack of helping around the house. However, she waited until they were relaxed together and then said:

You know, Chris, I wish we could spend more time together. However, I'm so busy with the house and it would be really helpful if you could lend a hand. I feel really left out when you go off to see your friends and I'm stuck here doing the ironing. It's not that I want to stop you going out but that I want to have more time, too. Look, I've worked out that, if you do more of the shopping and vacuuming I would have more time for myself. I'd really feel a lot better and not feel so taken for granted.

Of course, this may not do the trick straight away but it's a start. Sometimes it helps to rehearse what you want to say – that is, rehearse your assertiveness skills. Remember, it is a step-by-step process and does not have to go perfectly first time. By preparing what you want to say, rather than waiting until you get angry and rushing in with attacks, you are more in control and will often achieve more.

If you are prone to getting angry with yourself for not being as assertive as you would like to be, review the example of Roger on pp. 291–3. Work out if you are attacking yourself. Then rehearse the types of assertive things you would like to say. Say them out loud. Get used to speaking them and hearing yourself say them. Try to avoid brooding on your anger and on all the really nasty things you could say. You know that you probably won't say them so there is no point in rehearsing them. Try out only those things that you think you should say.

continued on next page

An important aspect of acting assertively is 'slowing your thoughts down' to give you space to think. If you get into a conflict situation, don't feel that you have to respond immediately. One way to do this is to ask the other person to tell you more about what concerns him or her, rather than trying to defend yourself immediately.

You then might say to the other person, 'I can see how you could think of it that way, but this is how I see it.' Try to be factual rather than accusing. Try to stick to the issue at hand rather than trade personal attacks.

Spend time thinking about forgiving others and letting go of the past. Write down the advantages and disadvantages of doing this. If you could let go of the past (and any desire for revenge you might feel), how would this help you? What stops you? What are your thoughts here? Try to use your rational/compassionate mind to challenge any negative beliefs you might have.

If you feel that some of the hurts from the past are very serious, and it is impossible for you to embark on this journey alone, think about seeking help. The moment you say, 'I no longer want to remain a victim of my past,' you are taking the first step up and out.

Try the Buddhist 'loving kindness' meditation. First, sit or lie down somewhere comfortable. Go through a relaxation exercise of the type given in Chapter 5. It does not have to be elaborate; just enough to get your breathing to subside to a calm rhythm. Now, think of yourself as a feeling, conscious being who needs loving kindness. Imagine yourself lying there and think that this person (i.e. you) needs loving kindness. Imagine the feeling of loving kindness directed at you. This may seem odd at first, but with practice, it may come. If there are things that you feel bad about, allow yourself to feel forgiveness for them. Admit to them and let them go. Sometimes people like to imagine themselves in a white or golden healing light. If you feel tearful, allow yourself to cry.

continued on next page

Whatever works for you, use it. The idea is to develop the inner art of forgiveness. Forgiving yourself does not mean an end to trying to improve. It just means that improving and changing will be easier for you if you don't hang on to things from the past that cannot be changed.

When you feel that you are succeeding at this, think of others close to you and of loving kindness directed at them. Gradually expand your feelings to as many other people as you would like. If others have hurt, you imagine forgiveness for them. This does not mean condoning their negative attitudes or backing down but rather letting go of destructive vengeance.

17

Dealing with Frustration, Disappointment and Lost Ideals

This chapter considers one of the most common reasons for anger – frustration. This usually involves the experience of being blocked or thwarted in the pursuit of something important. Both humans and other animals often react to frustration in specific ways, anger and irritation being the most common. Disappointment, also common to depression, is similar to frustration and usually involves some hope or expectation that does not turn out as desired.

Our emotional reactions to frustration and disappointment depend on the importance we place on things. Clearly, finding that we can't have things that we don't particularly want or value does not cause much upset, but if it is something we have set our hearts on, that's a different matter.

We can feel frustrated and disappointed about many things, but the most common are:

- When things don't work right or as we think they should.
- When others do not behave, or feel about us, as we want them to – e.g. don't show us enough affection, break promises.
- When we ourselves lack an ability to do or achieve something.
- When we feel certain things (e.g. feel depressed and lose energy, don't feel as positively about someone as we would wish, feel disappointed in ourselves because we lose the ability to feel affection or lose sexual feelings).

'Shoulds' and 'Oughts'

Disappointment is a major area where our 'shoulds' and 'oughts' come to the fore. We can believe that things, ourselves or other people 'should be like this and should not be like that.' The problem here is that, life being what it is, it will not respect our 'shoulds' and 'oughts'. Some people feel that we should not have to die, and instead of coming to terms with it, they rage about the fact that life 'shouldn't be like this.' Sometimes our 'shoulds' stop us from doing the emotional work we need to do in order to come to terms with things as they are and work out the best solutions for dealing with them.

We can develop a strong sense of 'should' when it comes to our own attitudes – e.g. 'I *should* work harder,' 'I *should not* make mistakes,' 'I *should not* be angry,' 'I *should* love my parents.' However, we can feel very disappointed when we don't turn out as the 'should' says we should. And 'shoulds' often involve anger and attempts to force ourselves to be different. When we strongly apply the 'shoulds' to ourselves, we inevitably end up bullying and attacking ourselves. It is as though we struggle to avoid accepting our limitations, setbacks or true feelings. The American psychotherapist Karen Horney called the shoulds 'a tyranny'.

When we apply 'shoulds' to other people, we often feel angry with them when they disappoint us. Instead of seeing them as they really are, we simply say 'they *should* be like this' or 'they *shouldn't* be like that.' Strong 'shoulds' often reduce our tolerance for frustration, and as we shall see shortly, 'shoulds' can lead to serious problems with disappointment. Indeed, Buddhism has recognized for thousands of years that much human misery stems from our frustrations and the way we think that we should have things or be a certain kind of person or that others should be a certain way. We can also become too attached to certain ideals and find giving them up painful.

Frustration Tolerance

Our ability to tolerate frustration can change for many reasons. You have probably noticed that, some days, you can cope with minor problems without too much effort, but on others, almost anything that blocks you can really irritate you. If we are driving somewhere in a hurry, we might see others on the road as 'getting in our way' and become angry. In extreme cases, we may even try to show them who is boss on the road. A situation such as this – called 'road rage' – becomes a primitive fight for dominance. As our feelings and attitudes become more urgent, we start to demand that things 'should be' different from the way they are.

Fatigue, tiredness and being under pressure are also typical everyday things that reduce our frustration tolerance. And depression itself can lower frustration tolerance.

The degree of frustration that a person feels can relate to a fear of shame. For example, Gerry lost his car keys on the day he had an important meeting. He became angry with himself and his family because the keys could not be found. In the back of his mind, he was thinking, 'If I don't get to the meeting on time, I will walk in late. Everybody will think I'm a person who can't keep to time and they will think I'm unreliable or careless.' At times, we may blame ourselves with thoughts like 'If only I were more careful, I wouldn't lose things.' Probably everyone could tell stories of how, when things are lost (e.g. the string or scissors are not in the drawer as expected), they became angry and irritated: 'Why are things never where they should be?'

Depression is commonly associated with blocks to major life goals. It is often helpful therefore, to explore in what way you feel blocked in your goals and/or feel socially thwarted, frustrated and disappointed. This frustration and disappointment will relate to your expectations, hopes, aspirations and ideals.

Lost Ideals

Perhaps one of the most difficult things in life is coming to terms with disappointment. In Arthur Miller's play *Death of a Salesman*, the main character cannot come to terms with the way his life has turned out and that he did not make it big. The American dream has eluded him and his sense of disappointment over this broken ideal destroys him.

We can be set up for disappointment because our ideals, hopes and expectations are unrealistic. Instead of coming to accept the world, other people and ourselves as they or we are, we try to enforce our standards and ideals on them and ourselves. Sometimes it is our values and ideals that lead us deep into frustration. At times, life can bring us down with a heavy bump. In Greek mythology, Icarus flew too high, the sun melted his wings and he fell back to earth. Like Icarus, our ideals can be overvalued and unrealistic. This can be a painful thing to admit to.

A serious thwarting of our life goals and ideals can trigger depression, especially if we see this as having a lot of social implications (e.g. loss of status, loss of a loving relationship) as well as implications for how our lives will be in the future. So to think about depression often means that we have to think about:

- What our ideals are.
- In what way we feel thwarted in reaching them.
- How we deal with the frustration and anger that comes when they are not met.
- What conclusions we can draw about ourselves, others and the future.
- Whether we are caught up in a strong sense of 'should'.

You can show this more clearly by writing out two columns of the ideal and the actual and then think about what I call the 'disappointment gap'. The disappointment gap leads to four possible outcomes: attack and blame the self; attack and blame others; give up; accept reality without seriously attacking either self or others

Because attacking is a common response to frustration, we can see that we have found a root source of our internal bully – none other than our frustration. The more frustrated we are with ourselves, the more we may tend to bully ourselves. The internal bully does not really exist at all! It is, in effect, often our 'attack self' response to frustration.

Let's work through some examples and see how this works.

Brian had set his sights on an important promotion. For over a year, he had worked hard to put himself in a good position, and his bosses had indicated that the promotion was within his grasp. He began to anticipate and plan how the new position would make his work easier and more interesting and how the extra money would allow him to move house. Unfortunately, two months before the promotion was due, Brian's company was taken over and all promotions were put on hold. Then, to make matters worse, the new company brought in some of their own personnel, and Brian found that the position he was going for had been filled by a younger man. He became angry and then depressed. All the plans, hopes and goals associated with the promotion seemed thwarted. He told himself that things never worked out for him and there was no point in trying to improve himself. His intense disappointment and anger in part fuelled his depression. He ruminated on the injustice of what had happened but had little power to change the situation – in effect, in his mind he kept fighting an unwinnable battle and thus saw himself as constantly frustrated and defeated. So his ideal–actual self looked like this:

Ideal	*Actual*
Get promotion	Didn't get promotion
Advance in career	Stuck in career
Move house	Stuck in same house

— Disappointment Gap —

- *Attack self*: I should have seen this coming. I should feel confident enough to try to get another job, but I'm not. If I were more assertive, I'd make them give me my promotion. I'm weak for not coping with this.
- *Attack others*: They're just using me. They're unfair, and they should be fair and realize that this promotion was promised to me by the old company. They have snatched an opportunity away at the last moment.
- *Give up*: I can't get out of this. Nothing will change. My future is ruined.

It is, of course, understandable why Brian felt bad about this lost promotion, but his anger and self/other-attacking made a bad situation worse. For him to come to terms with what happened – the fourth possible outcome – he had to recognize his sadness about it (rather than block it out with anger) and the depth of his 'shoulds', and stop attacking himself. He soon realized that he could not have 'seen it coming' and that it was not a matter of him not having been assertive enough. He gradually began to work out ways that he could get around this setback, waited a while and sought employment elsewhere. Coming to accept the situation and then working out how he could deal with it were important steps in his recovery.

'It's All Been Spoiled'

Depressed people often have the feeling that things have been spoiled. Susanne had carefully planned her wedding, but her dress did not turn out right and it rained all day. This was disappointing, but her mood continued to be low on her honeymoon. She had thoughts like 'It did not go right. It was all spoiled by the weather and my dress. Nothing ever works out right for me. Why couldn't I have had one day in my life when things go right?' She was so disappointed and angry about the weather and her dress that she failed to consider all the good things of the day, and how to put her disappointment behind her and get on and enjoy the honeymoon. She dwelt on how things had been spoiled for her. Later, when she considered possible positives in her life, she was able to give up her all-or-nothing thinking and to recognize that she was seeing the weather and the dress as almost personal attacks. She realized how her anger was interfering with her pleasure. She also acknowledged that many kinds of frustrations and disappointments in life are often activated by thoughts of 'everything has been spoiled.' She had to work hard to come to terms with her wedding 'as it was', but doing this helped to lift her mood.

The sense of things having been damaged and spoiled can be associated with the idea that things are irreparable and cannot be put right. In these situations, it is useful to work out how best to improve things rather than dwell on a sense of them being 'completely' spoiled. Of course, we might need time to grieve and come to terms with disappointments. I am not suggesting that one can simply rationalize disappointments away. The feelings can be strong indeed.

When we are depressed, we can sometimes feel that we are spoiling things for others or are a disappointment to them, or that they would be better off without us. Some children feel that they are a disappointment to their parents and live with feelings of guilt. They may think that they should have been different or better offspring. This can arise because they tend to focus on only the negatives and underestimate the positives. And it can be because they are actually disappointed in their parents – who did not praise them enough or give them enough attention. In a few cases, people can feel that they are spoiling things for others so much that they are a burden to them. To these individuals, suicide may seem like a good idea (see pp. 241–3).

If you think that something has gravely spoiled things for you or that you are spoiling things for others, it can help if you talk about these feelings openly – don't make assumptions. It is the depression that is the problem, not you as a person. So, once again, check out if you are thinking in all-or-nothing terms, overgeneralizing or discounting the positives in your life. Has *everything* been spoiled? Are there some things that remain good or even just okay? Are you seeing more damage in a situation than there is? Are you seeing yourself more negatively than other people do? Are you attacking yourself? Are you making overly negative predictions about the future? What possibilities for the future are you cutting yourself off from?

Loss of a Positive Relationship

When we fantasize about our ideal partners, we usually see them as beautiful or handsome, kind and always understanding. And when it comes to sex, we may think that they should be like an ever-ready battery that never goes flat. When we think about our ideal lover, we don't think about their problems with indigestion, the times when they will be irritable and stressed or take us for granted, or that they could fancy other people.

As an adolescent, Hannah had various fantasies about what a loving relationship would be like. It would, she thought, involve closeness, almost telepathic communication between her and her lover and few if any conflicts. She believed that 'love would conquer all'. This type of idealizing is not that uncommon, but when Hannah's relationship started to run into problems, she was not equipped to cope with them because her ideals were so easily frustrated.

The early courting months with Warren seemed fine and they got on well. Sex was good and Hannah was sure that theirs was going to be a good marriage and she had many hopes and ideals for it. However, after six months of marriage, they had a major setback. The negotiations for a house they wanted to buy fell through. Then, while they were trying to find another, the housing market took off and they found that they had to pay a lot more for one of similar size. Warren felt cheated by life, his mood changed and he became withdrawn and probably mildly depressed. Hannah, who was also upset about the house problems, was more concerned about the change in her relationship with Warren. The gap between her ideal and the actual relationship started to widen. This was how the discrepancy in her ideal–actual relationship looked:

Ideal	*Actual*
Have fun together	Can't go out, short of money
Have few conflicts	Increasing conflicts
Always feel understood	Don't feel understood
Feel close to each other	Feel increasing distance

— Disappointment Gap —

- *Attack self:* Maybe I'm doing something wrong. If Warren cared for me, he would talk to me more. Maybe he doesn't love me any more. I get irritated with him so maybe it's my fault. He's lost interest in sex, therefore I am not sexually exciting any more. I should be able to cope better. Maybe I made the wrong choice of partner.
- *Attack other:* This is a different side to him. He should cope better and recognize my needs. He's being selfish and moody.
- *Give up:* There's no point in talking about what's wrong. We can't change the housing market. I'm stuck.

Warren had had similar ideals and expectations about their relationship. The problem was that, when these ideals were not met, he and Hannah both tended to blame either themselves or the other – and this made the situation much worse. To move out of this position, they first had to give up attacking themselves and each other and unite to tackle their common problems. Second, they had to recognize that the ideals they had held were rather unrealistic – and that was painful to do.

Gradually Hannah began to recognize that their problems were not about love but the hard realities of living. There was nothing wrong with her as a person if Warren felt down, nor was there anything necessarily wrong with the relationship. They had to learn to deal with their problems in a different way by encouraging each other to talk about their feelings. Hannah had often avoided this for fear that Warren would blame her or say that she was, in some way, part of the reason why he was feeling down. She also had to give up attacking him when he did not give her the attention that she wanted.

She slowly moved away from thinking that all problems in their relationship were to do with a lack of love. Warren had to acknowledge that his anger at the house problem was damaging their relationship and that he needed to work through his sense of injustice and belief that 'This is unfair and it shouldn't have happened.' He also had to recognize the effect his moods were having on Hannah. They eventually learned to build on the positives in their relationship rather than fighting over the frustrations.

The Ideal 'Other'

We often have fantasies of an ideal 'other'. This may be an ideal friend, sexual partner, child or parent. But reality being what it is, these ideals are rarely met. If our ideals are too far from reality, we are going to be mightily disappointed.

Anna felt that her mother never really loved her, and so she created in her mind a picture of her ideal mother – loving, warm and kind. In many ways, this image was very helpful to her. In therapy, she was encouraged to dispute her negative self-attacking thoughts by thinking about what her ideal mother would say. Unfortunately, Anna also wanted her real mother to be more like her ideal mother – and this her real mother could not be. Anna thought: 'Why can't she be like my ideal mother? She should treat me better. Maybe if I tried harder, she would be nicer.' But, sadly, her real mother never was the way Anna wanted her to be.

It can be useful to create images of the kind of person we would like to relate to if this helps us challenge negative self-attacking thoughts. However, the moment we say, 'Others should be like this,' and confuse fantasy and ideal with reality, we are likely to run into problems. We will, at the least, feel terribly disappointed.

We may also feel a continuous sense of disappointment with other people, even when they try, to their best ability, to be reasonable and kind. If our ideals are too high, we will always find fault. Rather than take and show pleasure in what they do, we tend to focus on what they don't do. And if we are honest, we can get a little selfish about it. We focus only on how far the 'other' meets our standards of what they should be like. We may feel resentment when they don't come up to scratch.

Disappointment and Frustration with What We Feel

So far we have discussed how we can be disappointed in things and people that block our goals and affect our relationships. Another key area of disappointment centres around personal feelings. Some depressed people go to bed hoping that they will feel better in the morning, and it is a great disappointment when they don't. If they can say, 'Yes, I am disappointed about this, but it takes time to get out of depression. I will go a step at a time today and see how far I can get,' they may be spared some pain. Unfortunately, depressed people often feel (understandably) angry and deflated when they wake up and don't feel full of energy. But they also make matters worse by attacking themselves, predicting that the day will go very badly and telling themselves they 'should' be better. There are many other feelings that can be a source of disappointment. Let's look at some examples.

Don's problem shows clearly how difficulties can arise when our hopes and ideals are disappointed by our own feelings. Don had suffered from anxiety attacks for many years and, as a result, felt that he had missed out on life. He developed a strong fantasy that, if someone could cure his anxiety, he would be able to be like other people and especially more like his brother who was successful in the art world. When I saw him, I found that his attacks were focused on a fear of being unable to breathe and of dying. However, by looking at the evidence that he was not going to die when he had an anxiety attack, and learning how to relax to gain more control over his attacks, he made progress. In fact, he did so well that he went on a trip to Europe. But when he came back, he went to bed, got depressed, felt suicidal and very angry.

We talked about the problem as one of unrealistic ideals. Don had the fantasy that, if his anxiety was cured, he would do a lot of things and make up for many lost years. In his fantasy, he would be like others, able to travel, be successful and, in his words, 'rejoin the human race at last'. He believed that normal people never suffered anxiety. Also he had hoped that there would be some magic method that would take the anxiety away, and that once it was gone, it would be gone for good. He explained that, on his European trip, he had suffered more anxiety than he'd expected.

We wrote out two columns that captured this situation, headed 'Ideal me' (i.e. without anxiety) and 'Actual me' (i.e. how I am now).

Ideal me	*Actual me*
Like others	Not like others/different
Able to enjoy life	Life is miserable
Confident/successful	A failure
Explorative	Frightened

Our conversation then went something like this:

PAUL. It seems that you did quite a lot on your trip, but you feel disappointed with it. What happened when you got back?

DON. I started to look back on it and thought, 'Why does it have to be so hard for me, always fighting this anxiety?' I should have enjoyed the trip more after all the effort I put into it. I should have done more. It's been a struggle. So I just went to bed and brooded on how bad it all was and what's the point.

PAUL. It sounds as if your experience did not match your ideal.

DON. Oh yeah, it was far from that.

PAUL. Okay, what went through your mind when you found that the trip wasn't matching your ideal?

DON. I started to think I should be enjoying this more. If I were really better, I'd enjoy it more. If I felt better, I'd do more. I'll never get on top of this. It's all too late and too much effort.

PAUL. That sounds like it was very disappointing to you.

DON. Oh yes, very, terrible, but more so when I got back.

PAUL. What did you say about you?

DON. I'm a failure. I just felt totally useless. After all the work we've done, nothing has changed.

PAUL. Let's go back to the two columns for a moment and see if I've understood this. For many years, you've had the fantasy of how things would be if you were better. But getting there is a struggle and this is disappointing for you. When you get disappointed, you start to attack yourself, saying that you're a failure and it's too late. That makes the 'actual' you seem unchanged. Is that right?

DON. Yes, absolutely.

PAUL. Can we see how the disappointment of not reaching the ideal starts up this internal attack on yourself, and the more of a failure you feel, the more anxious and depressed you get?

DON. Hmm, yes.

PAUL. Okay, it was a disappointment to have anxiety again. Were you anxious all the time?

DON. No, not all the time.

PAUL. I see. Well, let's start from the other end so to speak. If you had to pick out a highlight of the trip, what would it be?

DON [*thinks for a moment*]. There were actually a few, I suppose. We went to this amazing castle set up on the hill . . .

As Don started to focus on the positive aspects of his trip, his mood changed. He became less focused on the negatives and more balanced in his evaluation of the trip. Now I am not saying that you should simply 'look on the bright side' but suggesting you focus on the possibility that there may be some positives on which you can build. It is easy to become focused on disappointment. By the end of the session, Don was able to feel proud of the fact that he had been to Europe, whereas a year earlier, that would have been unthinkable. He was not magically cured of his anxiety disorder but well on the way towards that goal.

Don was able to work with the links between his ideal, his disappointment and the attacks he made on himself. Because he was also prone to discount, or filter out, the positive things in his life if what he experienced did not match his ideal, we explored the successes of the trip. He saw his frustration and anger as 'destroying and ripping up' the good things that happened to him. This was all-or-nothing thinking fuelled by various 'shoulds'. For Don, the 'shoulds' were deep wishes, hopes and aspirations.

He began to lose his depression when he began to accept that his ideal might not be possible, and that he may have to grieve for some of the lost years. However, the more he focused on what he could do, rather than on how much he was missing out or how unfair it was to have anxiety attacks, the less depressed and self-attacking he became.

Disappointment with Oneself

We can feel that we have let ourselves down because we have not come up to our own standards or ideals. Here again, rather than accept our limitations and fallibilities – that maybe we have done our best but it did not work out as desired – we can go in for a lot of self-attacking. It is as if we feel we can't trust or rely on ourselves to come up with the goods. We start attacking ourselves like a master attacking a slave who hasn't done well enough. This frustration with oneself can be a major problem.

Lisa wanted to be confident like her friends. She wanted always to be in a good state of mind and never feel intense anger or anxiety or be depressed. She had two clear views of herself – her ideal and her actual self – and these would go hammer and tongs at each other.

Ideal self	Actual self
Relaxed and confident	Fearful and anxious
Hard-working	Lazy
Caring of others	Angry with others

— Disappointment Gap —

- *Attack self*: Oh God, I've let myself down again. Why do I have to be so anxious all the time? Why don't I just get on and do things? I am a useless, pathetic person.
- *Attack others*: Why do others always seem so confident? I hate them. They don't understand how difficult it is for me.
- *Give up*: I had better not try too much because it will not work out. I'm bound to fail and let myself down. I just can't rely on myself.

Both Lisa's ideal self and her actual self were unrealistic. Her ideal self could not be met all the time. Her actual self (which she identified as her depressed self) was prone to discount the positives, think in all-or-nothing terms and overgeneralize.

It may be true that we can't rely on ourselves always to be anxiety-free or make the best of things or be a mistake-free zone. The main thing is how we deal with our mistakes and disappointments. Attacking ourselves when we feel the anger of frustration is not helpful and, in the extreme, can make us very depressed. Learning to accept ourselves as fallible human beings, riddled with doubts, feelings, passions, confusions and paradoxes can be an important step towards self-acceptance.

Fiona had wanted a baby for about three years. She would fantasize about how her life would be changed with a child, and she engaged in a lot of idealized thinking of smiling babies and happy families. However, the birth was a painful and difficult one, and her son was a sickly child who cried a lot and was difficult to soothe. She found it difficult to bond with him and, within a short time, became exhausted and felt on a short fuse. At times, she just wanted to get rid of him. She took such feelings not as a natural (and indeed, not that uncommon) experience of women after childbirth, but as evidence that she was a bad mother. When her son could not be soothed by her efforts, she thought that he was saying to her: 'You're not good enough.' She thought that, if she had been a better mother, she would not have had a sickly child, and she would have been loving and caring from the beginning, regardless of her fatigue. She felt intensely ashamed of her feelings, and could not tell her family doctor or even her husband of the depths of her exhaustion or feelings of wanting to run away. She felt her feelings made her a bad person. The reality of life with her small son brought a whole set of ideals crashing down around her head.

We can explore Fiona's ideal of her motherhood and her depression.

Ideal self	*Actual self*
Happy and relaxed	Tense and fraught; many sleepless nights
Feel loving towards my child	Want to run away, feel aggressive
Be able to soothe him	He is difficult to soothe

— Disappointment Gap —

- *Attack self:* I thought that I was a caring person but I feel so awful when he starts crying. I just want to leave him, to shut the door on him so I can't hear him. I can't cope, therefore, I'm a weak, inadequate and bad person. If people knew what was going through my mind, they would hate me, lock me up or take my son away. Maybe I don't deserve to be a mother. I hate myself for feeling this way.
- *Attack others:* Why does my son have to cry so much? He doesn't like me. If he'd only sleep like a normal child, it would be better. It's not fair. Why do others seem so happy with their babies? I hate them. It's not fair.
- *Give up:* There's nothing I can do. I should just passively accept this state of affairs or get away. No one could understand me.

Depression and exhaustion after childbirth are not uncommon. If this happens to you, try your best not to be ashamed of it – you are far from alone. Speak to your doctor and tell him or her exactly how you feel – that you want to run away, feel aggressive or whatever. You may need expert help, counselling or drugs to help lift your mood. Or you may need to talk to other mothers who have had similar feelings. The moment you stop attacking yourself and recognize that you may need help, you are taking the first steps towards recovery. Becoming depressed after childbirth is intensely sad and disappointing, and you can experience many odd feelings, but try not to be ashamed about this. Try, to the best of your ability, to get your rational/compassionate mind to speak to you.

Inner bully says	*Rational/compassionate mind says*
You are not coping and are failing as a mother.	Many complex changes have taken place in my body.
You are useless/bad.	It is natural to feel tired and exhausted. Sometimes the changes that happen in childbirth produce some strange and odd feelings.
	If I'm not coping too well, maybe I need extra help. I will talk to my doctor and seek his/her advice and help.

I'm not going to listen to the bullying part of myself, which will simply run me down. I can take my feelings seriously and try to find out what I can do about them.

If I don't bully myself, I'm less likely to feel ashamed about my feelings.

They may be a great disappointment to me, but these feelings can and do happen to some women. There is nothing bad about me if I have these strange feelings – but I do need to try to obtain some help.

When we have these feelings of intense disappointment, there is often some bright spark who tells us to pull ourselves together, or who seems able to cope with everything. It may be someone in our lives who is being very critical of us, or who likes to tell us how well he or she coped with things and who can make us feel that, compared to him or her, we are failing. Try not to be too influenced by these people. What we feel is what we feel, and rather than attacking ourselves, it is preferable to look at the ways we can cope and sort out our problems in the ways that best suit ourselves.

Key Points

- We can be disappointed with things – e.g. blocks to major life goals, relationships and personal feelings.
- The anger and frustration of disappointment often set in motion a train of thoughts that are either self-attacking and/ or 'other' attacking.
- If we can learn to identify these thoughts early, we can take steps to challenge them and work through them.
- As the anger grows in us, there is a tendency to use many of the thinking styles we have met in earlier chapters (e.g.

continued on next page

---

all-or-nothing thinking, overgeneralizing, disqualifying the positives, dwelling on the negatives).

- Although disappointments are always upsetting, we can perhaps learn to limit their effects on us and try to prevent them from driving us into depression.
- In reality, the internal bully can be created by our own reactions to disappointment and frustration. It's the 'attack self' response.

Exercises

- Think of the last time you felt disappointed and angry about something. Then write down your 'Ideal' thoughts and your 'Actual' thoughts in two columns.

  Now find out if you do either of the following:

  Attack self: Write down any self-attacking thoughts that have been produced by this disappointment.

  Attack others: Write down any 'other-attacking' thoughts that have been produced by this disappointment.

- Now that you have worked out how you tend to react to disappointments, first acknowledge your anger. Ask yourself:

  Am I going in for all-or-nothing thinking?

  Am I discounting the positives? What remains good or okay?

  Am I saying that *everything* has been spoiled (i.e. over-generalizing).

  What would I say to a friend who had this disappointment?

  What would I like someone who cares for me to say to me?

  What evidence is there that shows I can cope with this? (Don't focus on the evidence against – which would be easy.)

continued on next page

- Note any negative thinking styles (see Appendix 2).
- Look out for 'It–Me' problems. Distinguish clearly between your actions and your 'self'. For example, ask yourself: If I fail an exam, does this make me – a person, my whole being, my totality – a failure? I might *feel* like a failure but this does not make it true. Are you saying, 'I only accept *me* if I do *it* well'?
- *'Shoulds' and 'Musts':* Explore the pressure of the 'shoulds' and 'musts' in your life and how they can produce more emotional pain.
- *Shame:* Are you disappointed because somehow you feel ashamed at not meeting your ideals? (If so, look at the shame exercises in Chapter 13).
- And finally, the most painful bit, in a friendly voice ask yourself, 'Are my ideals realistic?'

18

Perfectionism and Competitiveness, or How the Secret of Success is the Ability to Fail

Depressed people are often surprised when I suggest that 'the secret of success is the ability to fail.' So much in our society concentrates on succeeding and achieving things that we have actually become incompetent at failing. Yet, if you think about it, success, like love, looks after itself. Most of our problems don't come from succeeding or doing well but from failing and not doing well. The way we cope with disappointment and setbacks can do much to throw us into depression, especially if we spiral into self-attacking and self-dislike. Learning how to fail without self-attacking can be a useful means of exerting more control over moods.

One reason why failure becomes a serious problem is because, perhaps without realizing it, we have become perfectionist and competitive people to whom the idea of failure is a terror. I should also say that, while I will sometimes refer to people who are perfectionists, this is only for simplicity's sake, since it is more accurate to refer to perfectionist styles. Indeed, we can become more perfectionist in our thinking as we become depressed.

Before exploring perfectionism, it is useful to remember that failure is part of life. It is inevitable. Think of learning any new skill: learning to play the piano, tennis and so on, or a baby learning to walk. The chances are that, in the beginning, the failures will greatly outweigh the successes. If, for example, a baby gave up trying to walk the first time it fell over, it would never get going. But there are times later in life when we expect ourselves to get everything right from the beginning. This, of course, is not humanly possible.

If we can cope with failure and not be terrorized by it, we are much more likely to succeed and be more relaxed in the process. Perfectionism and competitiveness, along with unrealistic ideals, are reasons why failing can be so hard. If you hold highly perfectionist attitudes, you are going to run into many failures simply because it's tough being perfect.

Perfectionism

In some ways, perfectionism relates to having high ideals and believing that we must reach them or else we are worthless and bad in some way. However, perfectionism is a little more complex than this. Research by the Canadian psychologists Paul Hewitt, Gordon Flett and their colleagues suggest that there are three forms of perfectionism:

- *Self-orientated perfectionism:* Here the focus is on high standards and the need to be perfect. When people fall short of these standards, they can become highly self-critical and experience a lot of frustrative anger.
- *Other-orientated perfectionism:* Here people demand high standards of others. They can become angry with others if the latter are not up to the mark. The other-orientated perfectionist may look for how far people fall short of a standard rather than how good they are.
- *Socially prescribed perfectionism:* Here people believe that it is others who expect high standards of them and that they will be rejected or shamed if they don't come up to those expected standards.

At present, it remains unclear how far perfectionism drives certain depressions. One reason for perfectionism is the fear of failure. This is related to the competitive side of our personalities. It may be the fear of failure that is the real problem in perfectionism – especially if a person is prone to intense self-criticism. It is also possible that perfectionism leads to frequent instances of disappointment and 'defeat', and that this sense of defeat results in depression.

Competitiveness

Are you happy being average? If someone said that you are an average lover, wife, husband, doctor, driver or cook, how would you feel? There are probably some areas of your life where you would be content to be average, and if you are very poor at doing something (e.g. playing a game), being average might actually be good. However, would you be content to be average in all areas? If you cook a meal for people, would you be happy for them to say, 'Thanks for the average meal?' If you make love to someone, would you be happy to know that he or she felt your love-making was average? Well, perhaps, but often we want to feel special, at least some of the time and to some people (e.g. our parents or lovers). Most people might feel a little upset if they thought that their parents loved them no more than any other person. I think most people would recognize that this desire to feel special, at least some of the time, is normal. Indeed, telling someone that they are average is occasionally seen as a put-down: 'What! Only *average*?'

You can tell where your competitiveness lies by asking yourself two questions. First, in which areas of your life would you not settle for being average? And second, in what areas of your life are you concerned by what others have, are doing or are achieving? Your answers will tell you your areas of competitiveness. This competitive drive – to be socially successful, and seen as special – can play a role in depression.

Some forms of perfectionism are related to competitiveness. Competitive perfectionists tend to see life as a competition. There are two forms of competitive perfectionist styles. The first I will call 'keep up' competitiveness: these people strive to be as good as others, are highly focused on what others are doing or thinking, and are likely to say things like 'Other people can do this so, so should I.' They are running in a race to 'keep up', and their main fear is of not being as good as others and being seen as inadequate or inferior. Much of their thinking is dominated by social comparison, with negative thoughts and feelings being triggered when they see others doing better than themselves.

For example, Veronica discovered that her friend had decorated her bedroom and made new curtains. Veronica thought: 'My friend does things so easily. I ought to be able to achieve similar things. I don't cope as well as she does and am therefore inferior to her and inadequate.' Veronica was continually trying to reach standards set by others, and seeing what others could do became a driving force to achieve the same. Many people are like this to some extent, but perfectionists demand that they should always be at the same standard as others, or else they attack themselves. They drive themselves to reach high standards because they think others are already at this level. They may deny that they do this, but it is relatively easy to find in them a desire to avoid being seen as inferior. When they engage in this style of activity, they tend to take their standards from those around them and find it difficult to set their own.

The second style is 'get ahead' competitiveness – to be seen as special, unique and/or superior. Some people who are perfection-ist about their diets or weight are like this. Ursula had an eating disor-der and saw control over her body and its appearance as making her superior to others, and giving her an advantage over them. Edgar was a keen tennis player and the best at his club until another man joined who was better than he was. Edgar became preoccu-pied with his own playing and his need to be better, and became intensely self-critical if his performance was less skilled than the new member's. The motto of those who subscribe to the 'get ahead' competitive style is: 'There is only one place to be and that is at number one.' Of course, some people try to get ahead by cheating or 'wheeling and dealing', but although they may be highly com-petitive, they are not perfectionists. They will settle for whatever gives them an advantage. What marks the competitive perfection-ist is the focus on and drive to meet standards.

Competitive perfectionists do not always admit that their actions are designed to make them superior or special, but they certainly behave as if this is the case. They do not like to come second and can feel upset if others (and especially those who they regard as inferior) do better. Like the 'keep up' competitive person, their stand-ards can be taken from those around them and are not set by them-selves, and they are very sensitive to what others think about them.

Many of us have these aspects in our psychology to some degree. Indeed, from an evolutionary point of view, those individuals who were not competitive would not leave many genes behind them. As we have seen, most human beings want to keep up, have some means of impressing others, feel accepted and, at times, special. However, in the perfectionist, these traits are marked. To fail to reach those standards is, for them, to risk inferiority or a loss of admiration and approval. This results in anger, frustration and self-attacking.

It turned out that it was not just in playing tennis that Edgar was competitively perfectionist. A couple of years earlier, the man next door had put in a new kitchen. Before he went to see this, Edgar had had no thoughts of changing his own, but you can guess what happened. As soon as he saw the new kitchen, he had to have a new kitchen himself *and* it had to be better than the other man's. While he was putting it in, he became easily frustrated if it would not fit correctly. When I asked him to focus on the thoughts going through his mind, they were : 'I bet he didn't have this much trouble putting in his kitchen. I've got to make mine better than his; if not, I will feel that he has got one up on me and I will feel inadequate.'

Some people demand high standards of themselves even if these standards cannot be reached. Frank was an artist who thought that his work should be recognized by others as exceptional. He was intensely self-critical but also full of resentment at how others seemed to lack appreciation of his work. And if he heard of other painters (whom he regarded as less able than himself) winning prizes or gaining recognition, he would feel enraged and depressed. He always perceived people as trying to ignore him, put him down and prevent him from gaining the admiration he needed. At no time, before therapy, did he consider that his paintings were good but no more than that. They *had* to be great and others *had* to be full of admiration for them!

Perfectionist behavior can be activated in social situations that are seen as competitive. Many socially anxious people feel they have to be *really* interesting; to be boring or average is seen as a terrible thing to be. So they continually monitor their behavior for its 'interest' level, which increases their anxiety and makes easy conversation very difficult. Just imagine for a moment that you go to a party and every time you try to say something, you tell yourself, 'The others will find this boring. It's not interesting. I won't be able to hold their attention. They would rather speak to some-one else.' Eventually, you would get really anxious, which, of course, is what happens to the socially anxious person. Their ideals of being good conversationalists are extreme and they think that they will be rejected if they are not good at this.

Despite what many people think, perfectionism and constantly striving to keep up, win and succeed are not that helpful, at least not if you want to live a reasonably happy life. One thing research has shown us is that perfectionists don't have a good time. They are prone to get depressed, anxious, irritable and suffer from vari-ous other conditions such as anorexia and drink problems. And the reason for this is that failures and setbacks ignite much anger and self-attacking. These people take failures very badly.

Doing Your Best

Now, before we go any further, let's be clear about one thing. Most of us accept that trying to do our best is a good idea. If something is worth doing, it's worth putting some effort into it. The problem is: how much effort? Even if you work twenty hours a day, you might, in principle, say that you could have worked twenty-one hours a day. If perfectionists fail, they inevitably say they could have done more. The problem is clear – the goal posts keep moving.

It's similar for 'other-orientated' perfectionists. Even if you put a lot of effort into something, the other-orientated perfectionist will still say that you could have done more. Sara studied hard for her exams and got reasonable grades but not all top marks. Her par-ents indicated to her that she could have tried harder even though she had studied many hours a day. Sara was not able to see the unreasonableness of this but accepted their view and felt guilty and ashamed. It was as if her parents did not notice how much work she had done, but only focused on the comparatively few times when she took breaks from studying. Later in life, Sara may well have problems in judging what is reasonable effort and what is not.

So another problem with perfectionists is that they only judge themselves and others by the results and not their efforts. No effort is good enough if it does not produce the desired results.

Doing It All

Tina was often confronted by a feeling of being overwhelmed at home. There was the house to clean and the children to take to school, and never enough time. Her main belief was: 'I must do it all.' I used to feel exhausted just talking to her! Behind this belief were the following ideas: 'If I don't do everything, I will be letting others down. They expect it of me. Other women can do these things and go out to work. Therefore, I am inadequate, if I don't keep up.'

After some work together, Tina and I worked out some alternative thoughts:

- I am imposing these standards on myself.
- I can prioritize and recognize that I don't need to do it all.
- Frankly, some of this housework is boring and I'm lonely at home. That's why I don't feel like doing these things – it's not because I'm inadequate.
- I need to put time aside to do things I enjoy, such as visit friends – even if this means that I don't get everything done.
- I can go step by step and break down the chores rather than focus on all of them.

It also turned out that Tina could not let her husband help because she saw the home as 'her territory'. Moreover, although he was keen to help, when Tina allowed him to he was often less thorough than she was. Her perfectionist attitude meant that she was often dissatisfied with other people's efforts to help her. And she felt guilty and inadequate for needing her husband's help.

Letting others down and feeling guilty can be a driving force behind some perfectionist styles. So can a need to be 'in control'. Tina had the fear that, if she were not in control, 'everything will fall apart and disasters will happen.' This gave her some feeling of importance (i.e. she was needed) but not in a helpful way. The idea that 'others can't cope without me' is not uncommon in some perfectionist styles.

The Loss of Pleasure

Perfectionists can also cut themselves off from many positive pleasures. They are less likely to enjoy things for 'the thing in itself' but only focus on the results. For example, when painting pictures non-perfectionists may enjoy getting out in the fresh air to paint or simply putting paint on canvas. They may try out new things and have fun messing about with new ideas. Perfectionists, however, can enjoy few of these things, for in the back of their minds is always the question: 'Is it good enough?' Frank the artist told me how he would fly into rages and rip up his work if he could not make the image that he had in his mind appear on the canvas. Even in sex perfectionists may be more focused on how they perform than on getting lost in the pleasure of it. They have to 'do it right'. A patient of mine who used to go hiking complained that he could have been walking anywhere; what seemed to matter more was how many miles he covered. He would set himself tests – 'Can I walk twenty miles today?' Even if it had been a bright and beautiful day and the countryside had been in full bloom, he would hardly notice this, because he was so intent in doing his set number of miles – often as quickly as possible.

At one level, we may see this as 'gaining pleasure from achievement.' However, in depression there is often a sense of not achieving enough and certainly a loss in the ability to enjoy the simple pleasures of life.

The disappointment and dissatisfaction with performances that perfectionists feel can result in a number of difficult emotions: guilt, anger, frustration, shame, envy and anxiety. These negative emotions can make life a misery.

Perfectionism and the Internal Bully

One problem with perfectionism and competitiveness is that frustrative anger tends to get directed at the self by the actions of the internal bully. A competitive person can even 'adopt' the bully and believe that, unless they bully themselves, they will never do what is necessary to succeed. Consider Barry. He was well aware that there was a strong bullying and self-critical part to himself. He hated failure. Yet, although he knew that this was partly a source of his depression, and the reason why he had trouble with close relationships (he'd get moody if he had setbacks, or his lover did not come up to his standards), he was very reluctant to tackle the bully. When I invited him to 'let the bully speak', the bully 'said':

Barry is basically a lazy person. He needs me to kick him into action. Without me, he would never make anything of his life. He'd end up miserable and down and out. No one would respect him and he would constantly fail. He is basically a weak, useless person.

When Barry focused on these thoughts, he was at first surprised by their strength but they also seemed true to him – he agreed with his bully in a passive accepting way. On reflection, he realized that the bully was the voice of his father, so initially he felt unable to challenge it. But in time he learned to fight back. He came up with the following:

Actually, I'm not half as lazy as you think I am. To be frank, it is you, bully, when you hit me so hard, who makes me depressed. This depression causes most of my problems. You like to kick me when I'm down. If you are really as keen on success as you say you are, the best way to treat me is with kindness and support when things are tough. If I feel confident, I'm likely to do far more than if I'm full of fear, anger and disappointment.

It took a while but Barry finally began to bring his bully under control. The first step was for him to see how, for years, he'd accepted the messages of his inner bully and had never tried to fight back but only submitted to and placated it. But as I say to all my patients: Never try to placate bullies – they feed off that and only grow stronger.

If we don't control our inner bullies (which originate partly from frustration), they knock us down when we fail. Then it is difficult to recover from a setback and keep going. Moreover, they won't allow us to take time out to enjoy the simple pleasures of life. Their message is: 'Do, do, do, and when you've done, do more.'

Barry had also come to believe that he had no real motivation of his own, that there were few things that he was interested in or could aspire to – all his successes had been obtained because of the bully. This was very sad because, in fact, Barry was a very caring and passionate man. He would achieve more if he allowed himself to be motivated by his own inner desires rather than being bullied into action. Indeed, we can get so used to doing things because we are bullied into them that we lose the sense of our own joy of life, of excitement and the desire to succeed. Think about it this way. Suppose you have sex because you think you ought to, that this is what you are supposed to do. How can you then discover your own sexuality and its pleasures? How can you come to explore your sexuality and be motivated to satisfy your own desires? You can't. The most control you can exercise is to say 'No' to it!

When people decide that they don't want to do something, this decision can be seen as an act of rebellion against being bullied – not laziness. Many people find this out after leaving school. For example, I hated English and my teachers thought I was lazy – I had to force myself to do it. Later, without the pressure to pass exams I got to really enjoy writing and studying – but only after I did not have to do it.

So, if you only do what is expected of you by others, or because of your internal bully, you will tend to lose interest in doing that thing. You will, at one level, feel resentful at having to do it. Yet free yourself from this pressure (challenge that internal bully) and you may find a new source of energy that motivates you.

Hope for Success and the Fear of Failure

At times our competitive side can be carried away by fantasies of success. Ideals are set so high that they are impossible to achieve, so we live with a constant background sense of disappointment. Sometimes this reveals itself in the idea: 'I want to be a somebody rather than a nobody.' Anything that seems to block the path towards achieving these ideals is met with anger and frustration. Now, ideals are fine as far as they go, but if we fall into the trap of saying, 'I must reach my ideal, otherwise all else is worthless,' we are heading for trouble. We often fail to explore and enjoy the pleasures of living 'now' and focus only on where we want to go and how far from our ideal we are.

The other side to this is that 'hope for success' can hide a deep 'fear of failure'. What research has shown is that those people who have a high fear of failure tend to be:

- more attentive to the cues that signal possible failure rather than to cues that signal possible success;
- prone to self-criticism;
- prone to feelings of worthlessness;
- lacking in energy and concentration;
- likely to have difficulty in making decisions.

The constant fear of 'getting it wrong' takes a terrible toll.

Now there is one other important aspect to a 'fear of failure': sometimes it is not related to hope for success. I have found that people who suffer from a fear of failure rarely enjoy successes. Instead, they only feel a sense of relief from not having failed. For example, when Harry passed his exams, his main feeling was one of relief at not having failed, and he found it difficult to enjoy his classmates' celebrations. When he got married, his main feeling was: 'Oh, thank God, I got through that.' And when he obtained his first promotion, he thought: 'What a relief! I've made it through my first big test.' Harry rarely thought: 'Wouldn't it be wonderful if I succeed?' but rather 'Wouldn't it have been terrible if I failed?' Life was a constant struggle of dodging problems.

Proving Oneself and Self-Centredness

Some forms of perfectionism and competitiveness are very self-centred. Indulging in these types of behavior can actually block our ability to relate openly with others. Suppose you came to see me for therapy. Which would you prefer: that I am concerned to do all I can to help you because I am interested in you, or that I try to ensure that I do the best I can because I don't want to fail or be seen to fail – I am more concerned with my reputation than with you? Or suppose your lover has sex with you. Which would you prefer: that he or she wishes to share the experience with you, or that he or she makes love to prove that he or she is good at it?

Sadly, some perfectionists are so self-centred that they turn nearly all activities into reflections of themselves. If they fail, thoughts such as 'What does this mean about me?' dominate their thinking. Because they have not got control over their inner bully, they cannot afford to fail. It is not so much concern with others but how they feel about themselves. Of course, it is not quite as 'all or nothing' as I am making out – it is a matter of degree – but I hope that you see the issue here. The more you control your inner bully (and your frustration if you do poorly), the less self-focused you will be and the more you may be able to develop more satisfying relationships.

Perfectionism, Pride and the Desire to Impress Others

Sometimes we develop perfectionist and competitive standards as a way of dealing with shame. We have the motto: 'If we are perfect, we are beyond reproach, beyond shame or criticism.' Moreover, because we believe that our perfectionist standards are worthy of approval, we may only feel good if we reach them.

Kay, a dancer, was known to be a perfectionist. She was moody and rarely satisfied with her performance. At times she would push herself to the point where she would ignore small injuries, which would then become major problems. At these times, she would become depressed and angry with her body for letting her down. True, she did reach high standards but never seemed to enjoy her successes or, if she did, they were short-lived enjoyments. She had the motto: 'You are only as good as your last performance.' In therapy, we explored the origins of these standards and found that they came from her relationship with her father. She had always wanted to do something that her father would be proud of, and she was desperate to win his approval. Her father never showed strong feelings, either positive or negative, but Kay believed that, if she became famous or did something special, in some way he would have to take note of her and admire (and love) her, and so would other people. Gradually, as she moved into adulthood, she became less aware of how her father's approval was a driving force in her perfectionism.

Kay demonstrated a very common element in perfectionism – that it sometimes originates in the desire to do things to make someone proud of us, to see us as special and worthy of affection and attention. We are concerned to impress others. It may be that we think that they demand high standards or it may be that we think that achieving high standards is the way to their hearts.

Ask yourself: Why do I want to reach the standards that I've set myself? You have to be really honest in your answers. Here are some that others have given:

- I want to impress others.
- I want to be a somebody rather than a nobody.
- I want others to see how good I am.
- I don't want others to see the bad side of me or my flaws.
- I want to avoid being criticized and thought of as worthless.
- Life is pointless if you don't succeed.
- I must not let others down.
- There has to be something I am good at.

It does not matter too much what your wants, wishes and hopes are provided that you can cope with them not coming to fruition. If you say, 'I'd like to impress others,' that may be fine. But if you say, 'I must impress others, otherwise they will see me as inadequate and I will feel useless,' you have a problem. And the reason why is that failure and setbacks will generate such anger with yourself and others that this can drive you into depression.

Personal Pride and Perfectionism

Some people with eating disorders, who become very thin, are often highly perfectionist and competitive. However, they have a pride in themselves because they exert control over their eating and weight. Often the problem starts when they get on the scales, see that they have lost weight and feel a thrill or buzz of pride from the achievement. To put on weight produces a feeling of deflation and shame. They can become obsessed with every calorie and type of food they eat. This is an example of shame turning to pride. They may feel ashamed of their bodies or believe that there is not much about them to be proud of – but then they hit on the idea of weight loss, and the pride of losing weight drives them on.

When shame turns into pride, it takes a real struggle to change this. Helping these people to put on weight may be seen as taking away the only thing (losing weight) they feel good at. This kind of problem is a very different one from, say, panic attacks. Nobody wants panic attacks, so therapist and patient can line up together against the common problem. But anorexic people want to be thin; they want to maintain their perfectionist standards.

It is the same with all forms of perfectionism and competitiveness, be it cleaning the house, playing a sport well, working long hours and so on. *The person does not want to give up these things.* However, it is the reactions to failure and setbacks that have to be changed. If the sports person becomes depressed because he or she is not playing well and loses confidence in him/herself that is hardly helpful.

Pride and Confidence

Pride is actually quite different from confidence. In fact, we may call pride 'false confidence'. The reason for this is that pride depends on your performance – on what you think others will value. That is not confidence, although if you can reach your standards, you might feel confident. But this can be a fragile confidence. What happens the moment you fail? Your confidence disappears like the morning dew.

Real confidence comes from a belief in yourself as a person. That is, whether, succeeding or failing, you are able to cope without generating intense disappointment and anger that turns to self-attack or thoughts of hopelessness. You are neither carried away by success nor seriously deflated and depressed by failure and setbacks. You may have a strong desire to do well or look good and put much effort into these things, but your inner self is able to accept you as you are. This is the source of confidence – self-acceptance. You learn to be accepting of yourself for good or ill. Anything else means that you are only a fair weather friend to yourself. But real friendship and acceptance is standing by someone when the chips are down.

Envy and Competitiveness

Some styles of competitiveness can also generate envy of others and an inability to accept that others may, in some situations, be better and more capable than oneself. Alex, who was training to be a therapist, was an able student, but he took my suggestions on improving his skills very badly. I wondered if I was putting my suggestions across too critically. But every suggestion I made seemed to put him on the defensive and he would argue against it. After a time, I admitted to feeling rather irritated by him. He could take nothing from me and seemed to devalue whatever I said. I commented to him that he seemed to want to be a 'great' therapist without having to go through the difficult learning process.

After some difficult conversations, he reflected that his early life had been full of perfectionist and competitive demands from his parents. He had never been allowed to fail. So in his mind, if I showed him how he could improve, he viewed this as him 'not being good enough'. He had an easily activated sense of shame, and as a result, he was unable to acknowledge that others had things of value to offer him. In groups, he was envious, competitive and prone to run down others. If he had seen that others knew more than he did, he would then have had to acknowledge that he could improve, and to Alex that meant that he had to acknowledge that he was not perfect. A recognition of a need for something, like advice and training, was (to him) an acknowledgment of his limitations and thus not being (in his mind) good enough.

Shame-prone individuals who become competitive can be a problem to themselves and others because they go so easily on to the defensive. They feel bad if others criticize them or are more able than they are. Another person's gain is their loss. Competitive envy causes many problems in depression because it stops people acknowledging their need for others and their own vulnerabilities. They also begrudge the attributes, success, rank, status and attention accorded to other people. They may fail to offer assistance to those who succeed and try to undermine their efforts.

Envy can also come from a feeling of powerlessness and anger at being in that position. The American psychotherapist Althea Horner gives this example in her book *The Wish for Power and the Fear of Using It*:

> A woman who characteristically clung to a powerless position in order to force her mother to take care of her, as well as to protect

the mother against the hate of her own envy of the older woman's power, said of an associate, 'I hate her, and there's nothing that can be done about it. I spoil her by thinking her seams are crooked or that she only seems nice because she is so shallow. I am power-less with her. I do want to smash her, to get rid of her, to tell her what I think of her. And I hate you [the therapist] for being so strong. I feel impotent. I can't change you. I kiss ass and walk away hating you. It's a passive ragefulness.'

Although she used to think of herself as competitive, she came to understand the critical difference between competitiveness and envy. This difference resides in the degree of hostility and the wish to spoil or destroy that go with envy. One can value the competitive rival and have no wish to harm that person. In competitiveness, unlike envy, the only wish is to win.

If these are experiences you can identify with, you can try to change them. First, you can see that you are not alone in feeling this way. Second, by recognizing them, you are closer to understanding and challenging these thoughts. Try not to attack yourself if you realize that you have envious feelings, thoughts and attitudes. In fact, this is a step forward. When we are depressed, we can often feel envi-ous of those who are not. As one patient said to me, 'Sometimes I would just like to wipe the smiles off their faces and let them feel what I am feeling. Then they would not be so smug about it.' When you feel angry with others it can sometimes be that this anger comes from envy.

Challenging Competitiveness and Perfectionism

To challenge competitiveness and perfectionism requires us to first recognize them in ourselves. However, it is often the case that we don't always see these styles in ourselves.

One way of exploring your competitive and perfectionist styles is to write down the advantages and disadvantages of failing and to explore your fears (the disadvantages) of failing. Here's an example.

Pauline felt that she had constantly to keep up with the house-work but denied that she was a perfectionist. The very idea seemed a joke to her – 'That,' she said 'is the last thing I am.' But look at the advantages and disadvantages of keeping her house up to scratch that she wrote down. Her first thoughts were: 'There is so much to do and I must do it all.' If she did do it, then:

Advantages of keeping house tidy
- I'll feel I've achieved something.
- If I feel I have achieved something, I'll feel better about myself.
- I'll prove to myself that I am not lazy.
- I'll prove that I am as good as other people.
- The family expect it of me.
- They'll like, love and respect me more.

Disadvantages of not keeping house tidy
- I'll feel lazy.
- I'll have let my family down.
- I'll have shown once again that I cannot cope.
- My family will be disappointed in me and be angry – even if they don't admit it.
- I'll feel that I have failed.
- I'll feel useless.

You can see that showing through these advantages and disadvantages are perfectionist styles of thinking. There is the expectation that others (the family) will be disapproving of her; there is the feeling of being lazy and worthless for not succeeding; and there is a social comparison (others can do these things so I should also be able to).

It might be interesting for you to reflect on Pauline's thoughts and think how you might help her. What would you say? Would you agree with her? If your answer is 'Yes', then look at the implications. What this means is that, if you went to Pauline's house and found her sitting depressed in her kitchen, not able to get on and do things, you would say to her: 'Look, Pauline, you are being very lazy. Other people can keep their houses clean, so why not you? Your family expects it of you and you are letting them down. They are going to be rightly angry with you. You are not as good as other people and are worthless.'

The chances are that you would not treat someone who was depressed like this. You would probably not even think like this when dealing with someone else. (If your internal bully was in control of your thoughts, it's possible that you might think it, but you would not say it.) Why? You don't need to be a psychologist to know that it would push her further into depression.

So let's imagine that, when you visit Pauline, you come as a helper and healer. What would you say? First, you would be sensitive to her feelings.

> *Look, Pauline, you are feeling depressed right now, so all this must seem like a mountain to climb. Let's try to plan a couple of things that you might be able to do, and go from there. If you can do one thing, you are one step further on.*

Next, you might start to tackle her self-attacking thoughts.

> *You know that, when you feel well, you can do the housework okay. This problem has nothing to do with being lazy. If you were simply lazy, you'd put your feet up, read the newspaper and enjoy not doing anything. Maybe you're bored with house-work and this makes it even more difficult. Maybe you feel very lonely here on your own, struggling to do the housework when the family have all gone to school or work. If that's true, we can think about it and try to see what we can do to change the situ-ation. But first, you need to see that this is not about laziness.*

Next, you might deal with her habit of comparing herself to others.

> *Sure, other people can do housework when they are not depressed, but most people struggle when they are. By comparing yourself with others, you will feel worse. Let's focus on what you can do rather than what others can do, and move on from there.*

Next, you might discuss her family's expectations.

> *Could you ask them for more help? Ah, I see that you think that this will make you dependent on them or feel inferior to them. Well, right now the important thing is to get the help you need and to express your feelings. Sometimes we need to learn how to let others help us for a while. You think that your family will be*

critical of you for needing help? Do you have any evidence for that? Even so, maybe they are expecting too much. But the thing is, even if they are critical, this doesn't mean that you have to accept what they say as being true about you. Maybe they don't understand how bad depression feels. That's lucky for them, but then they are not in a good position to judge, are they? Of course, if you are angry with them and attack them for not helping, this will put them on the defensive, but if you are open and reasonable, they might understand. Have you tried that? Have you tried being thankful for help or have you always accepted it grudgingly?

Now you have an idea of how you might help Pauline. First, you would recognize the depression, then focus on doing small things, going step by step. Then you would try to help Pauline stop attacking herself and engaging in all-or-nothing thinking ('I have to do it all'). Then you might assist her to address the problem of asking her family for help because you recognize that their help could be useful to her. You might also focus on her thinking: does she discount the positives in her life or does she overgeneralize? The last thing you would want to do is to be negative towards her, for this would not work.

Now that you have seen how this kind of approach might help Pauline, you can use the same principles to deal with your own problems.

I have discussed Pauline's situation because it may not, on the surface, appear to involve competitiveness or perfectionism. But both of these styles were definitely in play, for two reasons. First, because if Pauline had believed that everyone had the same sorts of problems, she would have been less negative about herself. Second, because her thinking focused on trying to do everything rather than going a step at a time. Thus, it is preferable to learn to cope with being able to do less than one ideally would like. Another reason for using this example is because the problems it brings to light are relatively common in depression. Now in fact, it would not matter if we were perfectionist about our work or about achieving certain outcomes, such as a painting; the principles are the same. People often want to do more than they can, and it is when they fail to achieve their goals that problems begin. And to get out of these problems means coming to accept our limitations: that we are less than perfect; that we can survive failures and setbacks without attacking ourselves or becoming overly despondent. We may not be able to 'do it all,' but that doesn't mean we can't go some way towards doing some things.

It is not doing your best that is at issue. It is how we cope with failure and disappointment that may cause trouble. This is why the key to success is the ability to fail. When we fail, we have to learn to treat ourselves kindly. Anyone can feel good about themselves if they succeed. We have to find ways of minimizing our bad feelings if we don't do something well. We also have to learn to prioritize and decide what has value to us and what does not. Is it better to spend all your time making the house spotless, or is it preferable to be more relaxed about housework and focus on relationships with your family? Are achievements more important to you than relationships?

Key Points

- We can direct competitiveness and perfectionism towards ourselves or others or because we think others expect these styles of thinking of us.
- Some of our perfectionism is competitive – used because we want to avoid being seen as inferior or because we want to be seen as superior and special.
- It is sometimes a 'pressure to succeed' that reveals our perfectionist and competitive styles.
- We can become very self-centred if we drift into perfectionism. This is often because we have let our internal bully have too much control.
- The main problem with these styles of thinking is that they can lead to anger, frustration, guilt and anxiety about failing.
- These feelings can result from, and increase, the amount of attacking that we do to ourselves and others. This can spin us into a spiral of feeling more depressed.

continued on next page

- There is nothing wrong with high standards themselves, but it is how we cope with ourselves and others when, life being life, they cannot be met.

Exercises

- Your competitive and perfectionist styles will show up most clearly when you fail at something. So think about a time when you failed to achieve something. Now ask yourself the following questions:
  – What standard was I trying to achieve?
  – Why would it have been good if I had achieved that? What did I hope to get out of it?
  – Was I trying to avoid being seen as inferior or did I want to be seen as superior?
  – Are these my own standards or ones I think others expect of me?
  – Was I trying to impress others?
  – Am I a person motivated to succeed – seeking the pleasures of success – or am I someone who is primarily motivated to avoid failure? If the latter, I can start to learn to enjoy the pleasures of success by praising myself for small successes. If you think your successes are in some way 'fakes', review Chapter 10.
- Failing involves disappointment. So think back on the last chapter and explore what you do when you fail.
  – Attack myself (write down what you say about yourself).
  – Attack others (write down what you say about others).
  – Give up (write down why you give up).
  Remember: writing things down helps to make your thoughts clearer, rather than having them zoom about in your head (see pp. 113–17).

continued on next page

- Consider carefully the things you have written above and examine them for the typical depressive styles of thinking outlined in earlier chapters – for example, all-or-nothing thinking, discounting the positive aspects of your life, being overly focused on the negatives (see Appendix 2).
- Decide that coming to terms with failures and setbacks and learning how to fail are the real achievements here. Once you can fail, you are free to succeed. But if failure is a terror to you, the path to success becomes a dangerous and frightening place to be. So now, using your compassionate/rational mind to support you in your hour of need, answer the following questions:
  – What would you say to someone else?
  – What would you like someone who cares for you to say?
  – How can you challenge your negative thoughts about yourself?
  – What are some of the alternatives to your negative thoughts and feelings?
  – If you can't 'do it all,' is there some smaller part that might be achieved?
  – Can you go step by step, focusing on what you have done rather than what you haven't?

  Also consider:
  – Are there enjoyable things in your life or is it full of chores? Could you do one thing for yourself today?
  – How might you gain help from others?
- Try enjoying success. Allow yourself to say, 'That was good and I am going to enjoy my success.' Try praising yourself more, even for small successes. The more you experience this enjoyment of success, the more motivated you will be to try harder at achieving things. If you do something only out of fear, this can become very exhausting. It is useful to try to motivate yourself through rewards rather than through fear of punishment. You are using a different part of your

continued on next page

brain when you are motivated to succeed rather than to
avoid failure.
- Recognize that confidence comes from within. Try to avoid
  confusing it with false pride, which can be taken away from
  you the moment you fail. Pride may give us a buzz, but we
  can't depend on it.

19

Summing Up

Depression is probably one of the darkest winters of the soul. Researchers throughout the world are trying to work out why we have this capacity to feel as terrible as we do – and many have come up with their own explanations. In this book, I have given one view. This is that depression is a potential state of mind that evolved in our brains many millions of years ago. Our brains also evolved with a need to form social relationships. We are therefore highly motivated to be wanted, valued and have status in our relationships. When we obtain the signals that these things are coming our way, we tend to feel happy. But if we feel that we are not wanted or valued or if we lose status, our mood goes down, and it can slide into depression if we think that chances of our obtaining these 'social things' are low. So depression speaks to our need to live as social beings, in communities of familiar and trustworthy individuals. It is thus more likely in situations of social isolation and fragmentation. It is marked by inner feelings of being distant and cut off from others.

This does not contradict the idea that depression also relates to states of defeat and feeling blocked and inferior, for it is usually the social implications of a defeat that matter most to us. A defeat that does not lower your status or leave you feeling inferior or cause you to downgrade your self-esteem and social standing will have less impact on your mood than a defeat that does. This is when your thinking begins to play a part. The more a defeat or setback activates thoughts of inferiority and worthlessness, the more the depression will increase. Conversely, the more you are not inhibited by shame or are not grossly disappointed by unrealistic ideals, and you develop the ability to control your anger and stop putting yourself down, the greater are your chances of reaching out to others and getting out of the depression.

This linking of thoughts with internal evolved potential states of mind is only one approach to depression (see Chapter 3). There are others. Geneticists might see depression as related to some genetic disposition. They might point to the evidence of increased susceptibility in identical twins: if one twin suffers depression, the risks of the other one also suffering from it are higher than for the population in general. Those who study families might see depression as related to early family life experiences. Indeed, many of the most negative views that we develop of ourselves and others can often be traced to what happened to us in early life. Those who study the social environment might see depression as one consequence of the fact that our social environments no longer nurture us with long-term, committed relationships and because of our increasingly competitive and over-idealized expectations of how life should be. They may point to the differences in rates of depression in different countries and communities. Thus, there can be biological, psychological and sociological aspects to depression, each addressing different dimensions of our humanness. One, some or all these factors might apply to you.

I think that we do those who suffer from depression a great disservice if those of us who work in these fields become competitive about our theories. Depression is too complex and varied for there to be only one cause or one answer. In treating depression, one cannot be a 'one-club golfer.' One approach does not rule out another.

Nevertheless, I believe that, in many cases, people can become trapped in depression in part, at least by the way they think, and by the difficulties of facing up to things that have to be changed. This may well be the case for you. If you attempt some of the things suggested in this book, you'd be no worse off for trying – what have you got to lose? Try things out. See what works for you. Get your own evidence for what is helpful.

So I hope this book has given you some insight into the psychology of depression. It has been a long journey and no doubt you may want to visit various parts of it again. In closing, there are a few points that I would like to mention again.

- Depression is a very varied problem. It ranges from the mild to the severe. Some depressions are associated with much anxiety, others with much anger. Some come on slowly, others quite quickly.
- There is a psychological component to every depression, and indeed this book has focused on this, but this does not mean that psychological change is all you need to get out of it. Some people benefit from medication and others require a change in social circumstances.
- If you have a number of problems in your everyday life, it is possible that changing the way you think and behave can help you approach these in a different and helpful way.
- Self-help books can be very useful, but do not necessarily eliminate the need for professional help. It may be that reading this book has encouraged you to consider whether you might benefit from therapy or other forms of help. If so, contact your family doctor, who can refer you to a properly trained person. No self-help book can cover the richness of the experience of depression or all that goes on in therapy.
- Shame can be one of the main reasons why you may be reluctant to seek help, but try to remember that depression is one of the most common problems that mental health professionals work with. You are far from alone. A similar case can be made for talking with friends.
- Although you may need extra help, there are also many things that you can do to help yourself or at least avoid making your depression worse by the way you think.
- Getting out of depression often takes time, effort and patience.

The ten key steps that can help to control depression

1 Seek help if you need it – don't suffer in silence.
2 Go step by step.
3 Break problems down into smaller ones rather than trying to do everything in one go.

continued on next page

---

4 Introduce more positive activities into your life.

5 Become more attentive and aware of your thinking and the ideas that go through your mind when you are depressed.

6 Try to identify your typical thinking styles (e.g. all-or-nothing thinking, discounting the positive aspects of your life). Note especially what you think about yourself, and how you label and treat yourself. Look out for your internal bully. Remember that this can drive you further into, rather than out of, depression.

7 Try writing down your thoughts to aid clarity and to focus your attention.

8 Try to identify the key themes in your depression (e.g. your need for approval, shame, unhappy relationships, unrealistic ideals, perfectionism). This will allow you to spot more easily your personal themes when they arise – and to challenge them.

9 Learn to challenge your thinking with the use of your rational/compassionate mind. The more you treat yourself with compassion and give up thinking of yourself in terms of inferior, bad, worthless, and so on, the easier it will be for your brain to recover.

10 Try challenging negative thoughts and developing new ways of behaving. However, also expect setbacks and disappointments from time to time.

Finally, remember:

- Your depression may be a state of mind you are in, but your depression is not you.
- Your anxiety may be a state of mind you are in, but your anxiety is not you.
- Your anger may be a state of mind you are in, but your anger is not you.

These states of mind are to do with how your brain was designed over millions of years. They are part of human nature.

continued on next page

Whatever judgments of 'you' that your emotions come up with, they are about as reliable as the weather. The more compassionate you are with yourself, the less you will be a 'fairweather friend' to yourself. If you can stay a true friend to yourself, even though depressed, you are taking a big step forward. You're on the way up.

Appendix 1

Monitoring and Challenging Your Thoughts

These forms and how to use them are explained in chapters 5, 6 and 7.

Using Thought Forms

Chapter 7 introduced the idea of thought forms to help you monitor and record your key thoughts and also challenge them. At the end of the book you will find some blank forms for your own use (and you can photocopy them). You will also find some worked examples. Although the forms may look somewhat complicated, they are fairly straightforward when you get the hang of them. Remember, as we said in chapter 7, you can use a form that simply has two columns, one to record your negative thoughts and one to record your alternatives and antidepression thoughts. The thought forms here have five columns, which are used as follows.

In the first column write down any situation(s), event, memory, feeling or image that has sparked off feelings of anger, despair or depression, etc. In the third column (the 'feelings' column) write down what your feelings are/were and how intense they were. The reason we put the feelings in the third column is so you can see how your thoughts link the situation with your feelings – like a bridge between the two.

Now, for the second column, where it says 'beliefs and key thoughts', ask yourself some questions, such as *how are you seeing this event; what is going through your mind; what are you thinking about yourself (for example are you telling yourself you are no good);*

how do you think this event affects your future; what do you think other people are thinking about you? All these questions are designed to get at your key beliefs, those thoughts that really make you feel sad, down and upset, etc.

In the fourth column, labelled 'alternative challenges to negative thoughts and beliefs', try to stand back and think what you might say to a friend who had these negative ideas. Can you think of evidence of why your negative thoughts may be a bit distorted? Can you think of evidence against your negative thoughts and beliefs? What alternatives might there be? How might you best cope with this; what kinds of ideas would be helpful here? Again, it is important to get the idea that you are not going to accept your negative thoughts simply because your feelings of depression tell you to.

Now when you have taken some time to challenge your thinking, look at what you have written down and see if this has changed your feelings. If so, write down how much your feelings might have changed about that event now. By focusing on this possible change it may give you an opportunity to see that by stepping back from your thoughts, you can change your perspective and feel better.

Some people like to read what others have written and ways they have challenged their thoughts but don't just write out *their thoughts*. Do attempt it yourself – with your own thoughts. Try it out – after all what have you got to lose?

Compassionate Challenging

Do remember that one of the main reasons for challenging your thoughts is to help you *feel* differently about things and, in particular, not add to your stress. It is important to try to challenge with as much warmth and understanding as you can manage. Your challenges should not be cold, bullying or irritable in their emotional tone. The more you learn to have sympathy with yourself, while at the same time looking at the rational alternatives, the easier you may find it to change your feelings. Let your personal motto be *'inner warmth'*.

So, let's look at the forms now. The first form will provide you with some single (one-line) or basic challenges. Get the hang of this first and then you may wish to have more of a dialogue with yourself. Forms 2, 3 and 4 offer more complex challenges. Some of these examples were used in the first edition but I have changed them slightly here to make them easier to understand. I have also put in possible ratings for degrees of beliefs and feelings.

1. THOUGHT MONITORING AND CHALLENGING FORM

Triggering Events, Feelings or Images	Beliefs and Key Thoughts	Feelings	Alternative Challenges to Negative Thoughts	Degree of Feeling Change
Key Questions to help you identify your thoughts. *What actually happened?*	*What went through your mind? What are you thinking about yourself, and your future? What are you thinking about others?* *Rate degree of belief 0–100.*	*What are your main feelings and emotions?* *Rate degree of feelings 0–100.*	*What would you say to a friend? What alternatives might there be? What is the evidence against this view? How would you see this if you were not depressed?* *Rate degree of belief in alternatives 0–100.*	*Write down any degree of change in your feelings you now feel.*
Example 1 Friend at work snubbed me.	He/she doesn't like me. Sees me as inadequate. 70%	Upset, hurt, angry. 60%	Probably nothing to do with me at all. Friend can be quite moody and I have seen him/her do this to others. 50%	20%
Example 2 Forgot to take important file to work.	This is typical me. I am useless and a failure. 80%	Frustrated. Angry. 90%	I am bound to be a bit frustrated because it will hold up my work today. However, this does not make me useless. I won't even remember this event in three months' time. Accept my frustrations and try to relax. 70%	40%
Example 3 Just feeling down today.	I am always going to be depressed. Nothing will ever work for me. 70%	Depressed. Fed up. 80%	Moods do go up and down. This is normal. However, I have had better days than today. I am disappointed but I can see the sense of working with my thoughts, and in my heart I know if I keep going I'll feel better. 30%	20%

2. THOUGHT MONITORING AND CHALLENGING FORM

Triggering Events, Feelings or Images	Beliefs and Key Thoughts	Feelings	Alternative Challenges to Negative Thoughts	Degree of Feeling Change
Key Questions to help you identify your thoughts. *What actually happened?*	*What went through your mind? What are you thinking about yourself, and your future? What are you thinking about others?* *Rate degree of belief 0–100.*	*What are your main feelings and emotions?* *Rate degree of feelings 0–100.*	*What would you say to a friend? What alternatives might there be? What is the evidence against this view? How would you see this if you were not depressed?* *Rate degree of belief in alternatives 0–100.*	*Write down any degree of change in your feelings.*
Too much work to do.	I can't get it all done. I will never succeed. Others can do more than me. I am incompetent and a failure. 80%	Depressed. Fed up. 80%	I can focus on what I can do rather than everything at once. I am bullying myself with *all-or-nothing* thinking rather than supporting my efforts. I am assuming the worst before it happens. If I were helping a friend I would help them go step by step. I can break these tasks down into smaller, do-able tasks. If I am tired it is because I may be depressed, or just tired – not a failure. If I praise myself for small successes, I will start to feel better. I can learn to stop discounting my positives and focus on my actual abilities. 40%	20%

3. THOUGHT MONITORING AND CHALLENGING FORM

Triggering Events, Feelings or Images	Beliefs and Key Thoughts	Feelings	Alternative Challenges to Negative Thoughts	Degree of Feeling Change
Key Questions to help you identify your thoughts. *What actually happened?*	*What went through your mind? What are you thinking about yourself, and your future? What are you thinking about others? Rate degree of belief 0–100.*	*What are your main feelings and emotions?* *Rate degree of feelings 0–100.*	*What would you say to a friend? What alternatives might there be? What is the evidence against this view? How would you see this if you were not depressed? Rate degree of belief in alternatives 0–100.*	*Write down any degree of change in your feelings.*
Argument with partner.	I am going to end up rejected. It's all my fault. I must be very unlovable. 80%	Depressed. 75%	Hold on. There are problems in the relationship but I can't take all the blame. There are things that we are both unhappy with and need to sort out. If I take the blame then we can't work together. I am self-blaming and getting more depressed which actually stops me from trying to make the relationship work. It is upsetting to have arguments, but if I avoid all-or-nothing thinking about my lovability I am more likely to see them through. Anyhow, I have friends who like me, and we have had good times together in the past, so I can't be as bad as I am painting myself. 60%	30%

4. THOUGHT MONITORING AND CHALLENGING FORM

Triggering Events, Feelings or Images	Beliefs and Key Thoughts	Feelings	Alternative Challenges to Negative Thoughts	Degree of Feeling Change
Key Questions to help you identify your thoughts. *What actually happened?*	*What went through your mind? What are you thinking about yourself, and your future? What are you thinking about others?* *Rate degree of belief 0–100.*	*What are your main feelings and emotions?* *Rate degree of feelings 0–100.*	*What would you say to a friend? What alternatives might there be? What is the evidence against this view? How would you see this if you were not depressed?* *Rate degree of belief in alternatives 0–100.*	*Write down any degree of change in your feelings.*
Children need clean clothes, ironing not done, just too many demands on me.	I can't cope with the needs of my family. I just want to run away and leave it all behind. Can't be bothered with them. I must be a selfish, cold person for feeling this way. If I was a better mother I wouldn't feel like this. 80%	Overwhelmed. Guilty. Depressed. 80%	To be honest, I am feeling exhausted right now which is understandable given the demands on me. I need to create more space for myself, take some time out for myself if I can, and ask my family to help out more. I can break my problems down and just focus on things I can cope with. The world won't end if I don't get it all done. The desire to escape is a natural and normal feeling when one is exhausted and is not evidence of being a poor mother, indeed many mothers feel like I do from time to time. 60%	20%

Appendix 2

Quick Guides

To *identify* your negative thinking style, pay attention to your feelings (see Chapter 8 and 9). Then ask yourself:

- What is/was going through my mind?
- What am I thinking about me?
- What kind of judgments am I making about myself?
- What judgments or assumptions am I making about other people?
- What am I thinking about my future?

The way you think about things can affect the way you feel. Below is a summary of some typical ways of thinking that can worsen depression. If you can learn to spot these styles of thinking in yourself, then this is a good first step to disputing and changing them. We all use these styles of thinking from time to time; no one is 100 percent logical or compassionate all the time. But in depression they get taken to extremes.

Jumping to conclusions This involves the tendency to make decisions rapidly, especially when under stress. For example, you might jump to the conclusion that someone does not like you because they ignore you. You may predict the future, e.g. that nothing you do will work out. Jumping to conclusions means that you don't look at the evidence. Instead, you go for immediate gut reactions and assume these to be true.

Emotional reasoning This involves an over-reliance on feeling to guide judgments, e.g.: 'I feel this is dangerous, therefore it is.' You assume that negative feelings reflect the way things actually are: 'I feel it so it must be true.' Feelings are often poor guides to reality. The 'power' of feelings comes from our more primitive brains having more control over us than is often good for us. Remember to test out feelings: look for alternatives and explore the evidence for and the evidence against.

'I must'   These thoughts involve feelings of being compelled to do something. 'I must be in a relationship to be happy; I must achieve things to be a worthwhile person; I must never be criticized; I must never fail.' Try to turn musts into preferences, e.g.: 'I would like to do this, but if I can't then it does not mean that I am a no-good person or that I can't be happy.'

Discounting and disbelieving the positives   This involves the tendency to ignore or dismiss positive attributes, events or achievements. You either take them for granted or think 'anyone could do that'. When you disqualify the positives it is difficult to get started on the way up. Focus on what you can do rather than on what you can't.

Discounting and disbelieving others   This involves thinking that other people's (good) opinions of you don't count. You think that either they don't really know you or you have kept things hidden and deceived them. At other times you may think that others only say positive things to be nice; they don't, in their hearts, really mean it. This often involves a loss of trust.

Amplifying the negatives   When you are depressed it is all too easy to dwell on negatives and difficulties. They take on more importance and you are very attentive to possible rejections, put-downs or failures. You can easily lose perspective by amplifying negatives and dwelling on them. Try to regain perspective by generating alternatives and avoiding emotional reasoning.

All-or-nothing thinking   This is also called 'black-and-white' or 'polarized' thinking. You see things in 'either/or' categories. If your performance falls short of what you wanted, you see it or even yourself as a total failure. You may think: 'Either X loves me or s/he doesn't.' Or: 'Either I succeed or I fail.' However, life is full of indeterminate areas. Love is not either/or; there are degrees of love. Success is not either/or; there are degrees of success. Hence, it is more useful to think of the degree of success rather than the degree of failure.

Overgeneralizing You take a single negative event and see it as a neverending pattern of defeat. Here, one swallow does make a summer. You may think that things can never change, or that one failure means that everything you have done was a failure or faked.

A Quick Guide to Recognizing Your Self-Attacking Thoughts and Styles

Self-criticism This is when part of you becomes like an observer and a judge. You are constantly passing negative judgments on yourself, as if a critical parent were sitting on your shoulder. You are more focused on what you do wrong or badly, rather than on what you do well.

Personalization and self-blaming This involves the automatic tendency to assume that you are in the wrong or are responsible for negative events. You may not look at the evidence or consider alternatives, or reflect that most things are caused by a number of different factors.

Self-labelling This involves 'all-or-nothing' thinking about yourself as a person. If your behavior fails, you think you are a failure, unlovable or inadequate, etc. In depression this type of thinking involves blaming and name-calling (e.g. I am useless, inadequate, weak, a nuisance, a fake, worthless, bad, etc.).

It–me This involves the tendency to judge yourself rather than your behavior. You think that only your behavior matters; if that is not good, then you are no good. But behavior and self are quite different. A self is a conscious, feeling being, with hopes, desires and wishes. A behavior is just a behavior, that may or may not be disappointing.

Self-attacking This involves a degree of anger and hostility directed at yourself. It is more than being critical – after all, not all criticism involves hostility. But in self-attacking one is hostile with oneself.

Self-hatred This is an extreme form of self-attacking. It is more than just anger with the self and often involves judgments and feelings of being bad, evil or disgusting. Unlike self-criticism, which aims to improve through punishment, self-hatred can be about wanting to destroy and get rid of the self.

Social comparison Although social comparison is probably inevitable, try to be more aware of when you do it. Check out how your mood changes and ask yourself if the social comparison is valid. Does it help you? Are you engaging in envious thoughts? Do such thoughts help you?

A Quick Guide to Challenging Negative Thoughts and Styles

Once you have identified your depressing thoughts, consider:

• What would I say to a friend or someone I care about who was in the same situation?
• What would I like someone who cared about me to say to me to support and encourage me?
• Have I given enough weight to the fact that when I am depressed my 'brain-state' tends to look on the black side?
• How would I see this if I were not depressed?
• What might be a rational/compassionate way of thinking about this?
• Have I tried to look at alternative ways of seeing this? What might these be?

- Have I got enough evidence to support my view? What is the evidence that does not support my (negative) view?
- Am I letting my internal bully get away with too much?
- What are the advantages and disadvantages of thinking in this way?
- Did I put enough effort into trying to change or did I assume, from the start, that it would turn out badly? What have I got to lose by giving it a go?

See also Chapter 7 on 'Challenging Negative Thoughts and Feelings'.

A Quick Guide to Making Your Own Flash Cards

Throughout this book I have offered ways to challenge some of your thoughts. Here are some thoughts you could write down on flash cards to deal with common depressing ideas and feelings.

I Am Weak to Be Depressed

- Depression is a state of mind. Just as I can have other states of mind (e.g. happy, relaxed, angry, anxious), I can be depressed.
- Depression is unpleasant, but sadly many millions suffer from it because to the brain this is just one of its patterns for feeling.
- Depression can affect anyone – even people who are often regarded as strong (e.g. Winston Churchill).
- Depression is a horrible state to be in, but it is not evidence of weakness.
- Depression is most often about becoming exhausted, trying too hard, feeling defeated, losing hope. By understanding it more, I can try to bring my rational/compassionate mind to help tackle it.
- There may be very real problems in my life that have exhausted me and made me vulnerable to being depressed.

If I Need an Antidepressant Drug it Means I am Weak

- Depression is not about weakness, but can be about being exhausted.
- I need to get the evidence of whether an antidepressant would help me. If it can help me sleep better and boost my mood and

confidence, then that might help me to get on top of my depression.

- Millions of people take antidepressant drugs.
- Whether I choose to take an antidepressant drug or not is my own decision. I don't need to prove that I can cope without one as some kind of test of my strength.

If I Need some Therapy I Might Have to Reveal my Anger or Shame

- It is understandable to be anxious about revealing personal things to someone else, like a therapist.
- Properly qualified therapists are well aware that it is the things we are ashamed of that cause us problems.
- I have no evidence that a therapist will look down on me if I tell him/her the things that I am ashamed about. Indeed, just as a surgeon expects to deal with blood and guts, so therapists expect to deal with the less pleasant sides of life.
- The more I am prepared to face up to what I feel ashamed about, the more I may get to know myself and learn how to let these things go, or see them in a different way.
- A therapist can't force me to talk, so I can go at my own pace and decide whether the therapy is helpful.

I Can't Do What I Used to Do, Therefore I Am a Failure

- I am depressed right now, so it's natural not to have my normal drive.
- Even though I can't do what I used to, I can still do some things.
- I can praise myself for what I do do, rather than attacking myself for what I don't do.
- There is no way I am going to bully myself out of depression.
- I can go step by step.
- By praising my steps, no matter how small they may be, I am moving forward.

I Am Worthless

- To sum up a person (e.g. myself) in simple terms of good–bad, worthwhile–worthless, is all-or-nothing thinking.

- Just because I feel stupid and worthless this does not mean that I am.
- If I overidentify with feelings of worthlessness then I am more likely to get depressed.
- The idea of worth can be applied to objects like cars or soap powder, but not to persons.
- If I say 'worthless' is just one of a number of possible feelings that I, as a human being, can have about myself, then I can keep a perspective on these negative feelings.

I Am so Filled with Anger I Must Be Bad

- Anger is, like other feelings, something we are all capable of.
- High levels of anger usually point to high levels of hurt or vulnerability.
- My anger tells me that there is something I want to change and push against.
- True, flying into rages is not helpful, but I can learn to be more honest with my own needs and put them assertively.
- I can learn to understand my anger rather than just labelling myself as bad and trying to push my anger away.

I Am Not as Competent as Other People, Therefore I Am a Failure

- It is natural to want to compete in the world and feel that we are up there with others.
- All human beings are unique and need to go at their own pace. Just because some people seem more able than me does not make me a failure. I dare to be average.
- I can focus on what I can do and what is important to me, in my own unique life, rather than on what others are doing.

Nothing Ever Seems as Good as I Want it to Be, Therefore There Is No Point in Trying

- Disappointment is part of life and I can learn to cope with it if I keep it in perspective.
- I can learn to focus on what I do get out of doing things rather than how far short they fall of my expectations.

- I can check out whether I attack myself when I am disappointed and learn how to be kinder with myself.
- This type of thinking is rather all-or-nothing. Therefore I can learn to focus on what I enjoy rather than on what I don't.

I Will Never Get Better

- After reading this book, I realize that there are many ways to tackle depression and these work for many people (e.g. drugs, psychotherapy, family therapy, etc.).
- I don't have to suffer in silence.
- If I need extra help, I can talk to my family doctor and see what is available.
- I haven't always been depressed, so depression is a state of mind that I am in right now, but this does not mean that I'll always be depressed.
- I may have been trying to deal with my depression but, as this book points out, maybe I have been enduring it, trying to soldier on, rather than really tackling it.

Appendix 3

Antidepressants

If you are depressed, it is important to consider taking an antide-pressant medication. The evidence from research suggests that in severe depressions drugs work better than therapy alone. If you suffer from severe depression you may need to see a psychiatrist. Although depressed people often don't like taking drugs they can be extremely beneficial, even in less severe depressions. This is especially so if you're exhausted, can't sleep, feel bereft of hope and/or intensely anxious. Three common reasons that people do not wish to take drugs are:

- Beliefs such as 'I should be able to conquer this alone', 'It is shameful to take drugs', or 'I am weak for needing drugs'.
- Problems with side-effects.
- Fears of becoming addicted and not able to cope without drugs.

If the first of these applies to you, see the notes for the flash card on pp. 359–60. This appendix will explain why the second and third fears should not deter you from considering antidepressant medication, as well as giving you some background information on the kinds of medications that are available.

St John's Wort (*Hypericum perforatum*)

In the last few years there has been increasing interest in, and some excitement at, the possibility that St John's Wort, which you can buy in your local health food shop or chemist, could be a useful antidepressant for mild to moderate depressions. In Germany it is the first choice of treatment for depression and doctors only move on to other antidepressants if this does not work. In a recent paper (*Journal of Nervous and Mental Disease*, 1999 pp. 532–8) Kim and her colleagues looked at a number of studies on this herb. The data are encouraging, but more research is needed. Anecdotal reports also suggest that some people find this substance very helpful. We are not yet sure about the adequate dose: studies have suggested dosages varying from 200 mg to 900 mg (hypericum extract) per day. Also, while we know that established antidepressants take around three weeks to have an effect on mood (although they can help with sleep earlier), we don't yet know for sure what the corresponding time lag is for St John's Wort. You would probably need to stay on it at least a month, though, rather than expecting any immediate relief.

In 1996 the American psychiatrists Bloomfield, Nordfors and McWilliams wrote a book on hypericum which was published in the UK by the publishers of this book, Robinson, in 1998. The book is a good source of information on dosage, response times and the importance of getting 'good quality herb'. At the moment there appear to be low or no side-effects from this herb. If you think you are depressed or over-stressed, and you might wish to try hypericum, you should talk first to your doctor. This is because s/he can assess you and talk you through alternatives if this doesn't help you. Among these alternatives will be a course of antidepressants and/or some psychological therapy.

Antidepressants

You will need a doctor's prescription for an antidepressant; unfortunately, many people don't seek the help of their doctor because they don't want to admit to being depressed. Antidepressants are not addictive, but some people rightly worry that at times drugs can be used to deal with depressions arising from social and personal problems. The other side of this coin, however, is that if you feel less depressed then you will be better able to face up to your personal and social problems. If a drug helps you, this does not mean there aren't important personal and social issues to deal with. Nor does it mean that you could not benefit from therapy. As I stressed in the first chapter of this book, the treatment of depression should be biopsychosocial: that is, it should treat physical, mental and social issues together.

Only medically qualified professionals can advise and prescribe drugs. They should explore with you which ones will suit you best and what doses you may require, and check that you are not suffering from any physical disorder that may be contributing to your depression.

How Do Drugs Work?

For many years research has concentrated on three chemicals in the brain that seem to be involved with mood. These are dopamine, noradrenaline (called norepinephrine in the USA) and serotonin. Collectively these are known as monoamines. Antidepressant drugs work by increasing the levels of these chemicals and/or by changing how efficiently they work (on receptors) in the brain.

There are three basic classes of antidepressant. These are monoamine oxidase inhibitors (MAOIs for short); tricyclics; and selective serotonin re-uptake inhibitors (known as SSRIs). A fourth medication, lithium, is often used for people who have various swings in mood between depression and mania, as it helps to stabilize mood.

Most drugs have both a chemical name and a trade name. A trade name is given by the drug company which produces it. As trade names can vary from country to country, I will use only the chemical name here.

MAOIs include isocarboxazid, phenelyzine and tranylcypromine. These may be useful when anxiety (social and generalized) dominates the clinical picture. Patients taking these drugs must be extremely careful to avoid certain foods as these can cause very serious reactions. The list of foods to avoid includes cheese, red wine, yeast extracts and pickled herrings; your family doctor will provide you with information on what to avoid. You will also need to avoid certain medications such as decongestants and cough medicines.

Tricyclics work in a different way from MAOIs. The most common tricyclics are amitriptyline, clomipramine, dothiepine, imipramine and lofepramine. There are no dietary restrictions with these drugs, although alcohol should be avoided – as with all anti-depressants.

The SSRIs are a new group of drugs that came into use during the 1980s. Generally, they have fewer side-effects than the tricyclics, are safer and are increasingly becoming the drugs of first choice for depression. The most common ones are fluoxetine, fluvoxamine, paroxetine and sertraline. These drugs are believed to be more specific in their action than others, and primarily affect serotonin systems. They can be especially useful when obsessional problems are present.

I should point out that, as I write this guide, new antidepressants are appearing all the time. There is a new generation of drugs called SSNRIs, meaning that they work on both serotonin and noradrenaline systems in the brain.

Generally, antidepressants take three weeks or more to work on lifting mood, although they may help with specific symptoms such as sleep before this. The reason for this 'delayed action' has been the focus of much research. You should not use antidepressants as you might use a tranquillizer, because they have to build up in the body and thus need to be taken regularly. It is also important that they are taken at doses that are therapeutic. Too low a dose may not be helpful. Psychiatrists generally suggest that one should stay on a medication for six months or so after improvement.

All antidepressants have side-effects. Sometimes these will fade over the first few weeks. Tricyclics can give a dry mouth and affect sexual functions and weight. Different antidepressants have slightly different side-effects and your family doctor or psychiatrist will advise you on these. Sometimes, changing the time of day a drug is taken can be helpful.

There is also evidence that some patients do better on certain drugs than others; so if you find, after a reasonable trial, that a drug does not work for you, discuss this with your doctor. Don't give up if a particular drug does not suit you. Even within a class of drugs, e.g. the SSRIs, I have seen patients do better on one than another – although the research evidence for this is still being gath-ered. Very occasionally, some drugs increase irritability; if this is so for you, you should explore whether a switch to another medication would be helpful. It is extremely important that you and your doctor try to find a medication that you feel suits you, because choosing one that causes you too many side-effects increases the risk that you may not persevere with it, and thus lose the therapeutic effect. Around 60 percent of patients respond to antidepressants first time, although the figure climbs to nearer 80 percent if the treating professional tries different drugs to suit the individual. Looking at this another way, 40 percent of people may not respond well to the first drug used, but only 20 percent may have a disappointing response to antidepressants generally.

Once prescribed a drug, you should stay in regular contact with your family doctor so that s/he can monitor your progress. If things are not working out, or if you are having problems taking your medication, try to avoid thoughts like, 'Well, my doctor has done what s/he can. If this medication does not work, none will. S/he will get fed up with me. I just have to bear it.' Depression is a condition where we can easily give up if something doesn't work out quickly. However, treating depression is not always easy, and you and your doctor may need to work together to find what might best suit you and the help you might need.

If you want to know more about drugs and how they work, you can consult Spike Milligan and Anthony Clare's book, *Depression and How to Survive It* (Arrow, 1994). An excellent, quick overview which goes into more detail than I can offer here is given in David Burns's *Feeling Good: The New Mood Therapy* (Morrow, 1980). Dr Burns also explores eight common beliefs that stop people from using antidepressant medication and how to challenge these beliefs. In addition, you might find it helpful to consult one or more of the self-help organizations that I have listed in the Useful Addresses section below.

Finally, let me stress again that depression has many different causes and takes many different forms. The most important thing is for you to avoid feeling ashamed about being depressed. So, 'own' your depression and explore what you can do to change it or turn it off. Don't suffer in silence. There are many different types of antidepressants, and there are many different types of therapists and therapies. At the end of the day, it has to be your decision on how you will treat yourself. Professionals can only advise you.

Although there are no recipes for a pain-free life, and for some people life is full of hardships and difficulties, there are many things that can be done to ease the pain of depression.

Appendix 4

Useful Books and Addresses

Useful Books

A. T. Beck, *Love is Never Enough* (New York, Harper and Row, 1988) Useful book pointing out that it is often our beliefs about how relationships 'should' be and how others 'should' act that cause problems in relationships. Offers a practical guide for dealing with relationship problems.

David Burns, *Feeling Good* (New York, Morrow, 1980)
Old classic and still very popular. David Burns has also written a workbook (1986) and one on intimate relationships.

Dennis Greenberg and Christine Padesky, *Mind over Mood: A cognitive treatment manual for clients* (New York, Guilford Press, 1995)
Very practical step-by-step approach. Lots on recording thoughts and behavior.

Paul Gilbert, *Depression: The evolution of powerlessness* (Hove, Lawrence Erlbaum, and New York, Guilford Press, 1992)
This offers a more technical approach to understanding depression. If you are interested in the evolutionary aspects in general you might with to consult *Human Nature and Suffering* by me and the same publishers. Two excellent and fascinating books that explore the evolutionary approach are: Robert Wright, *The Moral Animal: Why we are the way we are* (Abacus, 1996); and Randolph Nesse and George Williams, *Evolution and Healing. The new science of Darwinian medicine* (Phoenix, 1996).

369

Hal Stone and Sidra Stone, *Embracing Your Inner Critic: Turning self-criticism into a creative asset* (New York, HarperCollins, 1993)
Explores in detail some origins and consequences of self-criticism. Not specific to depression.

Alan Stewart, *Tired All the Time* (London, Optima, 1993)
Explores common causes of tiredness, including things like allergy and diet.

Spike Milligan and Anthony Clare, *Depression and How to Survive It* (London, Arrow, 1994)
Mostly a psychiatrist's medical view of depression. Good on the role of genes and drugs (which types and how they work) and other physical treatments, less good on the psychology and self-help.

Richard Lazarus, *Stress and Emotions: a new synthesis* (New York, Free Association Press, 1999)

You might also wish to contact this publisher, Robinson, for details of other self-help books – e.g. on anxiety and on eating problems – in the same series as this one.

Useful Addresses

If you want to know more about self-help organizations here are some useful addresses.

MIND, The National Association for Mental Health
Granta House
15–19 Broadway
Stratford
London E15 4BQ

Tel.: 020 8519 2122

A very helpful organization that can offer advice on services for a wide range of psychological difficulties. It also has a wide range of literature.

Association of Post-Natal Depression
25 Jerdan Place
Fulham
London SW6

Tel.: 020 7836 0868

Manic-Depression Fellowship
8–10 High Street
Kingston-Upon-Thames
London KT1 1EY

Tel.: 020 8974 6550 and 020 8546 0323

Depression Alliance
PO Box 1022
London SE1 7GR

Tel.: 020 7721 7672 (Recorded information)

Institute for Neuro-Physiological Psychology
Warwick House
4 Stanley Place
Chester CH1 2LU

Tel.: 01224 311414

Seasonal Affective Disorder (SAD) Association
PO Box 989
London SW7 2PZ

(No telephone number available)

United States

American Mental Health Foundation
2 East 86th Street
New York
NY 1008

(Written enquiries only)

Association for the Advancement of Behavior Therapy
305 7th Avenue
New York
NY 10001

Tel.: 212 647 1890

The Behavior Therapy Center of New York
115 East 87th Street
New York
NY 10028

Tel.: 212 410 6500

Behavior Therapy Institute
San Francisco

Tel.: 415 989 2140

Behavioral Psychotherapy Center
23 Old Mamroneck Road
White Plains
NY 10605

Tel.: 914 761 4080

Institute for Behavior Therapy
137 East 36th Street
New York
NY 10016

Tel.: 212 686 8778

Institutes for Neuro-Physiological Psychology:
Dr Larry J. Beuret, MD
4811 Emerson,
Suite 209
Palatine
IL 60067
Tel.: 847 303 1800
and

Mrs Victoria Hutton
6535 North Shore Way
Newmarket
Maryland 21774

Tel.: 301 607 6752

Australia and New Zealand

Institutes for Neuro-Physiological Research:
Dr Mary Lou Sheil
80 Alexandra Street
Hunters Hill 2110
Sydney, Australia
Tel.: 298 796 596
and
Heather Jones
501 North Willowport Road
Hastins
New Zealand

(No telephone number available)

Index

A

abandonment, fear of 122, 123
abuse, histories of 16, 54, 63, 140, 147, 195, 213, 225, 227
activity
  deciding/embarking on 179–80
  increasing 72
  overcoming inactivity 126
  positive activities, planning 71, 82
addictions xv
adrenaline 5
adrenocorticotrophic hormone (ACTH) 19
affectionless-control parenting 54
aggressive behaviour 270–1, 285, 286, 287
agitation 5, 7, 72, 291
agoraphobia xiv, xv
alcohol 18, 75, 78
all-or-nothing thinking 132–4, 146, 174, 190, 191, 206, 229, 250, 274, 277, 279, 287, 292, 308, 313, 356–7
amitriptyline 365
anger 29, 49, 52, 89, 175–6, 181, 216, 263–83, 361
  anger attacks 267–8
  at failed assertiveness 291–3
  and blaming others 272, 273
  and brooding 274–5, 290
  bypassing 276–9
  compassionate anger 266, 277
  coping with 175, 263–83

  defensive anger 267
  envy and jealousy 265–6
  expansion of 4, 267–72
  and exploitation 265
  frustrative anger 263, 264–5, 327
  and grief 264
  and guilt 256–7, 260
  and hatred 273–4
  injury related 265
  in intimate relationships 293
  lack of attention and 265
  over lack of social conformity 266
  and pain 275–6
  and revenge 225
  shades of 266–7
  shame anger 271–2
  triggers 264–6
  turned inwards 263
  vulnerability beneath 267
  when using 'shoulds' and 'oughts' 272
anhedonia 4
animals, depression and xx, 3, 20
anorexia 332, 333
antidepressants 14, 44, 75, 76–7, 359–60, 363–8
  side-effects 76, 268, 366, 367
anxiety xiii, xiv, xv, 4, 5, 29, 43
anxiety spiral 89–90
anxious attachment 33
apathy 4
appetite gain/loss 6, 7

approval 187–91
 approval addiction 187
 approval-seeking behaviour 188,
  189, 191–2, 194, 236, 237, 238
 excessive need for 187–8, 189, 192,
  211
 nonverbal communication, conveyed by 202–3
 other people's judgments 189, 191, 203
 of others, showing 201
 pleasing others 194
 puppet behaviour 193
 relationships and 200–2
 subordinate approval trap 191
 see also subordination
assertiveness 104, 192, 271, 272, 277, 278,
  279, 284–93
 anger at failed assertiveness 290–3
 components 284–5
 focus on the issue 287, 288
 in intimate relationships 293
 respect for the other person 288
attachment losses 32
automatic thoughts x–xii, 85–7, 94,
  129–30
average, settling for the 322

B
Beck, Aaron xi–xii, xiv, 49
bed, staying in 70, 116
behavior therapy xiii–xiv
beliefs
 about others 56–7
 basic beliefs and attitudes 93–4
 core beliefs 50–4
 negative beliefs 50–1, 56, 93–4
bereavement 252–4, 264
'better safe than sorry' thinking 121, 217,
  267
biological factors 5–6, 13–17
biopsychosocial approach 13, 365
bipolar illness 7–8, 15
'black bile' 12, 13
the body
 caring for 75–82
 shame of 213–14, 222, 228

boredom, coping with 71–2
brain
 brain states, depression and xx, xxi,
  xxii, 6, 12, 13–14, 16, 20
 male/female compared 63
 and negative thinking 121
 structure and function xx–xxi, 16,
  42, 45
 see also thoughts
breathing patterns 79–80
brooding 274–5, 290
Buddhism 129, 145, 298, 303
bullying 203–7, 224
 at work 206–7
 direct attacks 220
 in intimate relationships 204–6
 put-downs 203, 204, 205
 see also inner bully; self-bullying
burnout 74, 238, 258

C
caffeine 78
cannabis 79
caring-healing nature 101, 102–4
catastrophizing 26
catnaps 75
causes of depression
 biological factors 5–6, 13–17
 evolutionary factors xx–xxi, 31–2,
  34–5, 42
 physical factors 76
 psychological factors 48–9, 63–4
 social factors 60–3
change
 blocks to 111
 disadvantages to 110–11
childbirth, depression after 150, 315, 316
childhood
 early experiences and traumas xx,
  xxi, 8, 16, 32, 50, 51, 54–5, 142,
  144, 217–18, 237, 297
 negative beliefs developed in 8, 50,
  51, 54–5, 144, 297
 sibling relationships 150–1
chronic depression 16
Churchill, Winston 5, 172

clomipramine 365
cognitive behavior therapy x–xii, xiv–
    xvi 48
    applications xv
    background xiv
    principles x, 49
compassionate mind 101–3, 105–6, 118–
    19, 128, 148, 172, 176–7, 178, 316–
    17
compensatory behaviour 222
competitiveness 42, 321, 322–5, 329–30,
    333–4
    challenging 335–9
    competitive perfectionists 322–3
    envy and 333–5
    failure, fear of 329–30
    'get ahead' competitiveness 323
    'keep up' competitiveness 322–3
    proving oneself 330–1
    success, fantasies of 329
    see also perfectionism
concentration difficulties 4, 7, 19
conclusions, jumping to 85, 122–4, 355
confidence 35, 161, 217, 333
confidence building 163, 197
conflicts and dilemmas
    clarifying 110–11
    conflict avoidance 142–3
    fear of 294, 295
conform, pressures to 219–20
control, taking 142
coping with depression
    initial steps 69–82
    ten key steps 345–6
    thoughts and feelings 84–98
cortisol 6, 19, 20, 34
counselling ix
cravings 129
creative visualization 81
crying 224, 230
cultural stereotypes 219

D
deception 164, 168
    sensitivity to 132
    see also fakery

defeat
    brooding on 37
    feelings of 37, 39, 343
    setting oneself up for 38
defeat states 37
defensive thinking 58, 121, 217, 267
delusions 8
depression
    adaptive functions 31–41, 44
    bipolar illness 7–8, 15
    causes 12–64
    chronic depression 9
    duration 9
    effects on life 4–6
    frequency of episodes 9
    gender and 9–10, 63–4
    incidence of xv, 3, 9–10
    major depression 7
    maladaptive depression 41–4
    mind–body link 12–13
    neurotic depression 8
    onset 9
    psychotic depression 8
    severity 9
    symptoms 4–6, 7
    triggers 74, 139, 305
    unipolar illness 8
deprivation, depression and 10
despair state 32
dexamethasone 20
diazepam 76
diet and nutrition 77–8
disappointment 133, 145, 160, 302, 320
    'attack self' response 263, 306, 309
    causes 302
disappointment gap 305, 306, 309, 316
    'it's all been spoiled' feeling 307–8
    lost ideals 304–7
    with one's feelings 311–12
    with oneself 314–17
    over relationships 308–10
    'shoulds' and 'oughts' 302–3, 313
disapproval, fear of 189
disloyalty, feelings of 278
distraction 72, 73, 95
distrust 58–9

Index

dopamine 14, 19, 20, 365
dothiepine 365
drugs
  antidepressants 14, 44, 75, 76, 76–7,
    268, 359–60, 363–8
  illicit drugs 79
  tranquillizers 76, 79
duration of depression 9

E
eating disorders xv, 180, 332, 333
efforts, disbelieving and discounting
  129–30
egocentric thinking 135–6
Ellis, Albert 49
emotional amplifiers 88, 91
emotional dampeners 88
emotional reasoning 126–8, 146, 160,
  355–6
emotions
  functions 29–30
  giving voice to 174–6
  managing 43
  of shame 211–12
  triggers 42–3
the empty self 159–61, 190
  challenging 161
entrapment, feelings of 5, 7, 33, 40–1, 244
envy 151, 265
  competitiveness and 333–5
escape, desire to 40–1, 244–5
events and meanings, distinguishing
  84–5
evolutionary factors
  anger and 263
  depression and xx–xxi, 31–2, 34–5,
    42
  shame and 210, 217
exercise 78
expectations, high 38
exploitation, feelings of 58–9

F
failure 144–5, 149, 160, 214, 320–1, 360
  ability to fail 320, 339
  fear of 321, 329–30

fakery 164–8, 242
  challenging 167
family histories 15–16, 344
fantasies, aggressive 225, 273
fatigue 7, 19
fear 4, 205, 235
fight/flight system 18, 40, 274–6, 291
flash cards 171–4, 359–62
fluoxetine 366
fluvoxamine 366
forgiveness 258, 259, 294–8
  forgiving ourselves 297–8, 300
  reconciliation 294, 295–6
  resentment and revenge 296–8
frequency of episodes of depression 9
Freud, Sigmund 263
frustration 31, 133, 134, 302–17
  'attack self response' 263, 306, 309
  causes 302
  frustrative anger 263, 264–5, 327
  with one's feelings 311–14
  with oneself 314–17
  tolerate, ability to 303–4
  see also disappointment
future
  pessimism concerning 125
  predicting 125, 355

G
genetic factors xx, 14–16, 344
goals
  blocked 304, 305
  setting 104–5
greed 246–7
grief 30, 31–2, 275, 276
  and anger 264
  and guilt 252–4
guilt 4, 7, 30, 33, 70, 73, 89, 162, 165,
    166, 234–62
  abandoning/separation guilt 251–2
  and anger 256–7, 260
  at good fortune 248, 249
  and caring behavior 235–9, 240, 242,
    253
  challenging 247
  compassion trap 243

and the desire to escape 244–5
existential guilt 254
focus 234
and forgiveness 258–9
and greed 246–7
grief and 252–4
guilt areas, recognizing 258
induced guilt 249, 254–5, 259–60, 289
and life dilemmas 243
projecting 288–9
punishment, expectation of 143
rescuing hero stance 237–9, 258
responsibility guilt 250–1
and a sense of deserving 245–6
shame and 226–7, 234–5
survivor guilt 247–8
tolerating guilt 255–6
triggers 258

H
hatred 149, 273–4
    self-hatred 147–9
high expressed emotion *see* put-downs
historic views of depression 12–13
holistic approach 13
honesty 164, 165
hopelessness 7
Horner, Althea 334–5
humiliation 224–6
hypochondrias xv
hypothalamic–pituitary–adrenal (HPA) system 19, 20

I
the ideal 'other' 310–11
ideals
    lost 304–7
    unrealistic 310–11, 312, 313, 314, 315, 343
identity, loss of 194–8
imagery of depression 5, 178–9
imipramine 366
inactivity, overcoming 126
inferiority, feelings of 9, 34, 35, 36, 39, 59–60, 150, 211, 270
    see also social comparisons

inner bully 152–4, 176–7, 178, 279
    'attack self' response 305, 316–17
    challenging 153–4, 229–30
    perfectionism and 327–9
inner compassion 45–6
irrational thinking 25, 26
isocarboxazid 365
isolation, feelings of 33, 36, 72, 212
it-me problem 144–6, 357–8

J
jealousy 29, 265–6

K
Kaufman, Gershen 213

L
life events xx, xxi, 15, 63, 69, 121
life scripts 182–3
limits, recognizing 73–4, 284
lithium 365
lofepramine 366
'loving kindness' meditation 298, 300

M
major depression 7
manic-depression *see* bipolar illness
MAOIs (monoamine oxidase inhibitors) 365
medication *see* drugs
meditation 81–2
melancholia 3, 12
memory 4, 19
men: at risk of depression 9, 10, 64
mind reading 124, 190–1
mind–body link 12–13
monoamines 6, 14, 365
motivation, effects on 4
muscular relaxation 80
'musts' 128–9, 356
    controlling 129
    turning 'musts' into preferences 356
    typical 'musts' 129

N
name-calling *see* self-labelling

needs
  openness concerning 163–4
  social and emotional 55–7
negative, dwelling on the 130–1
negative emotions, increase in 4
negative images, changing 178–9
negative labels 156–69
negative thinking bias 121
negative thoughts 23–4, 26, 46, 89, 90,
    355
  about emotional needs 56–7
  automatic thoughts x–xii, 85–7, 94,
    129–30
  brooding on 95, 96
  depressive spirals 52, 87, 88–9, 91,
    99, 121, 122
  developed in childhood 8, 50, 51,
    54–5, 144, 297
  styles 121–36
  triggers 91, 121
negative thoughts, challenging 99–120,
    122, 123–4, 126, 171–83, 193–4,
    358–9
  bonds, tasks and goals 103–5
  emotional reasoning, challenging
    127–8
  evidence gathering 105–6, 111–12
  exercises 119–20, 137–8
  experiments 111–13
  flash cards 171–4
  generating alternatives 106–9
  writing things down 103, 104, 107,
    109–11, 113–17, 178
neurochemistry 14
neuroses ix, xi, 8
neurotic depression 8
neurotransmitters 6, 14, 18–19
non-assertive behaviour 285, 286
  guilt projection 288–9
  sulking 289–90, 294, 296
nonverbal communication 202–3,
    204
noradrenaline 14, 19, 20, 365
nuisance, fear of being a 51, 162–3, 241,
    247
  challenging 162–3

O
obsessive compulsive disorders xv
onset of depression 9
overgeneralization 134–5, 167, 190, 191,
    287, 308, 357
  challenging 135
overwhelmed, feelings of being 326
overwork 42, 73

P
painkillers 79
panic attacks/panic disorders xv, 49, 90,
    215, 332–3
paranoia 49, 79
parent–child relationships 54–5, 201,
    240, 252
paroxetine 366
perfectionism 74, 165, 219, 320–21, 325–
    33
  challenging 335–9
  focus on flaws 165
  focus on results 325, 326–7
  and the internal bully 327–9
  loss of positive pleasures 326–7
  need to be in control 326
  'other-oriented' 321, 325
  personal pride 332–3
  pride and desire to impress 331–2
  self-centredness 330–1
  self-orientated 321
  in social situations 324–5
  socially prescribed 321
  see also competitiveness
persona 164–5
personal space 73, 74
personalization 140, 357
perspective, losing 39–40, 45, 121, 356
phenelyzine 365
phobias xiv, xv
physical activity as distraction 72–3
physical causes of depression 76
physiological changes 5–6
positive activities, planning 71
positives, discounting and disbelieving
    129–30, 131–2, 166, 172, 192, 199,
    279, 287, 356

powerlessness, feelings of 263, 276,
    334–5
praise, discounting 131, 132
preferences, recognizing 160–1
pride
    and confidence 333
    personal pride 332–3
problems, breaking down 70–1, 118, 125
projection 223–4, 288–9
provoking agents 61
psychiatry 76–7
psychoanalysis ix, xi, xiii
psychodynamic psychotherapy xiii
psychological factors 48–55
    cognitive approach 48–9
psychosis ix, 8
psychotherapy xiii, 8
psychotic depression 250–1
punishment, expecting 143
put-downs 203, 204, 205

R
rational mind 100–1, 105–6, 117–18, 128,
    316–17
recognition, lack of 218–19
reconciliation 294, 295–6
recurrence of depression 9
rejection, fear of 33, 123
relationships
    affection, expressing 215
    anger and assertiveness in 293
    approval in 200–2
    being open about needs 163–4
    bullying in 204–6
    conflicts in 39, 294
    depression, effects of 6
    disappointment and 308–10
    fear of losing 122–3
    idealizing 308–9, 310–11
    negative beliefs and 53–4
    with oneself 103–4, 139
    with others 55–60
    parent–child relationships 54–5,
        201, 240, 252
    and personal space 73
    reconciliation in 294, 295–6

shame in 212, 214–15
social needs 55–6
subordination in 194–9, 204
relaxation
    breathing patterns 79–80
    creative visualization 81
    difficulties 5
    meditation 81–2
    muscular relaxation 80
resentment 297
responsibility
    acknowledging 227
    burdensome 244, 245
    responsibility guilt 250–1
responsibility circles 141, 142, 205, 227,
    250
revenge 30, 225, 226, 227, 263, 297
risk factors xxi
road rage 304
ruminating 95

S
sadness 235, 275, 276, 306
St John's Wort 363–4
seasonal affective disorder (SAD) 77
self-acceptance 102
self-attack 46, 144, 146–7, 152, 153, 167,
        190, 197, 199, 211, 214, 258, 292,
        306, 309, 310, 314, 316, 320, 358
    styles 357–8
self-blaming 110, 111, 140–3, 205, 357
self-bullying 139–55
self-consciousness 228–9
self-criticism 38–9, 101, 143–4, 146, 147,
        176, 189, 190, 221, 357
self-disgust 147
self-esteem, low xv, 5, 7, 61, 239
self-hatred 147–9, 358
self-help books xv–xvi, 225, 345
self-judgments 145–6, 189
self-labelling 146, 156–9, 161, 172, 192,
        199, 274, 277, 292, 357
    challenging 158–9
    typical words 157
self-sacrifice 57, 198, 238
Seligman, Martin 20

Index

serotonin 14, 19, 20, 34, 365
sertraline 366
severity of depression 9
sexual abuse 54, 63, 140, 147, 195, 213
sexual feelings, shame of 215–16
sexual harassment 207
sexual jealousy 266
shame 27, 34, 38, 147, 187, 210–33, 345
    about competencies and abilities
      214
    anger and 216, 271–2
    avoidance 221–4
    dismissal of oneself 218–19
    emotions of 211–12
    feeling ashamed/being shamed 212
    focus for 213–17
    and guilt 226–7, 234–5
    healing 228–31
    humiliation 224–6
    origins of 210, 217–21
    in relationships 212, 214–15
    and responsibility 227–8
    and revenge 225, 226, 227
    self-consciousness 228–9
    shaming loop 220–1
    triggers 210–11
shame avoidance
    by blame and counter-blame 223
    by compensatory behaviour 222
    by concealment and distraction 222
    by violence/attack 222–3
'shoulds' and 'oughts' 245, 272, 302–3,
    313
sleep difficulties 6, 7, 74–5
social anxiety xv, 5, 49, 72, 89, 324–5
social comparisons 38, 59, 149–52, 161,
    358
    challenging 151–2
social conformity 266
social factors 60–3
    gender, depression and 63–4
    social roles 61–3
    vulnerability to depression 26, 60–
      1, 65, 187, 192, 238
    social isolation, feelings of 33, 36,
      72, 212

social patterns and lifestyles 61–2
social roles 61–3, 65
social withdrawal 220–1
SSNRIs 366
SSRIs (selective serotonin re-uptake
    inhibitors) 365, 366
standards, unrealistic 37–8
status and self-worth 59–60
stimulants 78–9
stress 17–27, 265
    chronic stress 44
    coping with 17, 21
    cumulative stresses 21–2
    depression and 17–27
    stress spirals 24–7
    stress/defence system 18–19
    stressful situations, preparing for
      173–4
    stress–depression linkage 17–27, 41
    thought patterns and 22–4
    stress hormones 6, 24, 34, 45, 46, 101
subordination
    enforced 34–5
    loss of identity 194–8
    in relationships 194–9, 204
    and self sacrifice 57, 198
    subordinate self 191–203, 285
    subordinate thinking 35–7, 292, 297
    to a way of life 199–200
success, addiction to 145
suicidal feelings 7, 241
sulking 289–90, 294, 296

T
talking therapies ix
teasing 220
therapy 103, 360
    see also cognitive behavior therapy;
      psychotherapy
thought monitoring and challenging
    forms 348–54, 384–91
thoughts
    about events and meanings 84–5
    about feelings and behaviour 89–90
    automatic thoughts x–xii, 85–7, 94,
      129–30

depressive spirals 52, 87, 88–9, 91, 99, 121, 122
  dwelling on 94–6
  emotional amplifiers 88, 91
  emotional dampeners 88
  externalizing 176–7
  extreme forms of thinking 5
  identifying 92–3
  monitoring and challenging 90–1, 348–54
  negative *see* negative thoughts
  writing down 90–1
tranquillizers 76, 79
tranylcypromine 365
traumas, early 54–5
tricyclics 365–6
triggers for depression 74, 139, 305
twins, depression in 15, 344

U
uncertainty, threat of 133

unipolar depression 8
unlovability, feelings of 50, 51, 52, 65, 277–8
useful books and addresses 369–73

V
values and attitudes, changing 180–2
vitamin supplements 78
vulnerability to depression 26, 60–1, 65, 187, 192, 238

W
weight changes 6, 7, 78, 332
women
  at risk from depression 9, 10, 60, 63–4
  boredom, vulnerability to 72
work
  bullying at 206–7
  overwork 42, 73
  and self-esteem 62
worthless label, challenging 192, 360–1

Extra Monitoring Sheets

THOUGHT MONITORING AND CHALLENGING FORM

Triggering Events, Feelings or Images	Beliefs and Key Thoughts	Feelings	Alternative Challenges to Negative Thoughts	Degree of Feeling Change
Key Questions to help you identify your thoughts. What actually happened?	What went through your mind? What are you thinking about yourself, and your future? What are you thinking about others? Rate degree of belief 0–100.	What are your main feelings and emotions? Rate degree of feelings 0–100.	What would you say to a friend? What alternatives might there be? What is the evidence against this view? How would you see this if you were not depressed? Rate degree of belief in alternatives 0–100.	Write down any degree of change in your feelings.

THOUGHT MONITORING AND CHALLENGING FORM

Triggering Events, Feelings or Images	Beliefs and Key Thoughts	Feelings	Alternative Challenges to Negative Thoughts	Degree of Feeling Change
Key Questions to help you identify your thoughts. *What actually happened?*	*What went through your mind? What are you thinking about yourself, and your future? What are you thinking about others?* *Rate degree of belief 0–100.*	*What are your main feelings and emotions?* *Rate degree of feelings 0–100.*	*What would you say to a friend? What alternatives might there be? What is the evidence against this view? How would you see this if you were not depressed?* *Rate degree of belief in alternatives 0–100.*	*Write down any degree of change in your feelings.*

THOUGHT MONITORING AND CHALLENGING FORM

Triggering Events, Feelings or Images	Beliefs and Key Thoughts	Feelings	Alternative Challenges to Negative Thoughts	Degree of Feeling Change
Key Questions to help you identify your thoughts. *What actually happened?*	*What went through your mind? What are you thinking about yourself, and your future? What are you thinking about others?* *Rate degree of belief 0–100.*	*What are your main feelings and emotions?* *Rate degree of feelings 0–100.*	*What would you say to a friend? What alternatives might there be? What is the evidence against this view? How would you see this if you were not depressed?* *Rate degree of belief in alternatives 0–100.*	*Write down any degree of change in your feelings.*

THOUGHT MONITORING AND CHALLENGING FORM

Triggering Events, Feelings or Images	Beliefs and Key Thoughts	Feelings	Alternative Challenges to Negative Thoughts	Degree of Feeling Change
Key Questions to help you identify your thoughts. *What actually happened?*	*What went through your mind? What are you thinking about yourself, and your future? What are you thinking about others? Rate degree of belief 0–100.*	*What are your main feelings and emotions? Rate degree of feelings 0–100.*	*What would you say to a friend? What alternatives might there be? What is the evidence against this view? How would you see this if you were not depressed? Rate degree of belief in alternatives 0–100.*	*Write down any degree of change in your feelings.*

THOUGHT MONITORING AND CHALLENGING FORM

Triggering Events, Feelings or Images	Beliefs and Key Thoughts	Feelings	Alternative Challenges to Negative Thoughts	Degree of Feeling Change
Key Questions to help you identify your thoughts. *What actually happened?*	*What went through your mind? What are you thinking about yourself, and your future? What are you thinking about others?* *Rate degree of belief 0–100.*	*What are your main feelings and emotions?* *Rate degree of feelings 0–100.*	*What would you say to a friend? What alternatives might there be? What is the evidence against this view? How would you see this if you were not depressed?* *Rate degree of belief in alternatives 0–100.*	*Write down any degree of change in your feelings.*

THOUGHT MONITORING AND CHALLENGING FORM

Triggering Events, Feelings or Images	Beliefs and Key Thoughts	Feelings	Alternative Challenges to Negative Thoughts	Degree of Feeling Change
Key Questions to help you identify your thoughts. *What actually happened?*	*What went through your mind? What are you thinking about yourself, and your future? What are you thinking about others?* *Rate degree of belief 0–100.*	*What are your main feelings and emotions?* *Rate degree of feelings 0–100.*	*What would you say to a friend? What alternatives might there be? What is the evidence against this view? How would you see this if you were not depressed?* *Rate degree of belief in alternatives 0–100.*	*Write down any degree of change in your feelings.*

THOUGHT MONITORING AND CHALLENGING FORM

Triggering Events, Feelings or Images	Beliefs and Key Thoughts	Feelings	Alternative Challenges to Negative Thoughts	Degree of Feeling Change
Key Questions to help you identify your thoughts. *What actually happened?*	*What went through your mind? What are you thinking about yourself, and your future? What are you thinking about others?* *Rate degree of belief 0–100.*	*What are your main feelings and emotions?* *Rate degree of feelings 0–100.*	*What would you say to a friend? What alternatives might there be? What is the evidence against this view? How would you see this if you were not depressed?* *Rate degree of belief in alternatives 0–100.*	*Write down any degree of change in your feelings.*

THOUGHT MONITORING AND CHALLENGING FORM

Triggering Events, Feelings or Images	Beliefs and Key Thoughts	Feelings	Alternative Challenges to Negative Thoughts	Degree of Feeling Change
Key Questions to help you identify your thoughts. *What actually happened?*	*What went through your mind?* *What are you thinking about yourself, and your future?* *What are you thinking about others?* *Rate degree of belief 0–100.*	*What are your main feelings and emotions?* *Rate degree of feelings 0–100.*	*What would you say to a friend?* *What alternatives might there be?* *What is the evidence against this view?* *How would you see this if you were not depressed?* *Rate degree of belief in alternatives 0–100.*	*Write down any degree of change in your feelings.*

Order further books in the *Overcoming* series

No. of copies	Title	Price	Total
	Anger and Irritability	£7.99	
	Anorexia Nervosa	£7.99	
	Anxiety	£7.99	
	Bulimia Nervosa and Binge Eating	£7.99	
	Childhood Trauma	£7.99	
	Depression	£7.99	
	Low Self-Esteem	£7.99	
	Mood Swings	£7.99	
	Panic	£7.99	
	Social Anxiety and Shyness	£7.99	
	Traumatic Stress	£7.99	
	P&P & Insurance		£3.00
	Grand Total		£

Name: ....

Address: ....

.... Postcode: ....

Daytime Tel. No. / Email ....
(in case of query)

Three ways to pay:

1. **For express service telephone the TBS order line on 01206 255 800 and quote 'CRBK'. Order lines are open Monday – Friday 8:30am – 5:30pm**

2. I enclose a cheque made payable to **TBS Ltd** for £...............

3. Please charge my ❑ Visa ❑ Mastercard ❑ Amex ❑ Switch

   (switch issue no. ....) £....................

   Card number: ....

   Expiry date: .... Signature ....
   (your signature is essential when paying by credit card)

Please return forms (*no stamp required*) to, Constable & Robinson Ltd, FREE-POST NAT6619, 3 The Lanchesters, 162 Fulham Palace Road, London W6 9ER.
Enquiries to readers@constablerobinson.com
www.constablerobinson.com